Advance Praise for Engine of Impact

"As a philanthropist constantly grappling with how I can achieve more impact, I found Jonker and Meehan's insights to be provocative and engaging. They go beyond the typical rhetoric regarding 'what the nonprofit sector can learn from business' and give these organizations their due—with great advice. Nonprofits are dealing with often intractable societal problems of enormous complexity and uncertain revenue streams. These authors appreciate the weight on leaders' shoulders, while offering a detailed roadmap to maximize their impact. A must-read."
—Jeff Raikes, Co-founder, Raikes Foundation, former CEO, Bill & Melinda Gates Foundation, and Chairman, Stanford Board of Trustees

"No one knows the not-for-profit sector and its most effective leaders better than Meehan and Jonker. Their book is a master class on what it takes to drive meaningful impact. In tackling the fundamental questions—strategy and focus, discipline and accountability—the authors get to the heart of what every mission-focused leader needs to understand. *Engine of Impact* is a book to read and re-read—the definitive guide for all who aspire to lead high performing and high achieving organizations."
—Sally Osberg, President and CEO, Skoll Foundation and co-author, *Getting Beyond Better*

"Bill Meehan and Kim Jonker have decades of experience in rigorously evaluating what makes organizations operate—or fail to operate—at a high level. In *Engine of Impact*, they leverage that deep knowledge to create a smart, compelling guide to doing good by leading well."
—Jamie Dimon, Chief Executive Officer, JPMorgan Chase

"*Engine of Impact* is an essential handbook for every aspiring social sector leader and philanthropist. Creating social impact is an art and a science, requiring investments of heart and mind. Meehan and Jonker's outstanding analysis combines the intense rigor of business strategy with the critical soft skills of courage and creativity to equip us with the toolkit necessary for transformative social change."
—Laura Arrillaga-Andreessen, Founder, laaf.org, author, *Giving 2.0*, Founder and Chairman, Stanford Center on Philanthropy and Civil Society, and Founder and Chairman, Silicon Valley Social Venture Fund

"Building and leading great non-profits is a socially vital—but managerially daunting—endeavor. Enter Bill Meehan and Kim Jonker who, in simple and lively prose, draw upon deep research and lived experience to deliver the essential field guide on how to do it right. All of us—donors, volunteers, board members, executives, citizens—are in their debt."
—Dominic Barton, Global Managing Partner, McKinsey & Company

"In an era when the work of nonprofits is ever more essential, Meehan and Jonker deliver critical insights, strategic guidance, and inspirational lessons from the front lines. Readers will benefit enormously from their candor and clear-headed wisdom. We're awash in business books, but the nonprofit sector has been wanting for its own evidence-based guide. In *Engine of Impact*, they have it. I strongly recommend this book for nonprofit leaders, funders, and anyone seeking to optimize humanitarian impact."
—Jacquelline Fuller, President, Google.org

Engine of Impact

Engine of Impact

ESSENTIALS OF
STRATEGIC LEADERSHIP
IN THE NONPROFIT SECTOR

William F. Meehan III and Kim Starkey Jonker

STANFORD BUSINESS BOOKS
An Imprint of Stanford University Press
Stanford, California

Stanford University Press
Stanford, California

Special discounts for bulk quantities of Stanford Business Books are available to corporations, professional associations, and other organizations. For details and discount information, contact the special sales department of Stanford University Press. Tel: (650) 725-0820, Fax: (650) 725-3457

Printed in the United States of America on acid-free, archival-quality paper

Library of Congress Cataloging-in-Publication Data

Names: Meehan, William F., III, 1952– author. | Jonker, Kim Starkey, author.
Title: Engine of impact : essentials of strategic leadership in the nonprofit sector / William F. Meehan III and Kim Starkey Jonker.
Description: Stanford, California : Stanford Business Books, an imprint of Stanford University Press, 2017. | Includes bibliographical references and index.
Identifiers: LCCN 2017006177 | ISBN 9780804796439 (cloth : alk. paper) | ISBN 9781503603622 (e-book)
Subjects: LCSH: Nonprofit organizations—Management. | Strategic planning.
Classification: LCC HD62.6 M44 2017 | DDC 658.4/092—dc23 LC record available at https://lccn.loc.gov/2017006177

Typeset by Newgen in 10.75/15 Sabon

Illustrations by Barbara McCarthy and Stephanie Gliozzo

Contents

Foreword

To build a truly great social sector organization, you need more strategic rigor than the average business corporation. This is unobvious to most people, says Bill Meehan, because nonprofits generally operate at a much smaller scale than enterprises that show up in the *Fortune* 500; but when you adjust for scale, a social sector organization is more complex, the problems more intractable, and the economic engine more uncertain than what companies face in rational economic markets. Simply put, it is substantially more difficult to build a great social sector organization than to build a great business corporation of similar scale. And that is why the best-run, most-impactful nonprofits stand as some of the most impressive enterprises in the world. "The best nonprofits are truly spectacular," said Kim Jonker in a conversation about this book. "They will take your breath away." And yet most nonprofits limp along, operating far below their potential impact.

So, what does it take to become a truly great nonprofit, one that can scale its impact? Certainly, we need Level 5 leaders—those who lead with a blend of personal humility and indomitable will in pursuit of a noble purpose. We need the right people on the bus, and in the key seats. We need to build a culture of discipline: disciplined people who engage in disciplined thought and who take disciplined action. And we need to construct a self-reinforcing flywheel that builds momentum: attract believers, build strength and capability, demonstrate results and impact, build a brand reputation, and then repeat the cycle, over and over again.

But even with all that, we need to know what to focus on, the few levers that most matter. That is precisely what Meehan and Jonker have distilled into these pages. Most nonprofit leaders are well intentioned and full of passion, but many lack a road map for how to harness their prodigious energies and limited resources to maximum effect. They jump in the car and just start driving with an idea of their intended destination; they'll get somewhere, but without a map, they are unlikely to end up someplace great. This book is, in essence, a detailed road map of disciplined thought and action for turning a good nonprofit into one that can achieve great impact at scale.

Imagine you seek to accomplish multiple gold medals in your chosen sport. What would it take? Within the small set of the most critical dimensions, you cannot have a weakness. If, as a middle-distance runner, you have awesome leg speed yet lack smart racing strategy, you will likely find yourself in poor position at the end of the race. If, as a gymnast, you have exquisite precision to hold balance on the beam yet lack the explosive power for a soaring vault or tumbling run, you will fail to win the all-around medal. If you do well in the water but fade in the run, you cannot win the triathlon. If you are physically gifted yet tend to collapse mentally under pressure, you will likely excel at lower levels of competition, but your weaknesses will show in the biggest events.

The same applies to building a truly great nonprofit: you have to know (and focus on) the elements of high performance that matter most. Meehan and Jonker have identified seven crucial pillars. And in these seven, you simply cannot have a single weakness, not one:

1. Your mission must be clear and focused.

2. You must develop a strategy rooted in the few strategic concepts that matter most.

3. You must figure out how to count what counts to ensure impact.

4. You must have insight and courage, bringing heart and soul to making and executing on hard decisions.

5. You must build a superb organization, a team of teams, that exemplifies the principles of high-performing organizations.

6. You must attend to money, as cash flow is like oxygen to breathe, by crafting a strategic revenue machine that includes the right donors.

7. You must achieve exceptional governance, building and nurturing a strong board that works.

The real key to getting the most out of this book lies in having the right mind-set and obsessive dedication—to set forth with the intention to not simply "get in shape" but to set out to win the world championship, to earn the gold medal of nonprofit impact. So, as you head into the text that follows, you might want to consider the following questions: Are you willing to demand nonprofit *performance*, not just good intentions? Are you willing to make rigorous fact-based decisions, even if those decisions run contrary to popular opinion or self-interested large donors? Are you willing to favor impact over recognition? Are you willing to scale proven innovations for widespread impact rather than just seeking to innovate on a small scale? Are you willing to bring your best, most intense, most creative, most disciplined self to your nonprofit work?

As Meehan and Jonker teach, the creativity and discipline required to build a great nonprofit substantially exceeds the creativity and discipline required to build a great business corporation. If you do your work well, the best business corporations should come to see your nonprofit as an exemplar of excellence from which they can learn. But even more important, you can change the lives—maybe even save the lives—of the people you serve. They are depending on you to get it right.

Jim Collins
Author, *Good to Great* and *Good to Great and the Social Sectors*
Boulder, Colorado, January 2017

Preface

We have been students of organizational performance—both corporate and nonprofit—for a combined sixty years. Most of the rich and varied case examples we present are of organizations and individuals we personally know from our advising, evaluating, teaching, and studying. We hope that their examples will enrich your lives and work as they have ours.

We have also benefited greatly from a long line of distinguished observers of organizational performance whose thinking has informed our own. We emphasize this because there is no settled view on how to assess an organization's performance; neither is there any general agreement on how to identify those attributes that correlate with, much less cause, that performance.

Our approach is perhaps closest to that of Peter Drucker, who simply didn't bother with measuring performance in any meaningful statistical way. Instead, he largely relied on his extensive knowledge of many organizations and mainly communicated his conclusions by using individual case examples. Nevertheless, his books, including *Concept of the Corporation* and *Managing the Nonprofit Organization: Principles and Practices*, have been foundational to organizational studies following World War II.[1]

Back when Bill Meehan joined the San Francisco office of McKinsey & Company in 1978, he met Tom Peters and Bob Waterman, who had just initiated their research for *In Search of Excellence: Lessons from America's Best-Run Companies*, an early business blockbuster that helped carve out a category of popular books on organizational performance.[2] In an era when strategy, analysis, and quantification were ascendant, Peters and Waterman, among many other things, reinforced that there was no formulaic approach to creating and sustaining a great organization. And oh, by the way, people and culture were essential elements too!

In 1996, looking to learn what great students of management and organization were thinking about the drivers of corporate performance, Bill convened a salon with a group that included Dick Foster from McKinsey and Jim Collins. As the first chapter of *Good to Great: Why Some Companies Make the Leap . . . And Others Don't* recounts, it was this salon discussion that inspired Jim's seminal book, for which the field and we are indebted to him.[3] His later monograph, *Good to Great and the Social Sectors*, has also been instrumental in the thinking between these covers.[4]

Three other studies of organizational performance have particularly swayed our thought and practice. In the early to mid-1990s, Mike Murray and Gil Marmol of McKinsey studied high-performing organizations.[5] Their summary of six attributes of high-performing organizations, while based mostly on their own insight, interpretation, and wisdom, is (in our estimation) on the same plane with what Drucker, Peters and Waterman, and Collins have described on the basis of their research. In 2001, Richard Foster, together with Sarah Kaplan, wrote *Creative Destruction: Why Companies That Are Built to Last Underperform the Market—And How to Successfully Transform Them.*[6] Foster and Kaplan's book set a standard for the statistical analysis of corporate performance by analyzing more than sixty variables to create a database of more than a thousand US companies in fifteen industries over almost four decades. Their key finding should guide everyone's thinking about organizational performance: over time, all undiversified corporate performance regresses to the industry mean. That is, of course, what competition and markets do. While we have a great appreciation for the quantitative power of Foster and Kaplan's work, we took a different page from Jeffrey Pfeffer and Robert Sutton, who relied on their personal experience—including interviews, informal conversations, quick observations, long-term ethnographic studies, and consulting engagements—to dispel management myths in *Hard Facts, Dangerous Half-Truths, and Total Nonsense: Profiting from Evidence-Based*

Management.[7] Our inferential conclusion: be afraid, be very afraid, of how data is misused but be grateful, very grateful, that evidence-supported management practices do exist.

Turning to the explicit study of nonprofit organizations, in conducting research for *Forces for Good: The Six Practices of High-Impact Nonprofits,* Leslie Crutchfield and Heather McLeod Grant outlined a survey and interview approach to research high-impact nonprofits.[8] Most recently, Mario Morino's *Leap of Reason: Managing to Outcomes in an Era of Scarcity* drew on his accumulated wisdom and the insights of others, including more than a dozen thought leaders and organizations, as well as essayists who contributed to the book.[9]

In our research, we have chosen to rely on our own insight and thinking instead of depending on the "wisdom of crowds" and have made no attempt to measure longitudinal statistical performance. Impact measurement of nonprofits, despite some progress, is nowhere close to identifying the key dependent variable that might be comparable to shareholder value for corporate organizations, so such an approach would have no merit. Our goal is to codify principles, offer frameworks, and spotlight nonprofits that we assess to be high performing—better than other organizations in their field—so that we may all learn from them. We are, in our roles in the nonprofit sector, empirical in mind-set, analytical in approach, and deeply moved by our heart-and-soul personal experiences in the social sector.

In Bill's case, this goes back to a serendipitous 1974 encounter that shaped most of the facts of his life from there on out. It was his last semester at Columbia University and he bumped into a classmate who introduced him to Bill Drayton, who was then working in an early version of McKinsey's Social Sector Practice. This led to Bill Meehan's first postcollege job and helped set the course of his professional life. Bill Drayton and his founding role in the social entrepreneurship movement set the standard for pursuing social impact and continue to define it.

Bill has taught a course on strategic leadership of nonprofit organizations at the Stanford Graduate School of Business (Stanford GSB), for eighteen years and counting, and during this time has frequently joined forces with Kim. Together, they have advised many nonprofits, written articles on the sector for *Stanford Social Innovation Review* (*SSIR*), and worked to develop the evaluation criteria for the Henry R. Kravis Prize in Nonprofit Leadership.

Kim, for her part, oversaw the Kravis Prize from 2005 to 2015. During that time, she had the privilege of learning and thinking about the topic of nonprofit leadership with a committee composed of knowledgeable, wise, and intellectually rigorous individuals. Marie-Josée Kravis, a respected economist specializing in public policy analysis, served as chair of the selection committee, which included Henry Kravis, cofounder of Kohlberg Kravis Roberts & Co.; James Wolfensohn, former president of the World Bank; Amartya Sen, Nobel Laureate in Economics; Josette Sheeran, president and CEO of the Asia Society and former executive director of the World Food Programme; Surin Pitsuwan, former secretary-general of ASEAN; Lord Jacob Rothschild, founder of J. Rothschild Assurance Group (now St. James Place); Ratan Tata, chairman emeritus of Tata Group; and Harry McMahon, board chair emeritus of Claremont McKenna College.

The notion of drawing out fundamentals in the field and steering organizations away from the siren songs of fads came into clear view in 2013, when Kim suggested that she and Bill lead a day of peer learning with all of the Kravis Prize winners. On this occasion, both were struck by how these top-performing, diverse nonprofits described what drove their high impact and growth and also by what presented them the greatest challenges. The factors they discussed were strikingly similar and are all captured in the pages that follow. Most recently, our work as funders with King Philanthropies with a focus on extreme poverty alleviation has deepened our insight into the sector and reaffirmed our takeaways.

Last, we have expanded and tested our personal knowledge by launching the 2016 Stanford Survey on Leadership and Management in the Nonprofit Sector.[10] Collaborating with GuideStar, BoardSource, the Stanford Center on Philanthropy and Civil Society, *SSIR*, and Stanford GSB's Center for Social Innovation, we received more than three thousand responses from nonprofit executives and staff, non-profit board members, donors, foundation executives and staff, foundation board members, and other stakeholders. This broader set of data has added depth and richness to our Drucker-inspired approach.

We do so hope that you, our readers, can learn from our thinking and writing. We expect and invite all of you to challenge, or even disagree, with our findings and conclusions. And we hope you will interact with our website, engineofimpact.org. Our primary goal as authors is to lend insight and energy to the vital and essential discussion of what drives maximum impact from nonprofit organizations. While we are no Peter Drucker, we aspire to have our thinking contain at least some of the durability and impact that his thinking has had.

As you will see, we believe that the nonprofit sector has a large and distinctive role to play if we are to reach our highest goals for society. To make it happen, those in the sector need a common language, a new way of thinking, and a clear approach—not the Tower of Babel that exists today. Strategic leadership is the dynamic vehicle for meeting those needs. Turn the page and let us show you how.

Strategic Leadership in the Impact Era

We are at the dawn of a new era—the Impact Era—in which nonprofits will play an ever more vital role in supporting, safeguarding, and sustaining American civil society. All of us—nonprofit executives, philanthropists, grant makers, board members, and everyday donors and citizens—must answer a question that is fundamental to our collective future: do we want a robust, high-performing nonprofit sector, or don't we? If the answer is yes, then we must move forward boldly. We must adopt the kind of transformational leadership that typifies our most ambitious philanthropists and social entrepreneurs. We must direct an ever-greater share of our national wealth transfer toward nonprofits that will bring a rigorous focus on impact to the use of these resources.

Much is at stake as we enter the Impact Era. Indeed, given the centrality of the nonprofit sector to American life, the stakes of this shift could not be higher. In the United States, nonprofit and other civil society organizations fulfill needs that in most other countries are met by government or families—or not at all. Nonprofits, for instance, provide approximately 70 percent of all inpatient community-hospital care, and they serve about 30 percent of all students enrolled in four-year collegiate institutions or in postbaccalaureate programs.[1] (Most US postsecondary students, of course, attend public institutions of one kind or another.) In addition, nonprofits account for a large portion of the cultural programming provided by museums, theaters, and various performing arts groups. Moreover, even as US politics become ever more strident and divisive, Americans still come together to donate their money and time to charitable organizations that provide a range of essential human services, including foster care for children in need; support for the hungry, the homeless, and the disabled; nursing-home services for the elderly; and more.[2]

Americans even allow (with only modest public debate) tax deductions for personal contributions to any of the more than one million nonprofits designated by the Internal Revenue Service (IRS) as 501(c)(3) organizations. They support independent schools, universities, and arts organizations through both ongoing donations and endowment contributions. They work through charities to act on their deeply held values, and they give tithes and time to religious organizations ranging from the traditional—Jewish, Christian, Muslim, Buddhist—to the harder to categorize. Whatever their many differences, Americans still find common ground in their support of a highly diverse nonprofit sector.

The French political commentator Alexis de Tocqueville famously observed that "Americans of all ages, all stations in life, and all types of disposition are forever forming associations. There are not only commercial and industrial associations in which all take part, but others of a thousand different types—religious, moral, serious, futile, very general and very limited, immensely large and very minute."[3] Tocqueville made his observation in the 1830s during his epic, seven-thousand-mile journey across the young United States and recorded it in his classic work *Democracy in America.* "At the head of any new undertaking, where in France you would find the government or in England some territorial magnate, in the United States you are sure to find an association," he wrote.[4] Although nearly two centuries have passed, and our nation has changed immeasurably, his description of American civil society continues to ring remarkably true.

The United States has the world's largest nonprofit sector, with more than $1.7 trillion in total revenue—a figure that is equivalent to approximately 10 percent of US gross domestic product (GDP).[5] Further, US charities are more dependent on philanthropy than are similar organizations in other developed economies: from 1995 to 2000, philanthropy accounted for 13 percent of revenue for charitable organizations in the United States, compared with 9 percent in the United Kingdom, 3 percent in Germany, and 3 percent in Japan.[6] Often forgotten is that the US nonprofit sector is a major instrument of government for the delivery of social and other services. Many nonprofits, in fact, provide their services as contractors of government and require government grants and fees to survive; the relationship is frequently one of mutual dependency and benefit.

In truth, for all its importance, the charitable sector might best be characterized as the impoverished stepchild of business and government. It remains chronically underfunded, relies extensively and consistently on voluntary gifts of time and money—inconstant though such gifts often are—and delivers services that benefit society overall but whose natural supporters are disparate and unorganized.

Equally troubling, one of the foundational elements of American civil society—the willingness to form and maintain an association to tackle a shared interest or goal—may be at risk. This trend was articulated by Robert D. Putnam in his 2000 book *Bowling Alone: The Collapse and Revival of American Community*.[7] Putnam argued that Americans took part less often in social activities and volunteer work, voted less frequently, and were less likely to join labor unions, churches, parent-teacher associations, and fraternal, civic, women's organizations—and even bowling leagues!—than in the past. With fewer social ties and associations, Putnam suggested, many positive aspects of American life may be lost; even the performance of representative government, which is highly dependent on the norms and networks of civic engagement, could be affected. Eleanor Brown and James M. Ferris used data collected by Putnam and found that people who are engaged with congregations, alma maters, clubs, or other groups do, in fact, give more than those who are not.[8]

At the same time, Americans are on the cusp of the greatest transfer of wealth in history, with baby boomers—who are beginning to ponder the great white light in the lessening distance—taking the lead in that process. Between 2007 and 2061, according to one scenario in a recent study, the baseline amount of charitable giving for US households will come to about $19 trillion. Yet beyond that amount, according to the study, $59 trillion will transfer from households to a variety of entities either when wealth holders pass away or while they are still living. Slightly less than $7 trillion of that total will go toward estate taxes and estate fees. But charitable gifts, bequests to heirs (who in turn will direct some portion of those bequests to charitable causes), and other transfers during wealth holders' lifetime will account for the remainder.[9] The scale, timing, and focus of the portion that goes to philanthropy are still very unclear and subject to influence—which is one of our reasons for writing this book, and for writing it now.

Never in American history have the challenges posed to civil society been more striking. Never before has the potential of civil society organizations to create impact been greater. That twofold reality helps to define the contours of the Impact Era. It is our aim in this book to offer a plan of action that will help ensure that the nonprofit sector—the most *American* aspect of American civil society—will earn the right to expand its role and maximize its impact during this new era. Citizens working together in common purpose to provide for their community is one of the most essential elements for continuing a vibrant, diverse democracy, even more so as it seems to grow more divisive.

An Exceptional History

Much of what we still view as the essential infrastructure of the non-profit sector arose from uniquely American responses to the conditions of other eras, beginning when the titans of the Industrial Revolution turned their focus to society's broader needs.

THE INDUSTRIALIST ERA (1880S TO 1930S): THE SECTOR EMERGES

Civil society and the nonprofit sector in the United States have deep and long roots. Going back to the early nineteenth century, voluntary associations formed to oppose slavery and support abolition.[10] The esteemed statesman and escaped slave Frederick Douglass was a key leader of one such group. Later, women's associations formed to support suffrage, culture, and educational activity. The pioneering equal rights crusaders Susan B. Anthony and Elizabeth Cady Stanton founded one such association.

The US nonprofit sector as we know it today began to emerge in law and structure in the waning years of the Industrial Revolution. The first national law mentioning specific financial benefits for associations undertaking the work of social improvement was the Wilson-Gorman Tariff Act of 1894, which includes the earliest tax exemption in US statutes. However, this legislation was preceded by state laws, and a legal framework for tax-exempt organizations was in place in many states by the mid-nineteenth century.[11]

In the late nineteenth and early twentieth centuries the major wealth holders were Gilded Age industrialists like Andrew Carnegie and John D. Rockefeller, each of whom accumulated private wealth on a scale theretofore unknown outside royalty. Carnegie created the first of three foundations in 1905, and Rockefeller followed with his own foundation in 1913. Carnegie's writings, including his book *The Gospel of Wealth*, also provided some of the philosophical and pragmatic rationale for philanthropy and for the creation of a robust civil society.[12]

Privately endowed foundations were also created by other important, if less well-known, philanthropists. Margaret Olivia Sage inherited a fortune from her husband, the financier Russell Sage, in 1906. She immediately began giving it away and established the Russell Sage Foundation, dedicated to "the improvement of the social and living conditions in the United States."[13] Julius Rosenwald, who owned part of Sears, Roebuck & Company, celebrated his fiftieth birthday by giving away $700,000 and encouraging others to "give while you live."[14] He befriended the famed black educator Booker T. Washington, whom he credited for helping "his own race to attain the high art of self-help and self-dependence" and "the white race to learn that opportunity and obligation go hand in hand, and that there is no enduring superiority save that which comes as the result of serving."[15] Rosenwald founded a foundation (the Rosenwald Fund) that was designed to spend down all its money within twenty-five years of his death, and he was thus the first American philanthropist of note to require that his wealth be used for current needs, not banked for perpetuity.[16]

Also during this period, charitable organizations began to receive special treatment for their fund-raising efforts. The Revenue Act of 1913 established an income tax and exempted certain types of income earned by charitable organizations. Legislation since then has added tax deductions for gifts to charity by individuals (1917) and corporations (1936). The current structure of Section 501(c)(3) of the Internal Revenue Code dates to the Revenue Act of 1954. The IRS has responsibility for the review and approval of new applicant organizations, the compilation of data, and regular reporting (since 1985) for exempt organizations.[17]

Through two world wars, the Depression, and the growth of the US role in international affairs, donors of all kinds emerged—from young children collecting pennies for UNICEF to major grant makers such as the Ford Foundation. Charitable giving represented approximately 2 percent of US GDP,[18] funding activities from the congressionally chartered American Red Cross to grassroots groups like parent-teacher associations. National entities such as United Way (founded in 1887) and the March of Dimes (founded in 1938) formed affiliates or chapters and so built both national and local initiatives for fund raising and for supporting the needs of people in communities.[19]

THE INDEPENDENCE ERA (1960S TO 1980S):
THE SECTOR IS DEFINED

The 1960s and 1970s were a tumultuous period in American history, one that saw an overall decline in confidence in most institutions; this trend was so pronounced that social scientists gave it a name—the "confidence gap."[20] Charitable giving fell in parallel with confidence, declining to less than 2 percent of GDP,[21] and vociferous debates over tax laws included proposals to eliminate the charitable deduction. Private foundations also faced criticisms about their grant making and governance.[22]

In response to the growing criticism of private philanthropy, John D. Rockefeller III recommended the creation of a blue-ribbon panel to investigate and elucidate the role of private giving. With funding from Rockefeller and others, the Commission on Private Philanthropy and Public Needs was formed in 1973. It included foundation executives, scholars, and leaders from influential nonprofit organizations such as United Way of America, Metropolitan Museum of Art, and Boy Scouts of America and was headed by Aetna Life & Casualty chairman John H. Filer.[23] The Filer Commission, as it became known, compiled findings from more than eighty research projects and issued a report that defined the voluntary (aka philanthropic or charitable) sector as a "third" sector of American society, one distinct from both government and business—an independent sector. It defended the tax deduction for charitable contributions and noted that private support was "a fundamental underpinning for hundreds of thousands of institutions and organizations."[24] Such support, said the report, "is the ingredient that keeps private nonprofit organizations alive and private, keeps them from withering away or becoming mere adjuncts of government."[25] Importantly, the Filer Commission's report also helped stave off political intrusion into private philanthropy.

However, critics of the Filer Commission, which included some representatives of charitable organizations, argued that the commission had focused too narrowly on tax policy and the role of government in funding charitable organizations. They sought to explore larger issues that encompassed the desired societal impact of philanthropic investments. From these concerns arose the National Committee for Responsive Philanthropy (which Rockefeller also funded in its earliest stages).[26] Another outgrowth of the Filer Commission and its report was the 1980 founding of Independent Sector, which resulted from a merger of the Coalition of National Voluntary Organizations and the National Council on Philanthropy.[27] One of the new organization's first acts was to widen the tent of the sector by including religious organizations. Because the majority of Americans then participated in religious activities on a weekly basis, this move served to immediately enlarge the independent sector in terms of organizations, finances, and participants. Over time, many of these congregants began to look for accountability from their churches in regard to offerings, expenditures, and even outcomes that were consistent with what they sought in other charities.[28]

Sociologists and other scholars had begun to research various aspects of volunteering and giving even before the Filer Commission; in 1971 the Association of Voluntary Action Scholars was formed to share its members' findings. (It later became the Association for Research on Nonprofit Organizations and Voluntary Action, or ARNOVA.) Universities also established academic programs dedicated to the study of the independent sector. Universities first added managerial training and more recently added social science research to test nonprofit work for its level of impact. In the 1970s, major American universities such as Stanford and Yale initiated research and teaching programs focused wholly or in part on nonprofits and foundations; Case Western, Duke, Harvard, Indiana, and others followed later. Today, there are more than three hundred universities with organized programs that study nonprofits and foundations.

THE INFORMATION ERA (1990S TO 2010S): THE SECTOR EMBRACES FACT-BASED DECISION MAKING

The IRS began collecting data about nonprofits on the IRS Form 990—"Return of Organization Exempt from Income Tax"—for the 1941 tax year. The two-page form included three yes-or-no questions, a request for an income statement and balance sheet, and, in some cases, attached schedules.[29] The Tax Reform Act of 1969 required all types of charities except congregations and other qualified religious groups to submit the Form 990.[30] However, although the data were collected, once the paper forms were returned to the IRS, they received little or no scrutiny and were simply stored away. To conduct a financial analysis of a single nonprofit, much less to compare several nonprofits, was thus an extremely challenging endeavor that was rarely undertaken, except at the wealthiest foundations. This situation remained more or less the same for decades. Indeed, even as the Internet revolution was under way in the 1990s, many nonprofits continued to generate paper-based information that they stashed away in internal filing systems.[31] Only a few foundations had the financial means and the staff to collect and analyze the data on nonprofit performance. The typical donor or analyst had little objective data to use in making judgments about which nonprofits were more effective or efficient.

But then, as the Internet took hold, it transformed data storage, information sharing, and communications. It also transformed people's expectations, and the situation began to change rapidly. By 2000, it was possible to affordably share massive amounts of nonprofit data that could then be analyzed. And, like the Industrial Revolution a century before, this new era bred a generation of business leaders who sought more than financial success. Like their predecessors— Ford with the assembly line or Carnegie with vertical integration[32]— entrepreneurs who had made their fortunes in technology eagerly applied new methods to a variety of endeavors. The tech entrepreneurs, spawned in the world of start-ups and venture capital, brought a mind-set of "we are new, different; about the future, not the past" that in many ways is still with us today.

One of the seminal leaders of the Information Era was Arthur "Buzz" Schmidt, the founder of GuideStar, which today is the preeminent source of data on nonprofits (with eight million unique users in 2016).[33] Back in the early 1990s, Schmidt, then an executive at the development organization TechnoServe, observed that the nonprofit sector lacked even the most basic data to support informed and intelligent decision making. "There was no information base to help [nonprofits] become more sophisticated, more dedicated, or more accountable in what they do," Schmidt explained.[34] To begin remedying this, he determined to digitize the Form 990, which by then had become considerably longer and included valuable information. By 1999, GuideStar facilitated public access to PDF copies of the IRS Form 990 for more than two hundred thousand charities.[35] While its work has expanded since then, the organization remains focused on facilitating access to critical information about nonprofit organizations. As of 2016, GuideStar's mission is "to revolutionize philanthropy by providing information that advances transparency, enables users to make better decisions, and encourages charitable giving,"[36] and its strategic plan for 2014–2016 rests on the three pillars of data innovation, data collection, and data distribution.[37]

In addition to GuideStar, the Information Era saw the birth of Network for Good, which enabled users to make online donations to any nonprofit, and VolunteerMatch, which made finding volunteers and volunteer opportunities easier. Later came Charity Navigator, which grew into a popular and widely used guide for assessing non-profits—although its overreliance on ratios and efficiency remains controversial. Still, beyond this small set of organizations, the Information Era produced few other efforts of any scale or impact.

Metaphors and practices from the start-up and venture capital community began to enter the nonprofit sector, with calls for active engagement, innovation, transparency, and accountability. The idea of venture philanthropy took hold following the 1997 publication of "Virtuous Capital: What Foundations Can Learn from Venture Capitalists" in *Harvard Business Review*.[38] Advocates for venture philanthropy—like Mario Morino, a tech entrepreneur and a cofounder of Venture Philanthropy Partners—wanted to see the nonprofit sector adapt strategic management practices used by business in order to achieve a higher rate of social return on their investments.

There were many other attempts to leverage the Internet to propel the nonprofit sector to new heights. But none made much headway. Charitableway.com, for example, a for-profit, start-up version of the nonprofit Network for Good, burned through many millions of dollars in venture capital before spectacularly flaming out. And while it spawned several imitators that shared its aim of doing well by doing good (i.e., making a profit from online donations), almost all are now long lost to history.

Ultimately, the Information Era had less impact on the decision making and other behaviors of stakeholders in the nonprofit sector than some of us had hoped and expected. Venture philanthropy, for example, turned out to be a powerful metaphor, but it has had limited application because of the lack of a robust social capital market that could provide continuing funding for high-impact organizations and drain lesser ones. In the Silicon Valley model, start-ups are spurred by new technologies and experience hypergrowth through the creative destruction of slow-to-adapt, mature, and more costly existing businesses. But the nonprofit sector still lacks the measurement, transparency, incentives, and capital sources to support such creative destruction. Small, low-impact organizations linger; traditional nonprofits that deliver essential services struggle annually to gain funding. And some days it seems that any young, attractive social entrepreneur with an apparently fresh, if untested, idea for a social venture finds favor. Venture philanthropy remains active today, embodied in close to forty organizations around the world that carry some form of the label "social venture partners," and the movement continues to serve its original and most impactful purpose: to attract young business leaders to philanthropy.

Much of venture philanthropy's momentum is being subsumed today by the impact investing movement, which extends the possibility of social impact to private investment. On its face, leveraging private capital for social impact is a fabulous idea—or, more precisely, a fabulous set of ideas. But even more so than venture philanthropy, the impact investing movement has filled its very big tent with sources of capital, hopeful recipients, and pundits who have varying, sometimes different, and even competing mind-sets. While we applaud the efforts by respected thinkers like Antony Bugg-Levine, Paul Brest, Sir Ronald Cohen, Pierre Omidyar, and Matt Bannick to offer a much more focused definition of "impact investing," we see little impetus for the movement to yield to a single definition. And now that private banks and other investment firms have grabbed hold of impact investing, we can confidently predict that the scale of investment in this category will grow. Controversially, we are very uncertain about the incremental social impact of such investment.

Indeed, perhaps the most lasting impact of the Information Era has been in the increased engagement that many people, particularly philanthropists, are bringing to the social sector. While venture philanthropy in retrospect was more a metaphor than a movement, it did provide a new generation of business leaders with a way to engage in civil society that seemed new and distinctive, and that they felt belonged to them. In many ways, this reconnection of business leaders and civil society dates to 1980, when Bill Drayton launched Ashoka, and with it the pervasive global movement known as "social entrepreneurship"—the first major effort to apply the principles of entrepreneurship to social change.

We have learned many essential lessons from the Information Era, above all that starting, leading, evaluating, and changing nonprofit organizations can be very hard and will not yield to the first instincts of the well-intentioned, however talented or energetic they may be.

THE IMPACT ERA (2000S TO THE PRESENT):
THE SECTOR RECKONS WITH NEW CHALLENGES

In the current era, leaders in the social sector have an opportunity—indeed, an imperative—to build on their predecessors' work to achieve ever-greater impact. However, to ensure that the Impact Era will succeed where the Information Era fell short, they must step back, assess the lessons they have learned, and apply those lessons in a pragmatic, persistent, and patient way.

First, although information is now plentiful, donors still lack access to useful impact evaluation data. Nonprofits still rarely use rigorous, fact-based evaluation as the basis for decision making, and they share evaluation data even less often. Donors then default to a friendly recommendation, their own intuition, or deceptive measures of efficiency. Charity Navigator is almost certainly the most popular online source of nonprofit evaluation, but its ratings are largely driven by expense ratios (yes, still)—even though sloppiness or inattentiveness to costs is only a relatively small limitation to impact in the sector. Of course costs count, but credible measures of impact are what matter first and foremost.

Second, donors still give mostly in emotional response to a fundraising request. Strategic philanthropy, based on in-depth impact evaluations, affects only a few discussions rather than most decisions. And those nonprofits that have development or fund-raising departments focused on large gifts and major donors—a select group that includes museums, universities and colleges, high-end performing arts organizations, and hospitals—are already able to attract significant donations. Meanwhile, most nonprofits serving the neediest people in society struggle to raise major gifts. Recognition, rather than impact, is the coin of the development realm.

Third, foundations remain stuck in a "do as we say, not as we do" mode. They demand transparency but share little. They assert the need for impact-based decisions but fail to take the lead by sharing their extensive evaluations of individual nonprofits and of underlying needs. To be sure, organizations such as the Center for Effective Philanthropy, the National Committee for Responsive Philanthropy (through its Philamplify initiative), and the Foundation Center (through its Glasspockets initiative) have undertaken efforts to gather and share foundation data. But on the whole, foundations have minimal incentive or limited means to disclose anything other than the names of board members, asset portfolios, and grantee names and amounts.[39]

Fourth, funders have still to address the chronic need for sustained operational support. They often seek to fund specific programs that fit their areas of interests. In response, nonprofits present programs that appear to match those areas, perhaps creeping away from their core mission in doing so, and are often left to plead for funding to cover day-to-day operations as overhead. And many younger funders today prefer policy advocacy, innovation, or impact investing, leaving nonprofits that focus on service delivery struggling to fund their core mission.

Fifth, the leadership practices of nonprofit boards remain ineffective. Few boards seek to learn and apply best practices or hold themselves to high standards. Given that government oversight of nonprofits remains essentially limited to cases of outright fraud, effective board governance is a sine qua non for any nonprofit organization, and yet it continues to be the exception.

Sixth, significant differences in performance remain among nonprofit organizations, but the social capital market (i.e., the financial flows from all sources into the sector) does not yet reward high performers or withhold resources from lower performers. Nonprofits often compete in markets dominated by market failure. Consequently, increasing scale and impact often results in worse economics instead of better, thus increasing the need for philanthropy and lessening the reliance on earned revenue. Because most nonprofits are effectively subsidized by donations, subscale and less-skilled organizations can linger, making the economics less attractive for stronger nonprofits. New entrants can hurt even high-impact nonprofits, as can competing subscale organizations that have managed to develop a philanthropic funding base.

Seventh, the sector's sense of timing and the probability of success have been off. A venture-funded business start-up is expected to provide returns to its investors in, say, five to seven years, or longer—and, as a rule of thumb, only one out of every ten start-ups is expected to account for virtually all of an investor's return, whereas the other nine will end in death or mediocrity. But in social entrepreneurship, decades may pass before an organization delivers consistent impact or even defines what its impact is. Efforts to instigate social change or provide an important social service, meanwhile, often take decades to become fully effective.

The Need for Increased Philanthropy

Underlying all of these lessons is another insight regarding the course that nonprofit organizations will follow in the Impact Era: in brief, they will need more money, and lots of it.

Let's recall the basic dimensions of the US nonprofit sector. In total, the sector brings in somewhat more than $1.7 trillion in total revenue.[40] That total exceeds the value added by several major US industries, including information technology and communications ($983 billion), retail trade ($969 billion), and banking ($730 billion).[41] In aggregate, meanwhile, donations account for 13 percent of nonprofit revenue. Different subsectors rely on donations to different extents. Health care—mostly hospitals—is the largest subsector in dollar terms but differs from most other subsectors in its economics: hospital revenue is roughly half of the nonprofit, charitable sector total. (About 70 percent of inpatient days occur at not-for-profit hospitals.)[42] These hospitals in aggregate receive only a small portion of their revenue as donations because private insurance payments and government programs, including Medicare and Medicaid, allow earned revenues to provide a relatively strong financial base. Every other nonprofit subsector needs more than the aggregate average of 13 percent from donations: the next two largest subsectors, education and human services, require 16 percent and 21 percent, respectively.[43] The remaining subsectors—international affairs, arts and culture, environment, and religious congregations—rely on philanthropy as their largest source of financial support, ranging from 44 percent for arts to 80 percent for religious congregations.[44]

Our starting point for calling for more philanthropy—for levels of giving that significantly outpace growth in the sector itself, including growth of other revenue sources—is a problem generally known as the "nonprofit starvation cycle."[45] At its root is a usually implicit, sometimes explicit, lack of trust that nonprofits will spend and invest money well. So funders chronically give them less support than they need, and they endure a hand-to-mouth existence that forces them to adopt a short-term focus and to "cry poor" year after year while also stifling their appetite to try new things. This is hardly appropriate for organizations that exist to serve their communities.

There is nothing new about this starvation cycle. The most cogent summary is offered in "The Nonprofit Starvation Cycle," an article by Ann Goggins Gregory and Don Howard, who cite "funders' unrealistic expectations," "underfed overhead," and "misleading reporting" as the driving factors in this cycle.[46] Whatever the root causes, the solution is more generous and more flexible funding by foundations and individuals.

Despite much talk, there has been little progress in addressing those root causes: nonprofits still encounter significant reluctance to fund ongoing operating costs, or the costs of impact evaluation and basic infrastructure. In recent years, as more funders have demanded impact evaluation to demonstrate that interventions are effective, nonprofits have found themselves stuck in a chicken-and-egg situation.

Many funders demand impact data but will not fund the often extensive research that is required to provide such data.

Perhaps the most widely debated aspect of the starvation cycle is overhead. In summary, many nonprofits' financial and accounting systems don't provide accurate data on overhead costs; ironically, given that many foundations provide support only to fund programs, nonprofits have an incentive to allocate those costs to specific programs. Even with an overhead rate of 20 percent, funders often end up failing to cover a nonprofit's overhead costs—either because those costs are simply higher than 20 percent or because some donors restrict their gifts to specific types of costs. The negotiation between grantees and grant makers on this issue seems to have become intractable. The starvation cycle has a certain rationality to it: funders, not confident that they know which (if any) organizations are effective at achieving impact, hold back from funding grantees' full operational needs, perhaps on the assumption that this approach will somehow make the grantees more focused and more disciplined.[47]

In addition to the sectorwide starvation cycle, specific nonprofit subsectors suffer structural financial challenges, as William J. Baumol and William G. Bowen noted as early as 1966.[48] Think of a live orchestra performance: because an orchestra is unable to leverage significant economies of scale—it can sell only so many seats, its costs are largely fixed, and technology has provided no solution—there is no way to increase the productivity of its musicians. As a consequence, major US symphony orchestras, and many other performing arts organizations, have a negative contribution and operating margin—the more performances they play, the more money they lose. The future is clear: such organizations will require more philanthropy.

Funders have been pushing for financial sustainability for the past fifteen to twenty years; in essence, this is a call for more earned revenue. In some cases, when a nonprofit has something of value and a customer base that can pay for that product or service, financial sustainability can be an important part of the solution. GuideStar, for example, originated as a quintessential public good; as of 1996, it derived just 1 percent of its revenue from fees. But since 2010, earned revenue—most of which comes from user fees for premium tools, bulk data licensing, and custom data analysis—has accounted for roughly 85 percent of its total expenditures.[49] *Stanford Social Innovation Review*, similarly, generated between 35 percent and 45 percent of its budget from earned revenue in the years from 2004–2010. More recently, however, it earned nearly 100 percent of its revenue from subscriptions and other nonphilanthropic sources.[50]

But, by their very definition, many nonprofits provide most or all of their services to people who are in no position to pay. Pressure for earned revenue, moreover, is likely to lead to mission-distracting activities. At the same time, financial sustainability can cause short-termism and restrict an organization's ability to scale. Look at what has happened to retail banking and retailing companies over the past twenty years: growth, scaling to the national level, leveraging technology. Meanwhile, most US nonprofits that deliver social services remain either local or stuck in a sub-optimal national federation that lacks the investment capital and organizational incentives that only funders could provide—either by modernizing what exists or by supporting the creative destruction process by withdrawing funding from the old model and funding new ones to discover one that leverages technology and new value models.

How much funding will the US nonprofit sector need if it is to remain a robust, sustainable, and essential contributor to civil society? And will philanthropic or other funding match that need? We have conducted an extensive scenario analysis that takes into account multiple factors that will affect the future financial needs of the sector, including costs associated with likely demographic changes (e.g., seniors' steadily growing share of the population), subsector-specific cost changes, and the potential for increased spending to cover unmet societal needs in the United States and abroad. Our analysis also takes into account the growth in giving that might result from decisions by Giving Pledge signers and other high-net-worth individuals. (The Giving Pledge suggests that signers donate "a majority" of their wealth to philanthropic efforts. But we wonder why 90 percent is not a better target all around. Giving at that level would provide valuable resources to communities, and it would still leave a healthy amount for the givers' kids!) We modeled various increases in foundation annual grant payouts and various rates of return on investments, as well as various changes in subsector-specific revenue (including shifts in government funding and earned revenue).

Our major conclusion: by 2025, philanthropic donors are on track to contribute between $500 billion and $600 billion annually to the nonprofit sector. (The total for 2015 was $373 billion.)[51] In addition, because of growing needs among those who benefit from nonprofit services, as well as urgent needs that remain unmet now, we predict that the nonprofit sector will require between $100 billion and $300 billion annually beyond what it can expect to receive from known revenue sources. (We base this projection both on historical rates of change and on the demographic and cost factors that we discussed earlier.) We believe, therefore, that philanthropy on a scale that exceeds its historical growth rate is the only likely source of significant increased revenue to the sector. Those who think that government funding or earned revenue from insurance payments, admission charges, and so on will increase significantly—we certainly don't—can reduce this estimate accordingly.

Another conclusion: people in the social sector had better hope that investment returns will at least maintain their levels from the past couple of decades. If investment returns decline meaningfully in the future, perpetual foundations will struggle to meet their federally required 5 percent payout. Universities, museums, and other nonprofits that have grown accustomed to similar payout levels will also find that they face new challenges. Thus, even as the sector requires increased philanthropy, lower investment returns may exert downward pressure on levels of giving.

A Call to Action for the Impact Era: Strategic Leadership

To ensure that these hoped-for new levels of funding will achieve maximum impact, the nonprofit sector must embrace the essentials of *strategic leadership*.

The practice of strategic leadership involves not just doing good work but also doing that work in a highly intentional and highly effective way. The best way to explain this practice, we believe, is by comparing it to a high-performance engine (Figure 1). Like an engine, it consists of multiple components that each must function well in order to ensure that the mechanism as a whole will achieve its purpose. In the model that we have developed, strategic leadership in the nonprofit sector has seven essential components, and success in the sector depends on the ability to operate each component at a high level.

An *engine of impact*, as we call it, starts with the mission of an organization. That mission is the very air that people in the organization breathe as they do their work. The next essential component is strategy. Much like the compressor in a jet engine, a carefully honed strategy takes the "air" of mission and applies pressure to it;

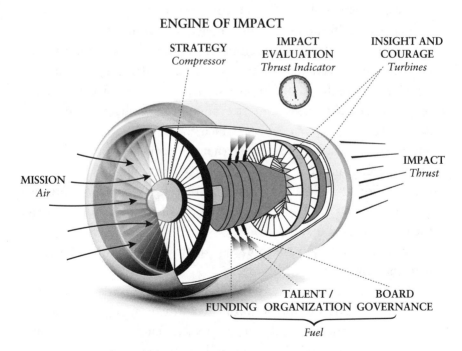

FIGURE 1 Engine of Impact: The components of strategic leadership
SOURCE: William F. Meehan III and Kim Starkey Jonker.

the result is an actionable set of goals that will govern the design and implementation of programs. Impact evaluation functions as the engine's thrust indicator—as a key instrument to gauge the performance of programmatic work. Impact evaluation allows an organization to compare its performance with its strategic goals, and, through a feedback loop, to adjust and refine its strategy (and on occasion its mission) over time. Helping to generate power for an engine of impact are the twin "turbines" of insight and courage. Those human qualities are what ultimately give an organization its dynamic force. To operate its engine of impact, meanwhile, an organization must draw on three varieties of fuel: well-managed talent and organization, sustained and sufficient funding, and effective board governance. When the engine works well, it creates thrust, or what we call impact.

Of course, the analogy between a nonprofit organization and an engine is inexact. But we offer this comparison to convey a vital truth: To make a significant and lasting impact, nonprofit leaders must engage with *all* of the essential components of strategic leadership in an integrated and comprehensive way. In particular, they must attain high levels of performance in both *strategic thinking* (which encompasses mission, strategy, impact evaluation, and insight and courage) and *strategic management* (which encompasses funding, talent and organization, and board governance). Strategic thinking pivots around a commitment to fact-based problem solving; it allows an organization to build and tune an effective engine of impact. Strategic management involves a keen-eyed focus on execution; it provides the fuel to propel that engine.

Strategic leadership, in short, equals strategic thinking plus strategic management.

Over the course of several decades, we have played virtually every role that exists in the nonprofit sector: executive, donor, grant maker, board member, adviser, even social entrepreneur. And we have been in active dialogue not only with many others who occupy those roles but also with an energetic community of thinkers, writers, speakers, teachers, and observers who work in universities or foundations, or within the sector itself. And on the basis of our extensive experience, we boldly proclaim that strategic leadership remains the most significant source of increased impact for the sector. Regardless of whether one is trying to maximize the impact of a traditional nonprofit or one that is highly innovative, greater impact begins and ends with strategic leadership.

We offer in this book what we believe to be a forward-looking synthesis of the best thinking and the best examples that relate to strategic leadership in the nonprofit sector. The core of the book is built on our own insights. But we have also tried to avoid being proprietary in a sector where virtually all intellectual property is held in common. So we draw freely on what we regard as the best thinking of others. Our goal is to inform and improve the ongoing, vigorous debate over how to maximize the impact of the nonprofit sector overall—and also to help all readers increase the impact of the non-profits in which they are engaged.

The basic structure of our book is straightforward.

Everything starts with mission. Chapter 1 posits that, despite that central principle, most nonprofits fail to start their strategic thinking process by ensuring that their mission is clear and focused. Having a focused mission statement is a critical tool for fighting "mission creep," which we believe pervades the nonprofit sector.

To achieve your mission and goals, you need a strategy. Strategy can seem like an arcane discipline that only management consultants and MBAs can understand. In Chapter 2, we describe—in a language accessible to all nonprofit leaders—the strategic concepts (such as theory of change) you need to build your engine of impact.

Rigorous impact evaluation provides critical feedback on whether an organization's strategy is working. Yet few topics provoke more intense debate than measuring and evaluating impact. In Chapter 3, we offer no simple answers, but we do show that approaches to impact measurement have advanced significantly. We then put forward specific ideas to move impact measurement and evaluation forward as a basis for decision making by nonprofit executives, board members, and philanthropists.

Even though we embrace fact-based analysis, we want to acknowledge that behind every high-impact nonprofit is a leader with exceptional human qualities, starting with insight and courage. This is the topic of Chapter 4. In fact, insight and courage are as essential as a focused mission, a clear strategy, and rigorous impact measurement to a nonprofit's ability to "earn the right" to seek philanthropic support.

While the first part of the book focuses on the components that you will need to build and tune your engine of impact, the second part of the book is all about fueling this engine. That simply isn't possible without talent, the subject of Chapter 5. Talent is a critical source of fuel for every organization, but talented people will thrive in an organization only if they have strong and responsive leadership. To this end, we recommend an organizational approach known as "team of teams." In this chapter, we also review several enduring principles that any high-performing nonprofit organization should follow.

Nonprofit leaders must recognize that if they want to save the world, they have to knock on doors and ask for money. In Chapter 6, we show you how the best fund raisers do it and argue strongly that building a strong major-donor function can provide essential fuel for human service, poverty alleviation, and other types of organizations that traditionally have allowed elite universities and high-end cultural institutions to monopolize that form of philanthropy.

Many in the sector sit on nonprofit boards—and find those boards to be ineffective in some important way. In Chapter 7, we show you how to build and sustain strong board governance. As a process shaped by the behaviors of individuals with varying skills, biases, and personalities, board governance follows no one formula. But an effective board does require leaders to engage more fully and demand more from one another, as well as from executive staff. This chapter provides lessons on how to initiate such engagement.

Along with building a well-tuned engine of impact, nonprofit leaders face another challenge: they must determine how far that engine can take them. They must ask, in other words, whether and how they can scale their organization. Many organizations try to scale too early, before they have "earned the right" to do so by building and

tuning their engine of impact. In Chapter 8, we offer a new managerial tool—one that draws on concepts discussed in the preceding
seven chapters—that will help nonprofit leaders assess their organization's readiness to scale.

The essentials of strategic leadership may seem uncontroversial.
Yet within the nonprofit sector, they remain subject to widespread
neglect. For this book, we conducted a survey—the 2016 Stanford
Survey on Leadership and Management in the Nonprofit Sector—that
drew nearly three thousand respondents. These respondents play a
wide variety of roles in the sector, and they represent virtually every
type of nonprofit. We asked them, "What do you think are the *top
challenges* facing the overall nonprofit sector as a whole today (not
just your own organization)?" In response, they indicated that the
top challenges are (in order of those most cited) "inadequate and/
or unreliable measurement/evaluation of organizations' impact and
performance," "weak or ineffective management," and "weak or
ineffective board governance."[52]

By their own admission, moreover, most social sector organizations struggle with at least one essential component of strategic
leadership. In our survey, about 80 percent of respondents indicated
that their organization faces significant challenges with one or more
of these essentials. We believe that an inability to master even one
component can prevent an organization from achieving its goals. The
chapters that follow serve as a guidebook for conquering such challenges. By using these chapters to help build, tune, and fuel their engine of impact, all social sector organizations can achieve the massive
and enduring impact to which they aspire and for which we hope.

PART I

Strategic Thinking

Build and Tune Your Engine of Impact

CHAPTER I

The Primacy of Mission

"A fish rots from the head down," says the ancient proverb. When it comes to nonprofits, the rot usually starts with a vague and unfocused mission. That's because nonprofits are, by definition, mission-driven organizations. The leaders of a typical corporation can assert that its primary purpose is "to maximize shareholder value." From that core purpose, any stakeholder can infer how the corporation's performance will be measured and how its leaders will frame strategic decisions and trade-offs.[1]

Nonprofits, however, lack such inherent clarity of purpose—and the market discipline that goes with it. They frequently have multiple stakeholders who have various, sometimes conflicting, perspectives and agendas that may change over time. A focused mission that is encapsulated in a clear and concise statement, therefore, is the foundation on which nonprofit organizations must build their strategy for achieving impact. A clear mission statement should serve to guide all major decisions that a nonprofit organization makes. These include inevitable trade-offs; sources of funding to seek; and which skills and leadership the organization needs in order to attract and retain its executive staff, board members, and even funders.[2]

The concept of mission has been applied to the nonprofit sector for more than a century. Indeed, the notion of accomplishing an organization's mission appears as early as an 1895 book of writings about Hull-House,[3] a settlement house cofounded in 1889 by Jane Addams (the first American woman to receive the Nobel Peace Prize, in 1931) to provide social and educational opportunities for working-class people. In the 1950s, the legendary Peter Drucker emphasized the importance of having a clear mission, a message he delivered throughout his career of more than fifty years as a management scholar. As Drucker asserted in his 1990 book, *Managing the Non-profit Organization: Principles and Practices*, "The first thing to talk about is what missions work and what missions don't work, and how to define the mission. . . . The first job of the leader is to think through and define the mission of the institution."[4]

But, despite the long history of applying the concept of mission to nonprofit organizations, the use of this essential tool suffers from widespread neglect throughout the sector. To date, there is no major study of the application of mission or the use of mission statements in this supposedly mission-driven sector. What evidence does exist reveals a mixed and confusing commitment to developing a strong mission statement.

In our 2016 Stanford survey, at least 75 percent of nonprofit executives and staff reported that their organization's mission statement was either "good," "very good," or "excellent," in terms of being "clear," "focused," "reflects what my organization does," and "reflects my organization's skills."[5] These data would be heartening if they didn't conflict so strongly with our own experience that most nonprofit mission statements don't guide stakeholder decisions or engagement. In 2014, as part of a webinar that we presented for *Stanford Social Innovation Review*, we surveyed participants from the social sector about their organization's mission statement. In a sample of more than one thousand registered participants—including nonprofit executives, staff, and board members—87 percent said that their organization's mission statement was not well crafted, 63 percent that it was unfocused, 59 percent that it was unclear, 87 percent that it was not memorable or sticky, and 76 percent that it was uninspiring.[6]

Over the past eighteen years, about one thousand students in Bill's course on strategic leadership of nonprofit organizations at the Stanford Graduate School of Business (Stanford GSB) have completed a session on organizational mission in which they are asked to choose a nonprofit of personal interest and analyze the effectiveness of its mission statement. They then interview a half dozen of the organization's stakeholders—executive staff, board members, donors, clients, and so forth—to evaluate how well the mission is known, understood, and actually applied. Each year, about three-quarters of these students determine that the mission statement they are evaluating lacks rudimentary clarity and is, moreover, so broad that even a large, resource-rich organization would struggle to accomplish all the activities it purports to undertake, let alone do them with excellence and impact.

A mission-driven organization should pursue its mission like a lodestar that will always keep it on course. It would therefore benefit many—perhaps most—nonprofit organizations to start any strategic planning effort with a review and assessment of their mission and their mission statement. A well-conceived mission statement that can guide an organization in making key decisions should do the following:

1. *Be focused.* Many nonprofit missions are too broad and unfocused, for instance, promising to end global poverty, bring about world peace, and feed all the world's hungry people when in fact the organization has resources only to grant a few hundred microloans, teach a few thousand children about nonviolent communication, or feed a few thousand people in one county.

2. *Solve unmet public needs.* Nonprofits exist to address needs that markets and governments can't or won't tackle, which is why they are accorded singular status, starting with their special tax category. Their missions should thus aim to address public—not private— needs that corporations, governments, and other nonprofits will not otherwise meet.

3. *Leverage distinctive skills.* The nonprofit sector tends to draw people who have passion and high aspirations. But, to make an impact, they also need to develop specific skills and capabilities that are tailored to achieve their mission in ways that other organizations cannot or do not achieve.

4. *Guide trade-offs.* Mission statements can help guide nonprofit leaders in deciding which initiatives and activities to pursue and which to abandon or avoid. Funding opportunities or new programs that are compelling but not aligned with their missions should be resolutely

declined; instead, challenges that will take their mission to the next level should be accepted, even if this is harder than taking on an incremental, less focused activity.

5. *Inspire and be inspired by key stakeholders.* Nonprofits generally have multiple stakeholders—board members, staff, clients or customers, governmental agencies, and the public at large—whose interests may conflict. A great mission statement should respect and reflect these stakeholders' diverse interests, even as it balances them and, in the best-case scenario, inspires them.

6. *Be timeless.* Change is inevitable—nonprofits will invariably need to reengage their stakeholders' understanding of and commitment to their mission every three to five years. But the best mission statements endure through periods of change—and they should be fundamentally altered only in truly exceptional situations. (Here let us note that we see nothing wrong with sunsetting a nonprofit whose mission has been achieved or that has discovered its intervention is not as impactful as it had hoped.)

7. *Be sticky.* Mission statements must be more than a motto and less than a summary of an organization's strategy. They should be long enough and comprehensive enough to provide real guidance for stakeholders. But they must also be compelling enough and short enough to be memorable—or "sticky," as the best-selling authors Chip Heath, professor at Stanford GSB, and Dan Heath, senior fellow at Duke University's Center for the Advancement of Social Entrepreneurship, so memorably phrased it.[7] The most memorable statements are short and concrete but can extend to three to four sentences when suitably sticky.

The Danger of Mission Creep

Breadth of mission, often accompanied by vagueness, is a prevalent virus in the nonprofit sector and the cause of its most severe chronic disease, commonly known as "mission creep."

Mission creep can stretch an organization so thin and so wide that it is no longer able to effectively pursue its core goals—if, indeed, the organization's leaders can even remember what they are. In the private sector, it would seem preposterous for a company that creates specialty dark chocolate to jump into the medical device business or start manufacturing home furnishings. Yet nonprofits routinely extend themselves in equivalent ways—expanding their programs far beyond their core competencies—and no one raises an eyebrow.

Another factor contributing to mission creep is the misguided belief that broad and vague missions are more inspiring than those that are specific and concrete. An example of a well-intentioned but overly broad mission statement is this: "The mission of the Elks National Foundation is to help Elks build stronger communities."[8] Likewise, aspiring social entrepreneurs commonly assert that they plan to found an organization whose mission will be "to alleviate global poverty in our lifetime." While some—though not us—might argue that vagueness is more inspiring than concreteness, vagueness and its companion, breadth, are inarguably antithetical to focus, a core tenet of strategy. Indeed, when students in Bill's course conduct interviews at their chosen nonprofits, they often discover that many stakeholders do not even know their organization's mission, let alone understand or feel any degree of passion or personal commitment toward it.

The problem of mission creep is often caused or exacerbated by funders who insist on making grants to narrowly defined programs. This dynamic often causes nonprofits to shift their core activities beyond their preexisting area of focus in order to appear to fit a grant-making request for proposal (commonly known as an RFP). At the peer learning event we led in 2013 for recipients of the Henry R. Kravis Prize in Nonprofit Leadership, a prevailing theme was the importance of developing the capacity—and the courage—to say "no, thank you" to funders whose grants might foster that kind of mission creep.

If funders are generally to blame for the onset of mission creep, internal stakeholders are often complicit. Oley Dibba-Wadda, former executive director of the Forum for African Women Educationalists, offered a blunt description of such people during the Kravis Prize event. "I call them 'mission whores,' and they are at work within most organizations," she explained. "They are internal stakeholders of an organization who are willing to 'sell out' by excessively broadening the scope of the mission in order to obtain funding or other advantages."[9] Not every Kravis Prize recipient used such choice words, but most could cite instances in which a member of their organization had to lead a colleague away from the temptation of mission creep.

Focus Beats Diversification

In guarding against mission creep, it is critical that nonprofits shun the urge to diversify their program areas and activities. "Focus on your core competencies" has become a ubiquitous expression in the business world, but it took many decades plus hard data on financial returns to convince businesses to focus. The 1970s and early 1980s were the era of conglomerates (think ITT, Fortune Brands)—a time when industrial diversification was the name of the game. Companies that simultaneously ran hotels, produced sausages, sold insurance, and built dining-room tables were the darlings of Wall Street. Conglomerates claimed management skills and a lower cost of capital as advantages that enabled them to outcompete more focused companies.

But because public companies share a common and well-accepted performance measure—maximizing shareholder value—strategists, stock analysts, and finance professors could actually identify which companies' strategies performed best. And countless studies demonstrated that a strategy of focus beats diversification. Companies that performed best were those focused on a single business, or set of closely related businesses, in which their core competencies provided them with identifiable competitive advantage(s).

These well-settled findings from corporate strategy are useful starting points for nonprofits. In the nonprofit sector, organizations do not share a common performance measure, so data proving the greater effectiveness of focused organizations do not exist. However, some academic research that associates focus with efficiency—that is, with the percentage of funding going to programs—is compelling (even though we are the first to acknowledge that financial efficiency is not the most important metric on which nonprofits should be evaluated). For example, Geoffrey M. Kistruck, Israr Qureshi, and Paul W. Beamish analyzed panel data involving charitable organizations over a five-year period and found that the main relationship between product diversification (i.e., diversification in program activities) and efficiency is an inverted-U shape: "Charities that diversify into new related services experience some initial positive efficiencies at very low levels but then very quickly become more inefficient at increasingly unrelated levels."[10] This makes sense, in the same way that conglomerates typically have higher overhead than businesses with a single product or service.

We have heard most, if not all, of the arguments against focus and find none compelling. Take, for example, a funder that might offer a grant to "extend your organization's capabilities into a related activity." This, of course, is where your mission begins to creep—and you will get no sympathy from us when you have to face the consequences.

If anything, focus is more important for nonprofits than for businesses. When it comes to program activities, "more of the same" almost always trumps "more new kinds of programs." Most nonprofits are small and therefore highly limited in capacity; 93 percent of them have budgets of less than $1 million per year. Even the 15,500 largest nonprofit organizations (those with budgets of $10 million or more) are highly unlikely to have the skills, resources, or management to support more than one core strategy.[11]

Unfortunately, many nonprofit organizations today are unfocused, and diversification in the sector is far too common. Indeed, during the final decades of the twentieth century, charities experienced a large increase in the number of activities with which they became involved.[12] This has continued into the twenty-first century. In our 2016 Stanford survey, we asked nonprofit executives and staff, "Would you characterize your organization's program activities as focused or diversified?" and 37 percent responded that their organization was diversified to some degree. We also asked, "How focused or diversified do you think your organization's program activities *should* be?" and 24 percent indicated that program activities should be diversified to some degree.[13]

The National Court Appointed Special Advocates (CASA) Association is a rare example of an organization whose programmatic focus has remained tight even as it has scaled and grown across the United States over the past forty years. The CASA programs do one thing and have always done one thing, even as the association's network has expanded to forty-nine states and the District of Columbia: they provide support to efforts in which volunteers (and staff members in some instances) "are appointed by judges to watch over and advocate for abused and neglected children, to make sure they don't get lost in the overburdened legal and social service system or languish in inappropriate group or foster homes. Volunteers stay with each case until it is closed and the child is placed in a safe, permanent home."[14]

Over time, there have been numerous temptations to expand CASA programs into new activities that would be complementary but not necessarily core to the program. CASA has resisted those pressures. For example, because of its success creating and supporting a program of volunteer advocates for foster children, the National CASA Association has been approached to create analogous volunteer advocates programs for seniors, for juvenile delinquents not in foster care, and for the disabled.[15] Tara Perry, chief executive officer of the National CASA Association, reflected:

Some of these opportunities have been interesting, and even tempting at times, especially because funding for programs reaching children in foster care can be especially scarce. But we've resisted the pressures, and chosen not to chase the dollar. Instead, we are focused on the remaining unmet need within our niche. We are reaching 40 percent of America's foster children and youth who have experienced abuse or neglect, which is a large number, but we have much further to go. Recruiting, training, and supporting advocates for abused and neglected children before the court has been the core mission of our member programs from day one, and we will focus on that until the need is met.[16]

A Tale of Three Mission Statements

Landesa (formerly called the Rural Development Institute) is a high-performing nonprofit organization whose enduring success is rooted in its strong mission. The leaders of Landesa have spent half a century working with governments to secure land rights for the world's poorest; the organization has had an impact on more than four hundred million people in more than fifty countries.[17] It received the inaugural Kravis Prize in 2006, the Skoll Award for Social Entrepreneurship in 2012, and the Hilton Humanitarian Prize in 2015. Landesa's mission currently states: "Landesa champions and works to secure land rights for millions of the world's poorest, mostly rural, women and men to provide opportunity and promote social justice."[18] The focus and specificity of its mission statement have enabled Landesa to decline outside-of-focus projects and resist the allure of expanding into new issues and environments where it lacks necessary skills.

In 1998, for example, Landesa's leaders had the opportunity to take on an urban land rights project in the former Soviet Union that initially seemed compelling. Landesa's mission statement was worded a bit differently back then—"a nonprofit organization of attorneys helping the rural poor in developing countries to obtain legal rights to land"—but nonetheless focused on the same core mission of helping the poor obtain land rights. It was already working in the former Soviet Union on a grant that was about to expire, and the project would provide a stable new source of funding and enable it to continue using its expertise in Russian land law. These synergies were certainly attractive—except, of course, Landesa's mission explicitly stated that it helped "the rural poor" and the project was neither rural nor targeted at the poor.[19]

If Landesa accepted the project, its team would have to devote considerable time and energy to understanding urban land rights issues—which might ultimately cause the organization to stray from its specialization in promoting land rights for the rural poor. "There was so much work to be done in the rural setting," said Tim Hanstad, Landesa's executive director at the time (today Hanstad is a special adviser to Landesa). "In the end, we turned down the urban opportunity because we felt that it was outside of our mission. And we felt very strongly that on principle we shouldn't chase after funding that was not mission-focused."[20]

Looking back, Hanstad believes he and his colleagues made the right decision. Landesa eventually found other income sources, enabling the organization to remain focused on its mission and develop what Hanstad called "a strong presence in the former Soviet Union within our niche of rural land rights reform."[21] By the end of 2006, Landesa had helped governments provide legal land rights to poor rural families for more than 21.2 million acres of land in Russia, 2.9 million acres in Moldova, and nearly 69 million acres in Ukraine.[22]

Landesa's determination to stick to its mission has also helped it to maintain the motivation and clear decision-making criteria necessary for difficult undertakings. In 1999, for instance, Landesa's management team debated the merits of expanding operations into India, which had the world's greatest number of poor people and the world's highest concentration of landless, or nearly landless, rural households (sixty-two million households). Landlessness—even more than caste or illiteracy—was the greatest predictor of poverty in rural India, according to a 1997 World Bank report.[23] For these reasons, Hanstad and Roy Prosterman, Landesa's visionary founder, were greatly intrigued by the prospect of working in India. "It was the kind of opportunity that makes nonprofit leaders who aspire to make a difference absolutely starry-eyed," explained Hanstad.[24]

Yet this opportunity was also high risk. Landesa generally entered only those countries whose politicians were willing to develop and implement the organization's recommended initiatives. "The conventional wisdom in the 1980s and 1990s was that India had insufficient political will for land rights reform," explained Hanstad.[25] Moreover, Landesa did not have any funding earmarked for new operations in India, which was likely to be an expensive and challenging place to work. India did not possess just one central decision maker but had twenty-eight states, each with its own set of land tenure rules. This meant that Landesa would have to establish an office in India to coordinate work in multiple and frequently remote locales.

Further, some Landesa staff members were not enthusiastic about entering India. Landesa had never previously established an in-country office with its own funding, and some staff members feared that diverting funds to India would endanger their jobs. They advocated for focusing on less costly regions, such as the former Soviet countries, where there was "easy money" and where Landesa had an established presence. "It would have been a no-brainer to forget about India and stay in the former Soviet Union except for one major factor: We had already reached a point of diminishing returns in the former Soviet Union," said Hanstad. "India, on the other hand, was a vast, totally untapped market full of incredible need and potential."[26]

To tap that potential, however, would require Landesa to adapt its approach dramatically. In most other developing countries where Landesa had worked, it had aimed to provide the landless with "small farms," which in India would have meant an average of two acres for each landless family. Given the vast number of rural landless families in India, however, reaching all those families would require redistributing between 20 percent and 40 percent of the country's farmland—which was financially and politically impossible. To work in India, with its vast number of landless poor, Landesa would have to serve fewer people, decrease plot size per family, or redesign its approach in some other way.

After much deliberation, the management team made its decision: Landesa would reinvent its model and enter India. "Our mission is to secure land rights for the world's rural poor," explained Proster-man. "The sheer numbers of landless rural poor living in India meant that we simply could not avoid the country while staying true to our mission and our aspirations for impact."[27] To date, the program that Landesa created in India has been highly successful. Five Indian states have launched homestead allocation pilot programs with Landesa's assistance, and as a result more than 680,000 Indian families have become landowners.[28]

The American Museum of Natural History (AMNH) in New York City is another example of an organization whose mission statement propelled it to take on exciting (but mission-focused) new challenges. Established in 1869, this iconic institution is one of the largest museums in the world, with more than five million visitors per year. Its mission statement is both ambitious and inspiring: "To discover, interpret, and disseminate—through scientific research and education—knowledge about human cultures, the natural world, and the universe."[29]

This mission was front and center during discussions in 2004 and 2005, when, as part of its strategic planning process, the museum grappled with an unparalleled opportunity to take its emphasis on education to a new level by developing a PhD program in comparative biology. "This opportunity to grant PhDs seemed entirely consistent with the mission, but it was one that the board weighed carefully," commented AMNH president Ellen V. Futter.[30] If it pursued this path, AMNH would become the only stand-alone PhD-degree-granting museum in the Western Hemisphere, and an amendment of its charter would be required. The museum's leadership and board of trustees considered whether creating a PhD program would constitute mission creep or an opportunity to more deeply pursue the mission's focus on education.

Although AMNH was a museum and not a university, it had been supporting postdoctoral research and hosting visiting students from partner universities since 1908. Futter explained:

We already had a very porous set of walls between us and the academic community. We had been running a fairly large program for graduate and post-graduate students at the museum for many years, and we had relationships with several universities (such as Columbia, NYU, Cornell, etc.) for a while. . . . Consequently, we viewed the opportunity to create a graduate school as consistent with history and not a creep, just a formalized version of existing activities in ways that were reinforcing and enhancing other museum activity even outside the graduate program and research.[31]

In deciding to offer the PhD program, AMNH placed considerable emphasis on its assessment of the organization's core assets and on how to best leverage those assets. Futter explained: "In decision making, nonprofits need to explore what assets they have and what sort of objectives they're trying to reach for, and map back to those assets. The risk for any organization, of course, is to take on a hobby.

The way we ensured against that was by grounding our decision making in the surest asset we had, which was our intellectual core."[32]

In 2006, AMNH established the Richard Gilder Graduate School, which includes a PhD-granting program in comparative biology within the museum;[33] a master's program in science teaching was subsequently added. On September 30, 2013, at the inaugural commencement ceremony, President Futter said, "Today we celebrate not only the graduation of our very first doctoral and Master's candidates . . . but also a deeper and more profound integration of the Museum's twin missions of science and education."[34]

The Afghan Institute of Learning (AIL) provides a third example of how an organization can develop an effective mission statement. AIL has provided transformative education and health care to thirteen million people in Afghanistan and Pakistan since it was founded more than two decades ago, and it has achieved significant reductions in mortality rates for both infants and mothers in the areas where it operates. We worked with its dynamic and courageous founder and CEO, Dr. Sakena Yacoobi, at the 2013 peer learning retreat for Kravis Prize recipients, part of which was devoted to reviewing mission statements.[35] Yacoobi bravely volunteered to have AIL's mission statement critiqued first. The polite consensus was that AIL's mission statement was, well, excessively wordy. Indeed, it was a half-page long, and its usefulness was largely obstructed by the fact that donors, staffers, and other stakeholders couldn't remember it.

But the verbosity provided an opportunity to craft language that would be more focused and inspiring. We worked with AIL to develop a pithier mission statement: "to provide education, training, and health services to vulnerable Afghans in order to foster self-reliance, critical thinking skills, and community participation throughout Afghanistan and Pakistan."[36] Yacoobi took this draft mission statement back to her staff so they could provide input, iterate, and reach consensus. The final mission statement in use today has not diverged significantly in substance, and to our great relief it continues to be only one sentence![37]

That said, in "Great Mission, Bad Statement," Erica Mills, a writer and professor who teaches people "to use better words to create a better world," provided suggestions for further improving the AIL mission statement.[38] Mills emphasized that it is advantageous for nonprofits to "expand [their] linguistic repertoire" and to "use better verbs" in mission statements. She noted that research on novelty by Russell Poldrack, professor of psychology at Stanford, and others suggests that organizations can garner more attention by using words that other organizations don't. So, in the example of AIL's mission statement, Mills suggested replacing the verb *provide*, which is used by 68 percent of nonprofit websites, with the verb *better*, which appears on only 0.1 percent of nonprofit websites.[39]

The Exceptions That Prove the Rule

AIL is an example of a nonprofit that was able to have extraordinary impact despite a suboptimal mission statement. Discussion of this point led to a debate among Kravis Prize recipients as to whether AIL's commitment to provide both health care and education services is too unfocused. After all, there seems to be little synergy between those two areas, and effective execution in each area requires very different skill sets and core competencies. Dr. Madhav Chavan, cofounder of Pratham, explained why his organization restricts its focus to education. "Providing health care and feeding kids are not educational programs, so we leave those services to other organizations in India," he said.[40] But others, including Yacoobi, argued that a nonprofit is justified in taking a more holistic approach, especially if it works in a severely underresourced country such as Afghanistan and if the unmet needs are interrelated. "How can our students learn well if they are hungry or sick?" she asked. "In addition to these obvious 'here and now' considerations, education and health are linked over the long term. For example, a child born to a mother who can read is fifty percent more likely to survive past age five."[41]

This debate encapsulated a critical issue facing the sector: when is a holistic approach that spans multiple program areas appropriate, and when is it a threat to organizational focus? It is our view that the temptation to adopt a holistic approach to programs should be resisted in favor of focus. But there are exceptions to every rule, and some organizations effectively earn the right to be an exception. BRAC, for example, has gained a well-deserved reputation as a high-performing organization despite having a wide array of programs (in Bangladesh and ten other countries) that cover education, health care, microfinance, and even road safety.

Damon Runyon, a legendary American raconteur and writer, is credited with saying, "It may be that the race is not always to the swift, nor the battle to the strong—but that's the way to bet."[42] For almost every nonprofit, our principles apply. However, there are rare exceptions that prove the rule. We suggest that a nonprofit should consider four main factors when deciding whether it makes sense to pursue a more holistic approach.

1. *Inextricable linkages in unmet needs.* Every nonprofit must ask if the various needs that it seeks to address are both interrelated and inextricably linked. For example, if you are running an education program for severely impoverished children who are so hungry they cannot concentrate and learn, then the needs for education and for food could be viewed as inextricably linked; it might not be possible to provide a high-impact education program without also providing a free breakfast and lunch program.

2. *Relatedness, with overlapping core competencies.* Another core issue is whether the proposed program areas are not only related but also mutually reinforcing. Nonprofit leaders must be able to make the case that each program area makes other areas inherently and significantly stronger. Moreover, the skills and core competencies required to execute on each program must overlap in significant ways.

Major universities, for example, have been built on the notion that teaching and research are closely interrelated and mutually reinforcing. For example, Steven A. Denning, chair of the Stanford University Board of Trustees from 2012 to 2017, explained:

Stanford, like other elite American universities, has a dual mission of world-class research and excellent teaching. We believe strongly that each mission enriches the other. Being taught and advised by the very best teachers and researchers, whether in the humanities, engineering, sciences or social sciences, sets a standard for our undergraduates and graduate students, as well as exposing them to the latest thinking in their field. And many of our professors who are top in their field as researchers are also excellent teachers. They are motivated by the opportunity to push the frontier of their field as well as by the opportunity to translate what they know into their teaching and pass on their knowledge to the next generation.[43]

3. *Lack of other organizations that have better skills.* Another key consideration is whether your nonprofit is working in a severely underresourced geographic area where no other organization is willing and able to do the work of your intended programs. Does your organization have a distinctive skill or core competency in each program area that other organizations do not and cannot possess? If you lead an education nonprofit, please do not consider providing health-care services if there is already an effective health-care nonprofit working down the street!

4. *Extraordinary talent and unusually strong capacity to execute.* To justify highly disparate program areas, a nonprofit organization must possess extraordinary talent and an unusually strong ability to execute. Is your organization's founder or executive director of the same caliber as, say, BRAC founder Sir Fazle Hasan Abed? Does your organization have a "one in ten thousand" ability to perform at a high level even when it is spread thin across disparate program areas?

A focused mission can come with a price. "Once, when I tried to protect us from mission creep, I lost a multi-million-dollar funding opportunity," said Yacoobi of AIL. "That was significant for us, because our total budget is only $3 million. I said to the funder, 'I'm not going to do what you are telling me to do, since it is outside the scope of our mission. I am doing what our beneficiaries need me to do.' And I lost that funding."[44] The price of saying no can be very high—but smart nonprofit leaders understand that the cost of saying yes can be even higher.

Embracing Mission-Aligned Challenges

At the same time, nonprofit leaders must embrace new challenges that will take their mission to the next level—however daunting that move might seem. Many Kravis Prize recipients recalled instances in which they had accepted the opportunity to tackle an outsized challenge that was aligned with their mission. Making such decisions was never easy, but these leaders invariably saw those decisions as having enabled them to increase their impact dramatically. In such instances, pressure from funders can have a positive effect. Chavan provided an example of that dynamic. "We have many long-term donors who noted our success with elementary education but kept asking, 'What about vocational training? Wouldn't this complement Pratham's other programs?' Our management team came to realize that they were right—that we needed to launch vocational training services because it was part of the continuum of education and supported our mission," Chavan said.[45]

But, even in the process of making this major decision, Pratham never lost sight of its admirably brief and well-focused mission statement: "Every child in school and learning well."[46] Pratham had a compelling rationale for developing such wrap-around services as vocational training and children's-book publishing, and it was clear that these services would complement its learning programs for elementary school children. But it was also evident to all that these initiatives would exceed the scope of its mission statement.

This created a dilemma: Pratham needed a solution that would allow it to expand its services while at the same time adhering to its mission statement. It resolved the problem by creating two separate organizations, Pratham Books and the Pratham Institute for Literacy, Education & Vocational Training. A separate board was established for each organization, with Pratham functioning as a holding company for these distinct yet closely aligned entities. Each of the new organizations naturally had its own mission statement, carefully fashioned not only to incorporate its connection to Pratham's core mission but also to reflect its individual goals and to inspire everyone who hears the statement. That of Pratham Books, in particular, offers a classic example of what a well-crafted mission statement looks like: "A book in every child's hand."[47]

In very special cases, creating separate organizations that take the form of brand extensions (as they are called in the corporate world) can help a nonprofit to avoid mission creep even as it pursues new and appropriately aligned initiatives.

"Mission" Versus "Vision" and "Values"

Closely related to the topic of mission statements is the question of whether and when to create vision and values statements. With their provocative and important book *Built to Last*, Jim Collins and Jerry I. Porras set the standard for how companies should approach this question. Collins and Porras explained that "a visionary company articulate[s] a core ideology," which consists of a firm's basic values (its essential and enduring tenets) and its purpose (its fundamental reason for existing).[48]

A recent trend has emerged in which nonprofits develop separate statements explaining their mission, their vision, and their values. We, unsurprisingly, believe that mission must be primary. Our against-the-grain view is that nonprofit organizations should stop spending so much time on vision and values statements, and funders should stop requesting and expecting that nonprofits include such information in grant requests. A mission statement is critical for a nonprofit—but vision and values statements are not. When mission, vision, and values statements are all included in a single communication, stakeholders are apt to lose sight of what is most important.

A vision is exactly what it sounds like: a description of a desired end state. In the nonprofit sector, a mission statement and a separate vision statement are usually redundant: they use different words to say the same thing and are therefore potentially confusing. If you think that your organization's vision is an essential element of its mission, then include it in your mission statement. But for many nonprofits, it's not essential—and a statement of vision can even distract from the primacy of mission. A statement of values, meanwhile, can serve a very important internal function—for example, as part of a team-building exercise. But these days, the values of many organizations are similar, if not the same. We're all in favor of values like excellence, collaboration, diversity, and leadership. So why make a special point of it? That said, if you believe that a certain value helps define your organization, then put it in your mission statement.

The effort of trying to convey an organizational mission in one, two, three, or four sentences—in a way that is compelling to both internal and external stakeholders—is an excellent exercise. It forces you to consider the key underlying trade-offs and compromises that characterize your organization.

Mind Your Mission

A clear and focused mission statement is a necessary foundation for becoming a focused and effective organization—one that will never rot (unlike the proverbial fish) but instead will flourish for years to come.

But, no matter how well crafted it may be, a mission statement alone is not sufficient. "For the ultimate test is not the beauty of the mission statement," wrote Drucker. "The ultimate test is right action."[49] Those involved in a nonprofit should remember these immortal words. They should live and breathe their organization's mission statement and allow it to guide each step they take. They should use it to evaluate every opportunity and program area—to direct them toward actions that serve the mission away from those that do not. "Does this new opportunity align with our mission?" should be a question regularly heard at staff and board meetings.

Of course, there's a simple way to measure the extent to which an organization lives by its mission: just *ask* staff members and other stakeholders. Discuss the topics raised in this chapter on mission at your next staff retreat, or have someone at your organization put together a survey. (Quick, electronic surveys such as those provided through SurveyMonkey are relatively easy to execute these days and remain far too underutilized by nonprofit leaders as a tool to help them assess their organization's strengths and weaknesses.) Surveys can include questions such as the following: What is our organization's mission? Do you think our organization is staying focused on this mission? Would you characterize our organization's current programs and activities as broad or focused? Do you think we are experiencing mission creep? Should we alter our mission? If so, what do you believe our mission should be, and why?

A mission statement goes far beyond the creation of inspiring language to use in fund-raising materials or in the "About Us" section of a website. It is a critical but sorely underused directional and defensive tool that nonprofits must wield wisely and well. With a clear and focused mission statement—and a strategy to implement it—you will be on your way to achieving deep and far-reaching impact.[50]

CHAPTER 2

The Few Strategic Concepts
That Matter

Once it has an effective mission statement in place, every nonprofit must ensure that its strategy can and will enable it to achieve its mission. We define a nonprofit's strategy as a planned set of actions that are designed to achieve its mission. By contrast, the strategy of a for-profit business is a planned set of actions that aim to maximize shareholder value by achieving sustainable competitive advantage.

Fortunately, academics and consultants have developed many tools and frameworks to guide leaders in their strategic thinking. These tools and frameworks—which include the Boston Consulting Group four-box growth-share matrix and the GE-McKinsey nine-box matrix[1]—were originally developed for companies and collectively constitute a discipline that we now call business strategy. More recently, we have seen the emergence of a significant industry of strategy consultants who aim to assist nonprofit and philanthropic organizations in applying such tools and frameworks. This approach was spurred by the 1999 launch of the Bridgespan Group, an affiliate of Bain & Company, with the encouragement and support of Joel Fleishman, then president of Atlantic Philanthropies, and others. McKinsey & Company, FSG, and other consulting firms have followed suit, each with its own variation.

Now, since we are career-long strategy consultants, we have a secret that we must confess at the outset: strategists, like many knowledge-based professionals, are prone to make their knowledge appear more complicated than it is. However, we are not writing this book to further muddy the waters with more obscure concepts that will likely leave you scratching your head or impressed with how smart we are. On the contrary, we believe that the nonprofit sector has an urgent need for clarity and simplicity in its strategic thinking—and that it can benefit from adapting the concepts of business strategy.

Not everyone agrees with us on this topic. In fact, some respected longtime sector leaders believe that nonprofits have already borrowed too much from business. Bruce R. Sievers, for example, is a visiting scholar both at the Haas Center for Public Service at Stanford University and at the Stanford Center on Philanthropy and Civil Society. In a 2004 article, he writes:

Unlike businesses, philanthropic and nonprofit organizations operate in two worlds. One of these is defined by instrumental objectives such as financial stability [or] number of people served. The other world, however, is defined by different end goals of human action: education, artistic expression, freedom of thought and action, concern for future generations, and preservation of cultural and environmental legacies. . . . These ends are the goals and aspirations of the human experience and are not reducible to the same kinds of categories that define profit margins and make for the most efficient production of widgets.[2]

We admire Sievers's eloquence, and we share his values. But we respectfully contend that nonprofit organizations and philanthropists can—and should—increase their impact through better strategic thinking. To be sure, choosing the next great social entrepreneur requires judgment and intuition. (The same goes for identifying the next great business entrepreneur.) And, to be sure, strategic thinking will not guide the next great performance of a Mahler symphony, nor will it teach empathy and compassion to a new nurse, physician, or social worker. But when it comes to understanding the impact or cost-effectiveness of an arts, educational, or social services organization, we believe in starting with facts and evidence, costs and benefits—and strategy.

Nonprofits are, above all, organizations that serve a social purpose as part of the fabric of civil society. But they are also organizations to which the basic principles of economics apply, and strategy essentially consists of developing a plan that reflects those principles. To understand the economic principles that underlie nonprofit strategy, consider the following points, which we have borrowed in part from an article by Henry B. Hansmann:

1. All nonprofits compete in markets, albeit widely varying ones. In some cases, these markets behave much like fully competitive markets and yield to strategies that closely resemble those of businesses in those segments. "Commercial nonprofits nearly always share their market with for-profit firms providing similar services," Hansmann writes.[3] Hospitals, day-care centers, and private nursing homes provide examples of areas in which for-profit and nonprofit organizations compete.

2. Many nonprofits, such as those in social services, compete in markets defined by market failure, which occurs whenever the production or allocation of goods or services by a market is highly inefficient. In such situations, businesses cannot thrive, subsidies from governments and donors are essential, and strategies for competition therefore differ greatly from those of an efficient market.

3. Many nonprofits—although not all—structurally lose money performing their core mission-driven activities; whatever earned revenue they receive is less than their direct costs and sometimes even less than their variable costs, too. For a profitable business, generally, the more successful it is, the more products or services it sells, and the more profits, cash flow, and value it creates. In the case of nonprofits that compete in markets dominated by market failure, success may well result in worse economics and result in the need for more subsidies! At the same time, subscale and less effective organizations can linger for as long as philanthropic or government subsidies continue.

4. Nonprofits lack the financial incentives that drive businesses to compete aggressively. As Hansmann writes, nonprofits are defined by the "non-distribution constraint"—they can generate a surplus or profit but cannot distribute it to related parties.[4] As a result, once an effective strategy is developed, a nonprofit must consider how to create the appropriate culture and incentives for salespeople to sell, development professionals to raise more money, professionals to balance quality services with cost, and managers and organizations to excel.

Given that they are economic organizations, nonprofits can benefit from using concepts that originated in the discipline known as business strategy. These concepts sometimes require adaptation, but fortunately leading academics and consultants have already done much of that work. Here, we summarize this knowledge and synthesize it for nonprofit and philanthropic leaders. Our goal is to acquaint you with the few strategic concepts that truly matter for social sector organizations: theory of change, Oster's six-forces model, assessing core competencies, and strategic planning processes.

Theory of Change: Tying Mission to Strategy

Theory of change is a highly useful strategic concept that has gained popularity in the nonprofit sector in recent years. Put simply, a theory of change is a logical description of *how* your organization's strategies will help achieve its mission. While other key strategic concepts have their roots in business strategy, this one originated in the social and government sectors. Although the term started to become prevalent only in the 1980s, the notion of a theory of change was put forward decades earlier. It appeared, for example, in discussions of how to evaluate government programs in the 1960s during the War on Poverty.[5] Numerous writers have asserted over the years that evaluation efforts are challenging in the absence of a clear understanding of program goals and their underlying logic.[6] For example, Carol H. Weiss "hypothesized that a key reason complex programs are so difficult to evaluate is that the assumptions that inspire them are poorly articulated."[7] Weiss's 1995 work with the Aspen Institute is recognized by many as formalizing the theory-of-change concept and disseminating it widely.[8] Weiss popularized the term *theory of change* "as a way to describe the set of assumptions that explain both the ministeps that lead to the long-term goal of interest and the connections between program activities and outcomes that occur at each step of the way."[9]

Many definitions for theory of change are used in the sector today. According to Paul Brest and Hal Harvey in *Money Well Spent: A Strategic Plan for Smart Philanthropy*, a theory of change is an analysis of the causal chain that links your philanthropic interventions to the goals you want to achieve.[10] Brest, writing elsewhere, further explained: "A theory of change is a comprehensive description of the theory that underlies all or part of an organization's work . . . [It] contains an implicit analysis of the causes of, or at least possible solutions to, the problem [that the organization seeks to address]."[11] We see the notion of theory of change as posing these fundamental questions: How are you planning to achieve your mission? Is there empirical evidence that makes you think your chosen approach will work?

Interposing a rigorous theory of change helps ensure that an organization's strategy is logically and empirically sound. Indeed, an organization needs a logical hypothesis about how its desired impact will be achieved before it can begin using empirical data to test and confirm that impact. As Brest and Harvey underscore, "A theory of change is only as good as its empirical validity. An intuitively plausible theory of change is better than none at all—but the not-for-profit sector is littered with programs based on theories of change that seemed intuitively plausible but were not valid. Therefore, the more tested the theory of change, the sounder its use as the basis for strategy."[12]

Despite the importance and usefulness of having a theory of change, only about half of nonprofit organizations actually do have one, according to *State of the Nonprofit Sector*.[13] And not all organizations that have a theory of change have one with empirical validity. In our 2016 Stanford survey, only 10 percent of nonprofit executives and staff said that they "strongly agree" with the statement that their organization's theory of change is "empirical/evidence-based."[14]

A theory of change can take a wide variety of forms. In the simplest form, the essential theory underlying an intervention may be distilled into a sentence or two; the most complex form might include graphical pictures using boxes and arrows to diagram how various assumptions, activities, strategies, and expected outcomes fit together and how an intervention will succeed. Numerous helpful resources have been prepared by experts in the field to provide organizations with guidance in developing theories of change. These include resources from the Annie E. Casey Foundation, the W. K. Kellogg Foundation, the Aspen Institute's Roundtable on Community

Change, the Foundation Center's GrantCraft, and Grantmakers for Effective Organizations.

A theory of change is similar to a logic model, and the terms are often used interchangeably even though there are differences. We will spare you this esoteric debate and use the term *theory of change* in lieu of *logic model*. We recommend that you join us in this—and if you ever find yourselves caught in a debate about these terms' usage, we suggest you leave the room immediately. We do.

Two organizations that stand out for the logic and rigor of their theories of change are the Center for Employment Opportunities and Landesa.

CENTER FOR EMPLOYMENT OPPORTUNITIES

The Center for Employment Opportunities (CEO) is a nonprofit with headquarters in New York that has spent the past thirty years providing employment services to those who have recently been released from prison. CEO has an excellent mission statement that clearly explains its raison d'être: "The Center for Employment Opportunities (CEO) is dedicated to providing immediate, effective and comprehensive employment services to men and women with recent criminal convictions. Our highly structured and tightly supervised programs help participants regain the skills and confidence needed for successful transitions to stable, productive lives."[15] CEO also has a clear and logical theory of change grounded in empirical evidence: "[It] posits that if the employment needs of persons with criminal convictions are addressed at their most vulnerable point—soon after conviction or when they are first released from incarceration—by providing life skills education, short-term paid transitional employment, full-time job placement and post-placement services, they will be less likely to become re-incarcerated and more likely to build a foundation for a stable, productive life for themselves and their families."[16]

Recidivism is a serious problem in the United States. Two out of every three released prisoners undergo rearrest within three years of their release.[17] Incarcerating such prisoners, moreover, costs society more than $30,000 per inmate per year.[18] As chief executive officer

Sam Schaeffer explains, "CEO's theory of change hones in on the *timing* of the intervention as a lever to reduce recidivism—meeting employment needs when the person is at his or her most vulnerable point because data shows that timing makes a critical difference."[19] The journalist Tina Rosenberg notes in an article about CEO, "Recidivism is highest the first year out of prison, and then drops; within a few years, a former prisoner's risk of committing a new crime is no different from that of others of the same age."[20]

Schaeffer continues, "CEO's theory of change is also grounded in the assumption that recidivism can be decreased by providing a unique mix of services [and offering them] together."[21] On the basis of this theory of change, CEO provides a road map (as depicted in Figure 2) for helping participants maintain their freedom and become members of the legitimate workforce.[22]

Empirical data have demonstrated the validity of both CEO's theory of change and its programmatic approach. In 2004, for example, the independent evaluation organization MDRC began a randomized study that enrolled 977 CEO participants and followed them for three years.[23] Individuals in the study group had extensive histories with the criminal justice system, with an average of seven prior convictions and five years spent in state prison. The evaluation found that CEO significantly reduced recidivism, with the largest impact seen among participants recently released from prison. Former prisoners who started the CEO program within three months of their release experienced a reduction in recidivism of 16 percent to 22 percent. These results are impressive when viewed in context: there are many transitional jobs programs in the United States, but these programs often fail to demonstrate recidivism reduction in randomized evaluations. As Rosenberg explains: "A reduction of one-fifth might seem like nothing to write a column about. But in fact, it is remarkable."[24]

LANDESA

Landesa, an organization that works to obtain land rights for the rural poor, has also adopted a compelling theory of change. That

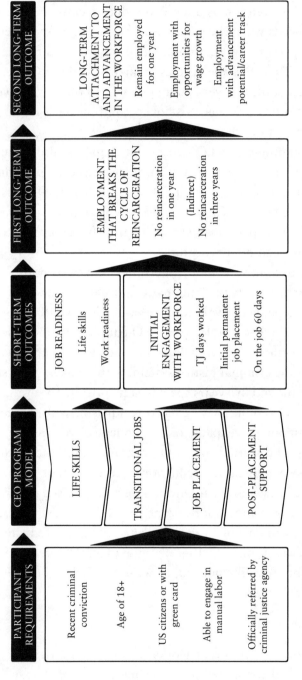

FIGURE 2 CEO's program model

SOURCE: "CEO Theory of Change," Center for Employment Opportunities, accessed August 31, 2016, http://ceoworks.org/about/what-we-do/mission-vision. Reprinted with permission.

theory of change is reflected in a sequence of five logic steps, each of which is informed by empirical evidence:

1. Land is the most critical resource for a majority of the world's poorest people.

2. The lack of secure and equitable land rights is a root cause of global poverty and gender inequality.

3. Secure land rights provide a foundation for economic opportunity and better living conditions.

4. Law is a powerful and highly leveraged tool for social and economic change.

5. A small group of focused professionals working collaboratively with governments and other stakeholders can help to change and implement laws and policies that provide opportunity to the world's poorest women and men.[25]

Landesa's theory of change grew out of insights that Roy Prosterman, its cofounder and chairman emeritus, developed while studying farmers' land rights during the Vietnam War. Because these insights are both enduring and profound, they are as important today as when the organization was founded. "The insights underlying Landesa's theory of change were developed in the earliest days of our work . . . out of an instinct to be rigorous. . . . I approached the work as a social scientist, and especially as a lawyer looking for evidence about what works," says Prosterman.[26] Landesa also developed a graphical picture of its theory of change that uses arrows depicting causality to delineate specific goals, activities, outcomes, and impacts.

For Landesa, as for most organizations, the process of developing and obtaining stakeholder agreement on its theory of change has been as important as the end product. Tim Hanstad, cofounder and former CEO and president, reflects, "Some of our richest discussions as an organization—with management, staff, board members, and donors—have occurred during the process of developing a graphical depiction of our theory of change and specifically around causality and the arrows in the boxes. We are forced to ask ourselves as a group,

'What evidence do we have that our intervention will bring about the intended results?'"[27] (Today Hanstad serves as a special advisor to Landesa.) To engage a wide range of stakeholders, Landesa created a process that involved lengthy group discussions among multiple entities. These included a twenty-member team of leaders and staff, a blue-ribbon panel that gave feedback on the draft theory of change, a joint task force of staff and board, and a group of donors.

Possessing a sound theory of change is necessary but not sufficient. An organization must also use its theory of change. The best way to derive maximum benefit from a theory of change is to deploy it—in combination with a mission statement—as a filter to justify every project and program area (and thus to reject proposed projects and program areas that do not align with the theory of change or the mission statement). Hanstad explains:

We have been intentional about incorporating our theory of change into our day-to-day work [and about] allowing it to guide our project design and work processes. One mechanism that has been especially helpful is dividing all of our programs into projects, and ensuring that every single project ties back to the whole organization's theory of change. We have an internal process (called the Project Life Cycle process) that requires every new project concept and design to be justified by our theory of change. The process of holding up new project designs to the organizational strategy and theory of change has been especially helpful. Our theory of change helps us determine what to say NO to! And in this sense, theory of change plays a similar role to mission, but [it] also [plays] a distinctive role that is complementary to mission.[28]

Oster's Six-Forces Model: Assessing a Nonprofit's Competitive Position

In his 1980 book *Competitive Strategy: Techniques for Analyzing Industries and Competitors*, Harvard professor Michael E. Porter synthesized his five-forces model, and since then that model has become the essential means for assessing an organization's competitive position.[29] (See Figure 3 for an illustration of the five-forces model.) In 2008, Porter reaffirmed his model, arguing that it is the job of a

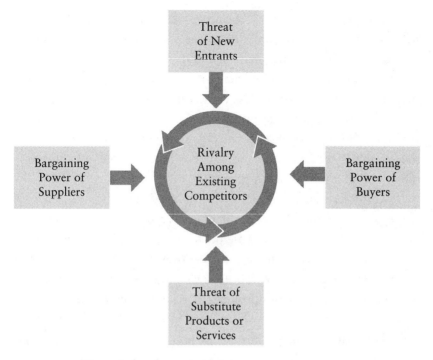

FIGURE 3   Porter's five-forces model

SOURCE: Michael E. Porter, "The Five Competitive Forces That Shape Strategy," *Harvard Business Review*, January 2008. Copyright © 2008 by Harvard Business Publishing; all rights reserved. Reprinted with permission.

strategist to understand and cope with competition. In many cases, he explained, "managers define competition too narrowly, as if it occurred only among today's direct competitors. Yet competition for profits goes beyond established industry rivals to include four other competitive forces as well: customers, suppliers, potential entrants, and substitute products. The extended rivalry that results from all five forces defines an industry's structure and shapes the nature of competitive interaction within an industry."[30]

Porter's model has survived and thrived in part because it is useful to such a wide variety of people—Ivy League economists, small-business entrepreneurs, and social workers can all find something of value in it. For example, if you have only one buyer and many suppliers, the power rests with the buyer who can play one supplier against others. (Think of a social service organization that relies predominantly on government contracts or grants. That organization has little or no power in its negotiations with its primary or sole source of financing.) Low barriers to new entrants or many possible substitutes make a market less attractive to enter or grow. (Think of college-prep programs that function in some ways as a substitute for high school.) Just observe the power of teachers' unions to limit the growth of the charter school movement and you can easily sense the bargaining power of suppliers.

Porter's five-forces model revolutionized the study of business strategy and "shaped a generation of academic research and business practice."[31] Then, in 1995, Yale professor Sharon M. Oster, who is one of the very few academics to research, write about, and teach nonprofit strategy, augmented Porter's model by adapting it to the distinctive dynamics of nonprofits. Her six-forces model (as shown in Figure 4) adds funders as a sixth force, in recognition of the critical role played by donors, grant makers, and governments, among others. It also changes the term "rivalry among" to "relations among" on the assumption that nonprofits often collaborate with one another to achieve their missions, whereas businesses typically compete with one another aggressively. Finally, it replaces the notion of buyers with that of users, who in the nonprofit context may or may not be the purchaser or payer.[32]

So, if a nonprofit were to use Oster's model to analyze its position in the market in which it "competes," it would first look at existing organizations that might attract both its users and its donors. It would then consider potential new entrants that might do the same. Next it would look at possible substitutes—are there other organizations, perhaps even for-profit ones, that might offer similar services or be more attractive to funders? Then it would consider suppliers— what kind of pressure are they placing on the organization? And, of course, it would examine users. Who are they, and why do they use our services? Finally, it would analyze donors. How many donors do we have, and how strongly do they support us? Why do they support us? Which other organizations do they support? What is the natural

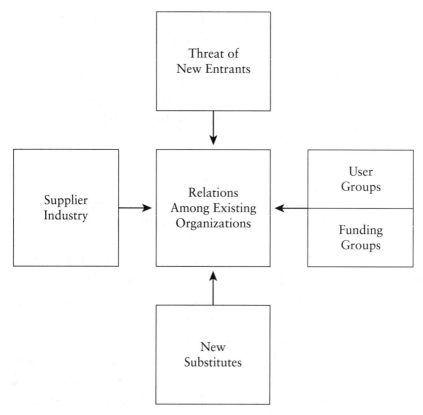

FIGURE 4   Oster's six-forces model

SOURCE: Sharon M. Oster, *Strategic Management for Nonprofit Organizations: Theory and Cases* (Oxford: Oxford University Press, 1995): figure 3.1, "Six Force Chart for Nonprofit Industry Analysis," 30. Copyright © 1995 by Oxford University Press, Inc. By permission of Oxford University Press, USA.

segmentation of our donors? Are they small but consistent in their giving? Are there a few major donors? Are donors inspired by our annual event?

To understand how applying the Oster model can clarify a nonprofit's strategic position, let's consider three examples. These examples—drawn from the fields of education, health care, and the performing arts—illustrate three competitive or market-based challenges that nonprofits commonly face: unmet public need, full competition (but worse), and the limits of earned revenue.

These examples, we believe, yield two major takeaways. First and foremost, most nonprofits compete in markets—but markets in which highly varying structures and forces are at work. Second, as nonprofit leaders undertake their organization's strategic analysis, they must apply a robust model for competitive analysis, such as Oster's six-forces model, in order to ensure that the strategy they are using to achieve their mission is sound.

EASTSIDE COLLEGE PREPARATORY SCHOOL: UNMET PUBLIC NEED

Back in 1996, East Palo Alto, California, was a city torn apart by gang violence and drug wars, struggling to recover from the dubious distinction of being the 1992 "murder capital" of the United States.[33] The prosperity of the surrounding Silicon Valley, with its booming economy and tech millionaires, seemed a world away. The economist Paul Krugman even used the city as an example of the polarizing inequality he saw cleaving the nation, contrasting "the grim environs of East Palo Alto" with the "well-tended lawns and flower beds" across the highway in Palo Alto.[34] Chris Bischof, who was then a recent graduate of Stanford University, observed the same spiraling inequality as Krugman, but his focus was education.[35] East Palo Alto had effectively become an educational desert since the Sequoia Union High School District had closed its only geographically proximate high school, Ravenswood High School, in 1976. Following the closure, East Palo Alto students were bused to high school in considerably more affluent neighboring communities. East Palo Alto students generally found themselves assigned to non-college-track classes in these new schools, which contributed to a dramatic and damning result: 65 percent of students from East Palo Alto dropped out of high school. Of the 35 percent of students who did graduate, less than 10 percent enrolled in four-year colleges.[36]

Bischof was convinced there was another way. As an undergraduate, he had started Shoot for the Stars—an after-school program for

East Palo Alto elementary students that linked participation in basketball with daily tutoring—and he believed he could do even more. Working with Helen Kim, a friend and a fellow Stanford graduate, Bischof founded Eastside College Preparatory School with the mission to "prepare our students to succeed at four-year colleges and universities and enable them to become leaders in their community and in the world around them."[37] Eastside Prep opened its doors in 1996 and by 2014 boasted fifteen graduating classes. The results were nothing short of remarkable: 100 percent of Eastside graduates were accepted to four-year colleges, and more than 80 percent of them had earned (or were on track to earn) their college degrees within five years of graduation.[38]

If a six-forces analysis had been undertaken for the proposed organization, it would have noted that Eastside Prep had no direct competitors when it opened. Indeed, a high school student in East Palo Alto had just three choices: travel thirty minutes to the remaining public high schools in the Sequoia school district; compete for a financial aid–supported slot at one of several elite private schools, none of which was geographically proximate; or drop out—a substitute, in strategic terms. Clearly, high school education in East Palo Alto was an unmet public need.

But Eastside Prep had to grapple with forces other than direct competition. It was an independent, tuition-free school founded before the charter school movement came to California. Funders—primarily high-net-worth individual donors from the venture capital industry—were a make-or-break element for Eastside Prep. Its teachers, who would be labeled "suppliers" in the six-forces framework, had to accept barely competitive salaries and yet be willing and able to sustain the school's education and culture. Moreover, Eastside Prep had to build its reputation, or "brand," among parents, students, and feeder middle schools in order to sustain and grow its enrollment. Later, specific assets like school buildings and dormitories would become essential to Eastside Prep's ability to maintain a strong competitive position, particularly following the rise of the charter school movement and an initiative by Stanford University to start a K–12 school within a few miles of Eastside Prep.

Eastside Prep was typical of many social service delivery and educational nonprofits: its focus was on providing essential services to an underserved population. But as our thumbnail six-forces analysis reveals, Eastside Prep remained subject to other important forces that affected its ability to build a strong and sustainable position that would allow it to achieve its mission: generous donors; highly competent, loyal teachers; and a reputation for excellence among parents and others who influence high school selection decisions. By the time Eastside Prep faced competition from East Palo Alto Phoenix Academy and East Palo Alto Academy, its competitive position was unassailable, allowing it to welcome its "competitors" without fear of losing its financial support, its teachers, or its reputation in the community.

STANFORD UNIVERSITY–UNIVERSITY OF CALIFORNIA AT SAN FRANCISCO HOSPITAL MERGER: FULL COMPETITION (BUT WORSE)

The health-care sector provides a classic example of a highly competitive commercial market in which nonprofits and for-profit companies compete.

Back in the 1980s, the health-care sector was under considerable pressure when it came to pricing and profits. Especially affected by this trend were university-based medical schools and affiliated teaching hospitals. Many of these hospitals faced financial deficits so significant that had they continued to grow, they could have threatened the financial stability of the universities themselves. Health insurers and payers, who largely controlled the flow of patients to hospitals via financial and other arrangements, were also under increasing cost pressure.

A crucial element of an academic medical center is its ability to provide so-called bench-to-bedside care, which brings newer and more complex tertiary and quaternary medical procedures from the laboratory to the patient. So, while you might go to your local community hospital for a simple gall bladder surgery, if you were in need of an organ transplant, you would likely seek a surgeon at an academic medical center with a specialty in the required procedure. Universities with medical schools needed their hospitals to train physicians and conduct research; given that academic mission, university leaders were unlikely to consider closing those hospitals. But the hospitals had to compete effectively, if not always efficiently, with a range of community hospitals. So many academic hospitals, despite their intended tertiary and quaternary focus, were serving patients with simple treatment needs that put these institutions in direct competition with nonacademic hospitals. Meanwhile, many nonacademic hospitals—envious of the academic medical centers' more richly reimbursed specialty procedures—took steps to build specialized clinics and surgeries. Often these community hospitals were nonprofits themselves, and they were forming partnerships that mirrored retail chains.

The competitive market situation for academic medical centers varied considerably by region. In some regions, including Boston, these centers were affiliated with, but not owned by, the universities whose medical students trained there.[39] As a result, circumstances paved the way for a fruitful merger between Massachusetts General Hospital (MGH) and Brigham and Women's Hospital (BWH) in 1994.[40] At first, many doctors saw MGH and BWH as unlikely partners, given their history of competing for physicians, students, and research funding. However, the main reason for the merger was very clear: to reduce price competition between the two hospitals. Payers and providers, after all, would need to give patients access to the tertiary and quaternary care available only at these academic medical centers.[41] Hence, once leaders from both organizations started a dialogue, the merger came together in months, and they were able to create a successful new entity, Partners HealthCare.[42] Although the hospitals initially did little to work together on clinical operations, they saved between 12 percent and 28 percent of costs from administrative consolidation. Today Partners HealthCare encompasses community and specialty hospitals, a managed-care organization, a physician network, community health centers, and other health-related services.[43] Its member institutions have a total research budget of more than $1.4 billion, and its flagship hospitals (MGH and BWH) are the largest private hospital recipients of funding from the National Institutes of Health.[44]

But, when two San Francisco Bay Area institutions, the privately owned Stanford University and the state-run University of California at San Francisco (UCSF), attempted a similar merger in the 1990s, the situation was different and so was the result.[45] Both universities had highly rated medical schools, and each institution owned, or was responsible for, the financials of its academic medical center. The two institutions considered a merger because they believed it could free them from competing for specialized, tertiary work (heart transplants, for example) and therefore stabilize the prices that insurance carriers paid.

The Stanford-UCSF merger was officially established in November 1997, but full integration of the two programs created a host of problems, notably in computer and information systems. The merger was also fraught with cultural challenges, some of which sprang from the fact that one institution was private and the other public: differences in the demands of their unions, their governance requirements, and their funding models proved difficult to reconcile. Both organizations were staffed at the physician level with powerful medical school faculty who relished their autonomy—and did not intend to give it up.[46]

A six-forces analysis of both situations would reveal that the key force at work was the relative power between insurers and the hospitals that compete for patients who need high-end specialty procedures. In Boston, Partners took a conservative approach. Although it made little effort to consolidate operational functions, it was still able to negotiate with health insurers from a stronger position. In the Bay Area, however, where an insurer required access to either Stanford or UCSF for many high-end specialty procedures, the underlying economic goal of the merger was to exert "niche" or "monopoly" power to extract higher prices for those procedures. But Stanford and UCSF undertook an operational merger, which resulted in a great many challenges and ultimately fell apart of its own weight. The merger lacked the stark cost reduction and financial incentives that fuel most corporate mergers, and it failed to motivate world-class academic physicians.

Applying a six-forces model to a case such as the Stanford-UCSF merger can generate new or counterintuitive insights. The leaders of those two organizations, for example, should have put greater focus on increasing pricing leverage and should have formed a holding company with no immediate expectation of near-term consolidation and cost reductions. In this way, they would have forgone the messiness of trying to get academic medical centers to behave like profit-maximizing corporations.

THE SAN FRANCISCO SYMPHONY: THE LIMITS OF EARNED REVENUE

The San Francisco Symphony (SFS) has long ranked among the world's top orchestras.[47] It is recognized internationally for its artistic accomplishments, educational outreach, and Grammy Award–winning recordings. The orchestra's reputation has grown under the leadership of music director Michael Tilson Thomas, a member of that increasingly rare breed—the classical music celebrity. In some circles, Thomas is known simply by his initials, MTT. As of December 2012, the SFS board of governors was led by Sakurako Fisher, a dedicated music lover who viewed the symphony orchestra as an integral part of any great city's ecosystem and civil society. But SFS's lauded artistic reputation has not translated to financial stability; on the contrary, like most of its peer orchestras, it has frequently run a budget deficit, with expense growth outpacing revenue trends in recent years.[48]

The forces pressuring SFS are common among US performing arts organizations, particularly those—like symphonies and opera and ballet companies—that practice the so-called highbrow arts. Although there are many musical groups in San Francisco, there is no other major symphony orchestra, and a new entrant to this market is highly unlikely; SFS thus faces little or no threat from either existing organizations or potential new entrants. The threat of substitutes, however, is high: classical music lovers may choose to access music digitally, for instance, or watch it on television or DVD. They may opt to listen to a smaller or less renowned—but still good—symphony that is closer to their home. Or, for that matter, they may go out to a movie or stay at home and binge watch *Game of Thrones*! Suppliers exert considerable cost pressure. SFS's unionized musicians, in particular, are vocal in their demands and have demonstrated a willingness to go on strike when those demands are not met. SFS, like top orchestras everywhere, has thus had to pay musicians ever-higher wages to retain talent. (Musicians' salaries and other artistic costs account for about 50 percent of total operating costs.[49]) Other costs, like marketing and development, constitute a smaller portion of overall expenses, but they have also been on the rise as orchestras have built up their ability to increase ticket sales, annual fund contributions, and endowment contributions.

SFS management and board leaders have struggled with the resulting structural deficit for more than two decades. Recently, genuinely worrisome declines in SFS's paid attendance have signaled that earned revenue has hit, or is beyond, its peak—and this at a time when most observers would say the orchestra under MTT has never played better and to more renown. But, as long as the unions of world-class musicians have bargaining power and the demand for concert tickets declines, the future of major US symphony orchestras lies increasingly with Oster's sixth force: funders, or in this case, donors.

Absent some generational sea change back toward concertgoing, the San Francisco Symphony, like other major orchestra, opera, and ballet companies, will face a future in which it has no choice other than to raise increasing amounts of money from philanthropy. The quality of high-end performing arts organizations—and that of elite research universities and museums—will be shaped significantly by how much money they can raise, particularly for their endowments, and by the return on endowment investments. Many such organizations still resist or deny this truth, but they would do far better to confront it head-on—for it is a matter not of hopes and dreams but of economics and strategy.

Core Competencies: Assessing a Nonprofit's Skills Across Its Value Chain

In 1990, C. K. Prahalad and Gary Hamel wrote a seminal article called "The Core Competence of the Corporation."[50] Its central argument was insightful, powerful, and simple, and we summarize it thus: an organization's strategy must be built on its distinctive skill, or skills. In practice, this means that nonprofit leaders must regularly ask, "Does our organization have the core competency or skill required to achieve its mission?" This is a leading question—one that can turn a nonprofit offsite on its head! We can imagine the response: "Skills, skills, of course we have the skills! Besides, if we don't provide [fill in the blank], who will?" But it is absolutely essential to make sure that you do indeed possess the skills required to carry out your mission. Equally important, you must ensure that these skills are assessed across your value chain, which is the set of activities that an organization undertakes to deliver a valuable product or service. The concept of a value chain is also derived from business strategy. To illustrate these linked concepts, let's consider the example of Equal Opportunity Schools.

EQUAL OPPORTUNITY SCHOOLS

Equal Opportunity Schools (EOS) was established in 2010 by Reid Saaris.[51] A former high school teacher, Saaris was haunted by what he called the "missing students" in the American education system: significant numbers of low-income students and students of color with strong academic ability who were "missing" from advanced classes, like Advanced Placement (AP) and International Baccalaureate (IB), in high schools across the United States. In 2007, he began research with the Education Trust that found that each year about 640,000 African American, Latino, and low-income students were about as likely as their white or higher-income peers to attend schools that

offered advanced classes, but they were much less likely to be enrolled in those classes.[52]

Saaris developed initial plans for EOS from 2008 to 2010, while
he pursued a joint degree program at the Stanford Graduate School
of Business and the Stanford Graduate School of Education. After
receiving seed funding of $80,000 from the Center for Social Inno-
vation at Stanford, Saaris established EOS to help schools and districts transition their missing students up to advanced classes. In its
first five years, EOS served more than twenty-five thousand missing
students in more than eighty school districts across the country and
developed a funding model wherein earned revenue covered 75 percent of program costs. This early success can be attributed to EOS's
ability to deploy distinctive skills across its value chain.[53] This value
chain (shown in Figure 5) has five core segments.

1. *Conducting rigorous research to identify the regions or districts
that present opportunity.* EOS draws from multiple data sources (e.g.,
National Center for Education Statistics, regional and national school
networks, Office of Civil Rights at the U.S. Department of Education)
to identify regions with high schools that fit EOS's criteria, which
include diversity in a school population, rigor of advanced classes
(the percentage of students taking and passing an AP or IB exam),
and significant numbers of students missing from such classes. Alexa
Llibre, manager of strategic initiatives for EOS, explains: "We have
enough data to say 'there are one hundred students who are white or
Asian at this school and 99 percent of them took the AP exam. But
there are one hundred students who are Latino and only five of them
took an AP exam.' Well, 99 percent of the Latino students should be
taking the AP exam if 99 percent of white and Asian students are."[54]
A region with schools that show both program quality and inequity
is potentially a good partner.

2. *Activating the moral agency of district leaders through sales
and marketing.* Getting school districts on board begins with getting
superintendents and other district leaders to attend in-person "educational leadership conversations." EOS excels at making these leaders
understand the "missing students" problem. It activates their "latent

Value Chain	1. Research Conduct rigorous research to identify the regions and districts and opportunity	2. Sales & Marketing Activate moral urgency and convert district leaders to obtain large district applicant pool	3. Selection Process Select the best district applicants	4. Execution Implement personalized programs with participating schools	5. Performance Measurement Assess and track progress and impact
Key Skills	• Leverage research expertise to analyze large variety of data sources	• Entice district leaders to attend in-person events with intriguing district level research • Use data to convince leaders of the magnitude of the problem, active their moral urgency, and persuade them to address it with EOS and turn moral urgency to action	• Analyze data to prioritize opportunities • Assess each district's leadership characteristics and potential	• Develop and execute a personalized plan for every participating school • Incorporate "growth mindset"	• Track and measure progress and impact at various levels: district, school, demographic group (low income, Black, Latino, etc.), and individual student • Apply feedback loop for continuous improvement

FIGURE 5 EOS's key skills across the value chain

SOURCE: William F. Meehan III and Kim Starkey Jonker, informed by William F. Meehan and Davina Drabkin, "Equal Opportunities Schools: Finding the Missing Students," Case No. SM-240, Stanford Graduate School of Business, 2015.

moral urgency" and persuades them to apply to partner with EOS by sharing EOS's deep knowledge, outlining its track record of rapid and cost-effective success, and highlighting partnerships with reputable organizations (e.g., Google, Education Trust, Stanford). After leaders attend one of these events, their district can submit school-level demographic and AP or IB data, and in return, EOS provides a customized analysis that benchmarks participation levels against state and national data. By applying research and data expertise to leaders' local context, EOS helps leaders turn their moral urgency into action. This combination of approaches enables EOS to achieve "outrageously high" conversion rates.[55]

3. *Selecting the best applicants.* EOS works to select district applicants that are the best fit for its criteria, because fit determines likelihood of success. For the 2014–2015 academic year, for example, EOS selected two-thirds of its applicants on the basis of how closely the applicants' data fit EOS criteria as well as the applicants' leadership characteristics.[56]

4. *Executing the program with participating schools, leveraging EOS's expertise in incorporating "growth mind-set," and developing insights for every student.* EOS has incorporated Stanford psychologist Carol Dweck's concept of growth mind-set.[57] With a growth mind-set, people believe that their most basic abilities can be developed through dedication and hard work. In contrast, under a fixed mind-set, people believe that those abilities are fixed traits. EOS has incorporated this concept across its entire program to broaden educators' understanding of student ability and to increase student engagement and motivation. In addition, EOS helps schools organize quantitative and qualitative data so they can develop personalized, growth-focused approaches for each student. Targeted districts, according to Saaris, are "so hungry to drive real progress and so often stymied in these attempts. We connect the dots—down to the level of individual student conversations between a given adult and a given missing student."[58]

5. *Measuring performance.* EOS has prioritized impact and performance measurement since its founding. It sets goals, tracks progress,

and then holds staff responsible for results by awarding bonuses and promotions connected to outcomes.[59] EOS measures progress and impact at various levels: district, school, demographic group (e.g., low income, African American, Latino), and individual student. It tracks AP and IB course enrollment rates and pass rates before and after program implementation, which enables it to measure changes over time and across groups. EOS also creates a Student Insight Card to monitor progress for each student. Today it is in the process of conducting the first random assignment (school-level) study of the impact of AP and IB on college completion,[60] as well as original research in collaboration with Stanford on growth mind-set and other learning mind-sets. These projects involve hundreds of schools and will provide a longer-term picture of EOS's impact, as well as insight into how schools can better identify, unlock, and activate previously overlooked student potential.

Strategic Planning: The Importance of Just a Few Scenarios

A leading theoretical physicist once lamented the decline of creative thinking in his field. "Since the advent of supercomputers, I think we have been losing our ability to think," he said. "We just run complex models." Both in business and in the social sector, similarly, we just find some intern who can make Excel sing with countless analyses; we pursue endless machinations of multiple variables that ultimately don't matter to strategic decision making.

But there is a better way: we can focus on a small number of scenarios that frame the range of likely outcomes. Scenarios are the most powerful way to deal with the irreducible uncertainty we all face when we look toward the future. The primary goal of building financial and strategic scenarios is to think deeply about the variables that might drive different financial outcomes and about how the relationship among these variables affects those outcomes.

The example of the San Francisco Symphony shows how scenarios can help us structure uncertainty and focus our attention on key strategic variables. For SFS, those variables include ticket sales, prices, musician costs, fund raising, and endowment payout. In 1993, when the exciting new music director MTT was selected, earned revenue—mostly ticket sales—accounted for nearly 60 percent of SFS's total revenue.[61] But by 2013, earned revenue had fallen to roughly 40 percent of total revenue.[62] Assume that major costs are from strong union-organized, well-paid orchestra musicians; that symphonies, like most high-end performing arts organizations, follow William J. Baumol's cost-disease principle of lacking economies of scale (only more so, as streaming music services provide some proxy for a live classical musical experience for free, or close to it); and that younger audiences, with far more ways to spend their leisure time and lower rates of musical education, do not seem to be gravitating to live orchestral experiences as their parents and grandparents did).[63]

Over the long run, how can a major orchestra like SFS address what has come to be known as its structural deficit? Financially, there are only two variables that matter: fund raising, including payout from an endowment above all; and a relative reduction in musician costs. Dynamic pricing, films with a live orchestral accompaniment, and chamber music in the park—while possibly valuable—will just not significantly move the needle. And boosting attendance will require cutting ticket prices, which may increase audience sizes but will do so at the cost of lower earned revenue.

DESIGNING STRATEGIC PLANNING PROCESSES

The two most important goals of excellent strategic planning are shaped by process rather than end product. The first goal is to build your organization's capacity for strategic thinking—its capacity for applying and adapting your key strategies to the inevitable changes and uncertainty you will face as soon as your strategic plan is final. And the second goal is to engage and align your key internal and external stakeholders in the process of developing strategy as a core tool. As a result, designing a strategic planning process that suits your organization and its context is essential.

Nonprofits face distinctive challenges in designing a successful strategic planning process. The following points can mitigate these challenges.

1. *Don't underestimate the time and effort required for an effective strategic planning process.* Most nonprofits have multiple stakeholders, often with competing interests and little incentive to resolve them. This means that the time and process needed to undertake effective strategic planning is significant. It might well require two years of task forces, meetings, surveys, and fact-finding for a large, complex nonprofit organization like a university or museum to start and finish its strategic planning process—often before the several years that might follow for the capital campaign to raise the money to fund it. Planning processes not only take longer in the nonprofit sector but also require sophisticated, even Machiavellian, skills. One must engage and energize a broad range of stakeholders even while keeping the strategic plan focused on the organization's core mission and making stakeholders feel that their ideas have been reflected or incorporated. Everybody's idea counts—at least, sort of. Perhaps as a result of how much time and effort is involved, many nonprofits conduct strategic planning only in order to prepare for a major capital campaign, and they tend not to see it as an essential leadership task.

2. *Remember that effective strategic planning is based on issues, not the calendar.* Many organizations—both business and nonprofit—have defaulted to an annual planning process, which attempts to address budgeting, operational planning, and strategy all at once. But strategic planning must take a longer view, certainly at least three to five years, and must focus on identifying and addressing three to five fundamental issues. Of course, an effective strategic plan must then be translated into budgets, operational plans, and the like. But it first requires a process designed to step back, take stock, and assess things objectively, including the basic and tacit assumptions that an organization is making.

3. *Don't forget to start with a fact-based, objective situation analysis.* Stakeholder engagement is not a substitute for objective,

dispassionate fact-based analysis, beginning with a deep understanding of the external environment in which a nonprofit operates. Just because all stakeholders agree on something doesn't make it a fact. The daylong offsite retreat, seemingly a mainstay of nonprofit strategic planning processes, can provide a great forum for brainstorming among selected stakeholders. Typically, such events include a SWOT analysis—an exercise in which people typically describe their impressions of the *strengths*, *weaknesses*, *opportunities*, and *threats* that characterize an organization and its external environment. But a SWOT exercise cannot substitute for a cogent view of the facts about whether and how the nonprofit organization is achieving its mission, how it could better compete or collaborate with other organizations, what it must do to sustain itself financially and organizationally, and similar crucial matters.

OREGON SHAKESPEARE FESTIVAL

Consider the example of the Oregon Shakespeare Festival (OSF), which has distinguished itself with strategic planning processes that are thorough, systematic, and well suited to the organization's unique context.[64] Established in 1937, the OSF is one of the oldest and largest regional theaters in the United States. It is situated in a small town in the largely rural Rogue Valley of Oregon, 290 miles from the nearest major urban center. Its founder, Angus Bowmer, was a populist who believed—correctly—that presenting entertaining, popular versions of Shakespeare in an Elizabethan format would be compelling enough to draw large audiences from miles away. Over time, OSF has come to draw some of the largest theater audiences in the country to an annual slate of a dozen plays, done in repertory, including Shakespeare, traditional theater, an occasional musical, and new or recent commissions. As of 2012, its in-residence attendance figures were almost 70 percent higher than the median for theaters with similar budgets.[65]

Notably, OSF has undergone seven strategic planning processes over the past forty-five years, all of which have helped its leadership team to step back and think carefully and strategically about the organization's aspirations for the future. Its most recent strategic planning process, which led to the formulation of the OSF Strategic Plan 2015–2025, had much in common with its previous processes but at the same time represented a deliberate departure from prior efforts. It differed most notably from the 2009–2013 plan, which was perceived to have important strengths—it was broadly participatory and had clearly defined components—but also drawbacks.[66]

The new OSF strategic planning process, which launched in 2014, was framed by a number of key elements. First and foremost, the process was driven more by artistic vision than by operational needs. It started when a few key board members approached the new artistic director, Bill Rauch—a talented, visionary, and ambitious man—and requested that he put his artistic vision on paper. Rauch, eager to inspire people's imaginations, wrote the vision document as if it were a snapshot from the future. This vision then guided the entire planning process and ultimately resulted in a much more expansive plan.[67]

Rauch, for example, coupled his strong artistic vision with a desire to make the OSF audience mirror the racial and ethnic demographic composition of the United States. There was also an effort to incorporate capital improvements left unfulfilled by the previous plan. The new plan thus called for redesigning OSF's Elizabethan Theatre and breaking ground on a new education center. Informed by external analysis of the changing landscape—the dramatic rise of digital, on-demand entertainment posed an existential threat to the live arts, and data underscored that challenge—OSF also made plans to pursue high-quality broadcasts and other digital solutions.

Importantly, the new plan prioritized the need for OSF to step further up into its national leadership role.[68] From 2013 to 2015, OSF had continued to see a massive expansion in its national reach. In 2014, for example, the OSF commission *All the Way*, by Robert Schenkkan, traveled to Broadway, where it won two Tony Awards, including Best Play. With this and other sources of visibility, OSF saw an unprecedented rise in both national and international interest in presenting touring or remounted versions of its productions. This momentum—coupled with the inspirational nature of the planning process itself—excited the board and staff and aligned them as they prepared to take OSF to new heights.

Dwight Eisenhower, when he was supreme commander of Allied forces in Europe during World War II, arrived at an essential insight about strategic planning: "In preparing for battle I have always found that plans are useless, but planning is indispensable."[69] Veterans of strategic planning—like those at OSF—understand that the value of planning comes at least as much from what you learn in the process as from the plan itself.

CHAPTER 3

Count What Counts

Early in the movie *Dead Poets Society*, Robin Williams, playing an English teacher named John Keating at a boys boarding school, introduces the topic of evaluating poetry. Keating leads his students through their textbook's ponderous teachings about how to evaluate a poem's meter, rhyme, and figures of speech and how to assess its quality using a graph with horizontal and vertical axes. Then Keating, suddenly changing his tone and manner, turns away from the chalkboard and begins to trash the tome that they have been reading, *Understanding Poetry* by J. Evans Pritchard. "Excrement," he says. "That's what I think of Mr. J. Evans Pritchard. We're not laying pipe, we're talking about poetry."

Keating's reaction perfectly captures the response of many nonprofit executives to the "art" of impact measurement: while they may not use Keating's provocative term, they regard the effort to measure impact as an exercise in which some analytical type, some J. Evans Pritchard, tries to turn their equivalent of poetry—be it a human service, a performing art, or an educational endeavor—into horizontal and vertical axes. A poem of love bastardized into an equation.

Most observers focus their concerns about impact evaluation on the challenge of quantification. To us, however, that is no longer the primary issue. Great progress is being made on multiple fronts to develop and apply rigorous methodologies for impact evaluation.[1] This progress is based on key concepts that are as straightforward as they are powerful: Start with a mission-focused theory of change, and design an evaluation process that demonstrates the linkage between your intervention and your desired impact.

A host of new players have emerged to assist nonprofits with measurement and evaluation. Prominent among these players are the

Abdul Latif Jameel Poverty Action Lab (J-PAL) at the Massachusetts Institute of Technology (MIT) and Innovations for Poverty Action (IPA), both of which specialize in undertaking randomized evaluations, which (despite the high cost of conducting them) are considered the gold standard of impact evaluation. These evaluations randomly assign participants to treatment and comparison groups, deliver a given intervention to the treatment group, and measure differences in outcomes between the two groups. Evaluators then identify those differences as the impact of the intervention. J-PAL, a network of scholars who test and improve the effectiveness of poverty reduction programs and policies, has more than eight hundred ongoing or completed evaluations and has trained more than one thousand practitioners in best-practice evaluation techniques.[2] IPA, meanwhile, has worked with more than five hundred seventy-five leading academics to conduct more than six hundred fifty evaluations.[3] IPA founder Dean Karlan has started a new nonprofit called ImpactMatters and we are cautiously optimistic about its potential. ImpactMatters conducts "impact audits," which are short-term engagements that have two objectives: First, it aims to "guide nonprofits to strengthen their use and production of appropriate evidence in order to deliver more effective programs." Second, it aims to "rate the impact of nonprofits for donors to provide guidance on which nonprofits credibly advance their mission."[4]

Many other initiatives are tackling some part of the impact evaluation and measurement challenge. Collaborative efforts are under way to generate tools that will help nonprofit practitioners. In addition, information intermediaries are working to identify interventions that appear to have strong impact. GiveWell, for example, identifies evidence-based interventions and recognizes organizations that have used them to achieve demonstrable impact. The International Initiative for Impact Evaluation (3ie) is a knowledge broker that synthesizes and disseminates high-quality evidence of what works, how, why, and at what cost in international development (in addition to its role as a funding agency that offers support and resources promoting evidence-informed policies and programs).[5] The National Institute of Justice has created CrimeSolutions.gov to share evidence-based information about "what works, what doesn't, and what's promising in criminal justice, juvenile justice, and crime victim service."[6] And the Foundation Center's Tools and Resources for Assessing Social Impact (TRASI) contains links to numerous tools, methods, and best practices that can help a nonprofit measure its impact.[7]

At the same time, management consulting firms like the Bridgespan Group and McKinsey & Company are helping nonprofits to create cultures of measurement and evaluation. And various centers housed in universities—such as Stanford's Center on Philanthropy and Civil Society, Harvard Business School's Social Enterprise Initiative, UC Berkeley's Center for Effective Global Action, University of Pennsylvania's Center for High Impact Philanthropy, and Arizona State University's Lodestar Center for Philanthropy and Nonprofit Innovation—actively support courses on evaluation, along with related research and initiatives.

We therefore conclude that the development and application of useful approaches and tools for impact measurement and evaluation are robust and ongoing. As Bill Gates wrote in a 2013 essay: "In the past year, I have been struck by how important measurement is to improving the human condition. You can achieve incredible progress if you set a clear goal and find a measure that will drive progress toward that goal."[8] He went on to cite numerous examples of the ways in which measurement had improved delivery of education, health care, and other vital services.

Gates also acknowledged that measurement is too rarely done. Indeed, while the tools and approaches needed for impact measurement and evaluation are increasingly available, the pace of implementation has been slow. In research that we conducted for the Henry R. Kravis Prize in Nonprofit Leadership, more than 75 percent of the organizations on which we conducted due diligence did not have reliable impact data. In our 2016 Stanford survey, moreover, we asked respondents to pick the top three challenges faced by the nonprofit sector overall. The challenge that they selected most frequently was "inadequate and/or unreliable measurement/evaluation of organizations' impact and performance."

What accounts for this gap between what is possible and what people in the social sector are actually doing? The answer is twofold. The first challenge is that the incentives for nonprofit executives to seek out impact measurement are mixed, at best. One might think that executives would welcome the rich feedback about their efforts that impact evaluation can provide. For many leaders, feedback is the "breakfast of champion," notes Joel Peterson, a professor of management at the Stanford Graduate School of Business (Stanford GSB).[9] Yet nonprofit executives often prefer to remain opaque about the effectiveness of their programs and are often reluctant to undergo rigorous impact evaluation. Many boards of directors, moreover, enable their executives' avoidant behaviors. An old cartoon comes to mind in which a cowboy says to his horse, "Well, you've been a pretty good horse, I guess. Hardworkin'. Not the fastest critter I ever come across, but . . ." And the horse impatiently interrupts, "No, stupid. Not feedback. I wanted a feedbag!"

The second challenge is that most donors, philanthropists, and grant-making professionals don't demand a more evidence-based decision-making approach and are reluctant to pay for it. In our Stanford survey, only 42 percent of nonprofit executives and staff indicated that more than half of their donors or grant makers demand performance measurement or impact evaluation. And only 5 percent of nonprofit executives and staff indicated that more than half of their donors or grant makers demand that their organization undertake preannounced randomized evaluations conducted by a third party.[10] Equally important, funders are reluctant to pay for evaluation. In a 2015 survey conducted by the Nonprofit Finance Fund, 69 percent of nonprofit professionals in senior leadership positions indicated that their funders cover impact measurement costs "rarely" or "never"! And only 9 percent indicated that their funders cover impact measurement costs "often" or "always."[11] In our Stanford survey, less than 10 percent of nonprofit executives and staff indicated that half or more of their donors or grant makers are willing to pay for randomized evaluations conducted by a third party. This is unfortunate. Laura Arrillaga-Andreessen, a philanthropy expert and lecturer in philanthropy at Stanford GSB, offers this astute advice to philanthropists: "It's not only about demanding a higher level of accountability and transparency about results [from grantees]; it's also providing the resources to help the organizations and individuals that you are funding to accumulate that data and disseminate it appropriately."[12]

Admittedly, there are methodological challenges that people in the field are working to address. For example, there remains no "unified field theory" of nonprofit impact measurement and evaluation. There are no common metrics within most subsectors of the field, or a common vocabulary of measurement and evaluation, or common systems for classifying organizations or standardizing data across information systems.

Yet, at the level of specific interventions, the tools and approaches for effective impact evaluation are available and within reach. Their use remains limited only because many nonprofit organizations are reluctant to embrace them and cannot afford them, and because many funders are unwilling to use them or pay for them. The best solution to this impasse, we believe, is for funders to start demanding—and paying for—impact evaluation. (After all, why should a funder invest its capital in a nonprofit whose work lacks empirical support?) In this way, we can finally end the state of gridlock in which nonprofits merely pretend to have impact while funders pretend to believe them.

In the spirit of pragmatism—unlike J. Evans Pritchard, we are not dogmatic about such things—we offer seven ideas to help move impact measurement forward as the basis for decision making by nonprofit executives and staff as well as funders.

Listen to Einstein!

As in so many contentious debates, each side of this issue asserts a "straw man" position that the other doesn't actually espouse, then finds that position lacking in some important aspect. The two sides—let's call them poets and analytics—seem to stand at opposite ends of social sector conference cocktail parties, smiling even as they disdain the other's narrow-mindedness. The poets say: "Those analytics think they can measure everything, and they focus on measuring whatever they can in the short term, with little or no understanding of how complex and long term most nonprofit interventions are. Why can't they just trust us wise elders? As funders, we have made grants totaling millions of dollars with little or no data, and we think the impact of those grants was great!"

The analytics, believing it self-evident that their approach is superior, respond: "Trust, but verify! Of course you can't measure everything, and in any case, the measurement has to be over a meaningful time frame in a range of contexts, using appropriately valid statistical approaches. Are you really asking us, as your potential funder, to give you millions of dollars and simply to trust your judgment—because you 'just know' what works? Reading scores, graduation rates, behavioral changes, recidivism rates, and the like are certainly not perfect, and some gamesmanship is inevitable. But these are very useful impact evaluation tools nonetheless."

Think of us as "analytics who love Yeats." We are able to sit in a church, visit a hospital, or attend a symphony concert without focusing on ways to measure the impact of that experience. And we take guidance from none other than Albert Einstein, who was a resident at the Institute of Advanced Study in Princeton, New Jersey, from 1933 to his death in 1955. It is said that Einstein—perhaps inspired by his search for a unified field theory in physics—had a sign hanging in his office at the institute: "Not everything that counts can be counted, and not everything that can be counted counts."

Drawing inspiration from Einstein, we wonder why some pundits in the nonprofit sector have grown impatient with efforts to quantify the impact of the many and various interventions into complex social systems. It is certainly important work to increase our knowledge even if those efforts result in imperfect measures or unhappy evaluations. That said, we do not defend—in fact, we selectively criticize—those who measure with data simply because that data is available, when its analytical connection with impact is spurious. The most obvious target in this regard is Charity Navigator, which spent many years convincing millions of website visitors that its system of awarding stars on the basis of two main criteria—"financial health" and "accountability and transparency"—was useful to donors in making their decisions. On the contrary, because Charity Navigator has not yet provided cross-organizational ratings of impact or cost-benefit analyses, its ratings have not been useful and have even been dangerous. It reminds us of the old joke about the drunk who searches for his lost keys under a streetlight because, he says, "that is where I can see"—all the while knowing that he lost his keys somewhere else. Charity Navigator plans to eventually add a category called "results reporting" to its rating system and to encourage charities to "publicly report their mission-related results."[13] We are hopeful that Charity Navigator will be able to execute on that promise.

The quest in the nonprofit sector to clarify what can be measured (and how) and what can't be measured (and why not) is yielding new insights. We urge you to join the impact evaluation movement. You are certain to learn a lot from it, as we have—including humility.

Translate Qualitative into Quantitative

Each of your impact measures should be quantifiable. Many nonprofits resist this truth, claiming that the qualitative nature of their work cannot be reduced to mere numbers. We nonetheless encourage them to try. An organization will learn things from the process of trying to translate qualitative factors into quantitative ones, and that process will likely strengthen its intervention considerably.

Consider the example of Willow Creek Community Church, which undertook a massive effort to translate touchy-feely qualitative things such as "spiritual growth" into quantitative dimensions that could be measured.[14] Based in suburban Chicago, Willow Creek is one of the best-attended and most influential churches in the United States. In 2003, executive pastor Greg Hawkins found himself thinking about the many activities that his church pursued and wondering which of them had the greatest impact. If a donor were to give Willow Creek

$100,000 to invest in helping parishioners grow into disciples of Christ, would he know what to do with the money? Would he, for instance, increase participation in small groups? Encourage congregants to serve more? Install a better sound system in the worship center? Hawkins had a gnawing sense that he would not know how to direct this imaginary donation because he did not know which of the church's many endeavors helped people the most.[15]

When Hawkins first joined Willow Creek, he was surprised by the extent to which its evaluation efforts relied on anecdotal feedback, sometimes from just a few people. As a Stanford MBA who had worked as a McKinsey & Company consultant, he was predisposed to relying on data. So, together with his team at Willow Creek, Hawkins embarked on a three-year process of research and analysis for which they enlisted the help of Eric Arnson, a consumer research expert with experience in conducting quantitative studies for private-sector companies. Hawkins and his team first determined that their ultimate objective was to foster spiritual growth and maturity in every congregant. They condensed several biblical precepts into the concept of "an increasing love for God and other people" and then sought to determine which activities were most effective in promoting that goal.[16] In 2004, the research team distributed fifteen thousand surveys to the Willow Creek congregation.

The results shocked church leadership: increased church involvement did not lead to significant increases in spiritual maturity; greater participation in church activities such as small groups, weekend worship, and volunteering did little to increase love of God or love of others. These findings invalidated one of Willow Creek's most basic assumptions, which had previously inspired its leaders to focus on increasing each congregant's involvement in the church. Instead, the research demonstrated that the number-one driver of spiritual growth was Bible engagement—not just reading or studying the Bible, explained Hawkins, but "reflecting on it, letting the words of it influence your life" in multiple areas.[17]

This research led Willow Creek to unveil a new vision and a new strategic plan in 2007. The new vision centered on the church's role in helping each congregant develop an individual plan to deepen his or her relationship with Christ. In this way, congregants would learn how to nurture themselves through spiritual practices rather than relying on the church to serve as a spiritual parent.[18] Since implementing these changes, Willow Creek has continued to survey the congregation and has found strong and encouraging results. The church has also led an effort to define church best practices and to survey a diverse cross-section of other churches. By 2014, this effort had spanned more than two thousand churches representing more than five hundred thousand congregants in the United States and Canada.[19]

The work of translating the qualitative into quantitative data also helps to inform the approach taken by Helen Keller International (HKI). HKI prioritizes its program activities by focusing on critical questions on which quantitative evaluation data can truly shed light. CEO Kathy Spahn explained that the organization finds it helpful to assess its effectiveness by asking a question originally posed by Jean-Pierre Habicht, a former board member: "Are we doing the right thing, for the right people, in the right place, at the right time, and in the right way?"[20] By asking this simple but incisive question, the organization is forced to carefully examine each component of its work and weigh that component against possible alternatives. Spahn explained:

To see if we are doing the "right thing," we look at the evidence base for a particular intervention (compared with the evidence base for alternative interventions) and include analysis of HKI's unique skills and expertise. Similarly, we look at the evidence base to determine who can benefit most from our intervention. Are we targeting the right people? The right geographic locations? Are we applying our intervention at the best point in the life cycle? How can we improve our implementation? We focus our impact evaluations to best inform us to answer these key strategic questions. This helps us prioritize and resist the effort to count things that could be counted but are less important.[21]

Deciding which metrics to use is not always straightforward and often evolves over time. Bill Drayton, founder of Ashoka, posits three different levels of impact that leaders must consider when deciding what to measure: direct service, pattern change, and framework change. "At the first level, direct service, one can consider, for example, a teacher in the classroom," Drayton explained. In that case, key metrics will focus on such questions as "How many kids did you teach?" and "How well did they test?"[22] The essential insight for the second level, pattern change, emerged from the doctoral work of Diana Wells, who is now president of Ashoka. Drayton explained:

> We measure what proportion of Ashoka social entrepreneurs have changed national policy after five years and discovered that the answer was over 50 percent . . . What proportions have changed the pattern in their field at the national level within five years? Three-quarters. And then a more indirect measure: what proportion have seen independent institutions copy the idea or the innovation in five years? More than 90 percent.

"The third level, framework change, differs yet again and requires different measures. In our early years," Drayton explained, "20 percent of Ashoka's effort was focused on framework change, which [involved] introducing the concept of social entrepreneurship very consciously. . . . To propagate the concept of social entrepreneurship, we worked with a small number at the universities and built up case examples, we made the examples clear, and we were insistent about the language."[23]

When Macro Fails, Try Micro

For decades, macroeconomists ran cross-country growth regressions to understand the factors that promote economic development and poverty alleviation, but this work did little to clarify which interventions were most effective in advancing those goals. Then, in the 1990s and 2000s, economists at MIT and elsewhere began developing and testing randomized evaluations (also known as randomized controlled trials, or RCTs) to understand which interventions worked, or didn't, in the field of international development. This turned out to be pathbreaking work.[24] Randomized evaluations are considered the gold standard of evaluation methodologies in development economics because they establish causality and enable a comparison between an intervention and the counterfactual case in which the intervention did not happen. RCTs are not suited to every intervention (for example, it is impossible to randomize the application of a national policy), and some economists criticize them on the basis of issues such as external validity, lack of generalizability, ethical challenges, and high costs. However, for many organizations, randomized evaluations can not only demonstrate impact but also guide strategic decision making. Randomization, as Esther Duflo of J-PAL explained to the *New Yorker*, "takes the guesswork, the wizardry, the technical prowess, the intuition, out of finding out whether something makes a difference."[25]

Over the past twelve years, Pratham, which works to foster literacy and raise learning levels of children across India, has completed eleven randomized evaluations to transform its operations for the better. "Randomized controlled trials have been tremendously helpful in allowing us to zoom in on the strategy that works and to change the model when it didn't work," said Dr. Madhav Chavan, cofounder of Pratham and former CEO of the Pratham Education Foundation. To illustrate the power of randomized evaluations, Chavan cited a Pratham program in India that uses volunteers to teach children to read:

We found that there was progress in the reading levels of the children that these volunteers were tutoring. But when we looked from one status report [that was a sample of the whole state] to the next year, [we saw that] there was no change in reading levels in the aggregate.

At first we had no answer to explain this puzzling discrepancy. But we got the answer from the RCT that was under way at the time. We confirmed that the volunteers were teaching successfully: the kids they tutored [had not been] able to read, and the volunteer's intervention got them to read. But we discovered that the volunteers were not sufficiently targeting the kids who needed the most help. Rather, the volunteers were teaching kids of high-income, educated parents who have some literacy themselves and are engaged. These kids would learn to read anyway at some point. The volunteer had no way of knowing that; the volunteer was just teaching. What was happening was that the data that we were seeing on monitoring was saying that the kids were learning and our intervention was creating improvements, but when we were looking at the state level, [we found that] the volunteers were teaching the kids who were going to learn to read eventually, even without the intervention.

Once we had this data, we altered our model significantly. Among other things, we worked to improve the way that we identified and targeted the kids most in need of our interventions. This example underscores the power of RCTs and the danger of trying to rely solely on monitoring data. The randomized controlled trial essentially isolates impact made by your intervention versus what the rest of the world is doing or what else is happening. And you can go and see, How much did *you* actually impact?[26]

In addition to enabling improvements in program strategy, randomized evaluations can instill a measurement mind-set. Chavan argued: "The RCT process is expensive, but the value is enormous because it builds internal capacity. After we started doing the RCTs, our entire organization started understanding data much better, and we acquired down the line a better understanding of how to think of impact."[27] Chavan and his team acknowledge that the RCT process has forced them to relinquish some control over program and evaluation design. But by investing in the best available form of external evaluation, Pratham has shown a definitive, causal link between its program and beneficiary impact—which in turn has unlocked millions of dollars in funding and a greater ability to scale.

Learn the Lessons of Cost-Benefit and Cost-Effectiveness Analyses

The nonprofit sector has historically viewed itself as distinct from other sectors and has often failed to draw on knowledge from other fields. In evaluation, nonprofits have not fully absorbed the lessons of cost-benefit and cost-effectiveness analyses. These economic evaluation methods have been used extensively in public policy since the 1960s. (A cost-benefit analysis uses monetary values, whereas a cost-effectiveness analysis weighs monetary costs against outcomes.) Many of the methodological strengths, weaknesses, complexities, and ambiguities we confront in the nonprofit sector were addressed long ago in the application of these approaches to other sectors.

Certainly, some nonprofits and foundations have undertaken cost-benefit and cost-effectiveness analyses, usually in collaboration with outside organizations like the RAND Corporation or Mathematica. But it has never become standard practice. A significant opportunity therefore remains for the nonprofit sector to learn and apply what is already known.

The core of any viable measurement methodology must include an analysis of costs and benefits. HKI, for example, pursues proven interventions that prevent blindness and malnutrition, and it prioritizes those that are low cost, thereby improving its ability to scale. In 2015, HKI's model allowed the organization to effect deep and lasting change in the lives of nearly three hundred million people.[28] Of course, the crucial analysis is the *combination* of costs and benefits—the benefit-per-unit cost. In some cases, organizations might intentionally and justifiably pursue high-cost interventions because the benefit-to-cost ratio is so great.

We must stop arguing over whether cost-benefit and cost-effectiveness analyses can be useful methods for nonprofit evaluation. They can. Of course we know that a human life can't be fully reflected in dollars and cents, but the history of cost-benefit and cost-effectiveness analyses has taught us that there is great decision-making value in applying lessons learned from such approaches. And the number-one lesson is this: the value of an analysis lies more in what you learn by doing it than in its specific result.

Use Evaluation to Create a Loop to Drive Strategic Thinking

Impact evaluation has the power to unleash a dynamic feedback loop that can drive strategic thinking. The resulting virtuous cycle brings together the vital concepts of mission, strategy—including theory of change—and impact evaluation. (Our next chapter adds poetry to our analytics by arguing that insight and courage are essential components of strategic thinking as well.)

For nonprofit leaders, strategic thinking involves a simple but powerful logic. This logic begins with mission—"the what and the why" of an organization, or in other words, its purpose. A nonprofit ideally starts with a clear and focused mission that is aligned with its skills and capacity; this mission is typically unchanging. The mission will in turn shape the organization's theory of change and its overall strategy. As we explained earlier, a theory of change sets forth the "logic of how." It describes how the organization will achieve its mission—and it incorporates evidence about why the theory works or can work. Theory of change drives the broader strategy, including the design of specific interventions or programs. Strategy is the "plan of how," a plan of action that translates the theory of change into how the nonprofit will actually achieve its mission. That starts with goals of organizational usefulness in a sensible time period—this could be three to five years, or a generation. Those goals are translated into plans, actions, and initiatives to achieve those goals.

And that is where impact evaluation comes into play. Impact evaluation reveals "what works and what doesn't." Impact evaluations are conducted at various milestones to evaluate progress against the organization's strategic goals, which, according to its theory of change, will over time enable the organization to achieve its mission. Impact evaluation enables a feedback loop mostly to strategy but also on occasion to theory of change: by discovering what works and what does not, an organization can refine and improve its strategy and theory of change over time. That is the virtuous cycle part. As the impact evaluation reveals what is working and what is not, then at a minimum your strategy, starting with goals, will have to change; in more extreme cases, you may have to rethink or reformulate your entire theory of change.

Strategic thinking cannot make real progress until it is supported by a feedback loop. The virtuous cycle that we have described here is nothing more or less than a closed loop system common to any well-run organization or project. In a *Wired* article titled "Harnessing the Power of Feedback Loops," Thomas Goetz notes that thinkers and researchers have been refining the basic framework for feedback loops for ages. Goetz traces the concept of feedback loops back to the eighteenth century, when engineers developed regulators to modulate steam engines and other mechanical systems. Goetz notes:

The potential of the feedback loop to affect behavior was explored in the 1960s, most notably in the work of Albert Bandura, a Stanford University psychologist and pioneer in the study of behavior change and motivation. Drawing on several education experiments involving children, Bandura observed that giving individuals a clear goal and a means to evaluate their progress toward that goal greatly increased the likelihood that they would achieve it. He later expanded this notion into the concept of self-efficacy, which holds that the more we believe we can meet a goal, the more likely we will do so. In the forty years since Bandura's early work, feedback loops have been thoroughly researched and validated in psychology, epidemiology, military strategy, environmental studies, engineering, and economics.[29]

Although the notion of a feedback loop might be prevalent in many disciplines, its use in the nonprofit sector is still surprisingly rare. Our Stanford survey found that only 57 percent of nonprofit executives and staff regularly use findings from their impact evaluation and performance measurement efforts to refine their organization's theory of change or its overall strategy. Getting all (or at least most) nonprofits to codify and implement these components of strategic thinking will be a major step in moving the nonprofit sector from good intentions to great impact.

Be Early, Be Managerial, and Consider External Evaluators

If possible, don't wait until your organization is firmly established to start measuring impact. Instead, start early and let evaluation results guide your program activities as you grow. BRAC, a trailblazer with respect to conducting rigorous evaluations, "invested very early in creating internal evaluation capacity, and that has continued to be a priority," explained its founder and chairman, Sir Fazle Hasan Abed. The organization maintains a research website that features more than one thousand publications related to the evaluation of BRAC programs.[30]

Starting early makes it easier to conduct impact evaluations because the stakes and the risks are lower. If an evaluation identifies a problem with a program, it is much easier to change course when the program is small and nascent than when it is large and has many stakeholders. This is especially important if an organization takes our advice and remains tightly focused on a single core mission even as it grows. Moreover, "investing upfront in evaluation capacity lowers the cost [of evaluation] down the road," notes Michael Faye, cofounder and chairman of GiveDirectly, a nonprofit that provides cash transfers to the extreme poor in developing countries.[31]

Early evaluation also instills a measurement mind-set that is crucial for any dynamic, growing organization. Small efforts can lead to big change: the measurement mind-set is often contagious within an organization, with staff learning to increasingly prioritize agreed-upon metrics. Top leaders can reinforce this mind-set by finding ways to signal the importance of measurement throughout their organizations. At BRAC, for example, the evaluation department is so important to the organization that it is known as a proving ground for senior leadership. (BRAC's current vice chair came from that department.) HKI uses a significant portion of its unrestricted funding to support experts in monitoring and evaluation in the field in Africa and Asia. "This speaks volumes to staff," said Spahn. "Everyone on our team knows that unrestricted funds are precious to us, and consequently everyone understands that evaluation is top priority for us as an organization."[32]

Evaluation should be more than a onetime endeavor that tells an organization whether to shut down a program or to keep it going. Instead, evaluation should occur frequently and should guide continuous improvement in the organization. As evaluations become more rigorous and reliable, their usefulness as an internal management tool will increase, providing an incentive to continue and intensify measurement efforts.

BRAC has a distinctively "failure-focused" approach to using evaluation as a management tool.[33] By using evaluation to identify points of difficulty, the organization is able to adjust its programs continuously. In 1979, for instance, it launched an oral rehydration program to treat diarrhea, a leading cause of death in children under the age of five. During its initial phase, the program was not meeting its goals, and an evaluation identified a host of challenges. Health workers, for example, weren't using the program methods at home with their own children—a clear sign of a more systemic problem. BRAC brought in an anthropologist who discovered that there was an underlying gender issue: BRAC hadn't persuaded men in the program's target households to use the treatment. The evaluation process also led BRAC to develop an incentive payment structure for health workers who promoted the oral rehydration therapy. "The program became enormously successful mainly due to continuous monitoring and evaluation of program effectiveness," said Abed.[34]

Measuring for management frees organizations from trying to attain the unattainable goal of perfection. "We look for organizations where if something goes wrong, they would know about it, and they would highlight it, and they would learn from it," Elie Hassenfeld of GiveWell told the *Huffington Post*. "If you're hearing some bad news, that's a good thing. If you're only hearing good news, that's a bad thing. You should hold organizations accountable to that standard rather than a totally unreasonable one of perfection."[35]

When creating a measurement culture, it is imperative to get the incentives right, or your efforts can backfire. In some schools, for example, an emphasis on standardized testing has had positive effects, but in others it has led to educators to "teach to the test" and neglect deeper learning. Regardless of your politics on this issue, it is undeniable that a failure to design incentives appropriately can cause problems for a measurement-oriented culture. Even businesses face this challenge: if you want a common example, ask a smart salesperson in any tech company how to game the company's quota system!

Measuring for management requires frequent monitoring. Taking a page from the best private-sector companies, Pratham tracks key metrics through daily SMS alerts and through weekly data uploads to a management information system from hundreds of staff members. In this way, the organization is able to identify and address problems before they spiral out of control. Measuring for management also entails staying abreast of data that emerges from outside an organization. For example, Landesa's measurement efforts not only include its own rigorous impact evaluation but also incorporate reviews of research done by other parties. "We stay current with the literature; this is extremely important. On occasion, 'other people's data' has led us to alter our program model and even our approach to measurement," commented Landesa cofounder Tim Hanstad. "For example, research in the mid-1990s increasingly showed the importance of women within the household obtaining legal land rights in order to achieve optimal outcomes for agricultural productivity and nutrition. . . . We realized that our theory of change and strategy needed to have a stronger gender lens and our measurement needed to break out the number of households to count women and men separately."[36]

Whether a nonprofit undertakes a randomized evaluation or another type of evaluation, it should consider inviting a third party to conduct it. External evaluators will have additional capabilities as well as a more impartial perspective.

Kravis Prize recipient Vicky Colbert, founder and executive director of Fundación Escuela Nueva, notes that her organization has benefited significantly from twelve external evaluations that it has undergone over the past two decades. "As Escuela Nueva has grown over the years, data and analysis from external sources have been extremely helpful in paving the way for us to scale," Colbert observed.[37] A research initiative led by Patrick McEwan, a faculty member at the Stanford Graduate School of Education, evaluated the effectiveness of the Escuela Nueva (EN) program in Colombia. McEwan found that the program had a positive and statistically significant effect on Spanish and mathematics achievement among third-grade students and on Spanish achievement among fifth-grade students. Yet his research also uncovered troubling variations in program implementation from one school to another: less than half of schools in the program were using official EN textbooks (learning guides), and one-third of those schools did not have libraries. Colbert and her team used that information to adapt the EN program. "Stakeholders, both internal and external, are less likely to dispute [program] changes when they are a response to real data obtained by an external evaluator," she says. "The improvements that we made, coupled with the many evaluations that demonstrated that our approach really worked, gave us momentum to scale."[38]

Youth Guidance, which works with at-risk youth in Chicago, found benefits from partnering with an external evaluator to conduct an RCT of its counseling and prevention program, Becoming a Man (BAM). Conducted by the University of Chicago's Crime Lab, the RCT confirmed BAM's impact by finding that among male students in Chicago Public Schools, BAM reduces violent crime arrests by 50 percent, reduces total arrests by 35 percent, improves on-time high school graduation rates by 19 percent, and increases school engagement.[39] Crime Lab research also notes that every $1 invested in the program results in $30 in societal gains from reductions in crime. In theory, moreover, increases in participants' future earnings resulting from the effect of BAM on high school graduation rates would make the return on investment even higher.[40] Michelle Adler Morrison, CEO of Youth Guidance, reflected:

Utilizing an outside evaluator makes a tremendous difference. However, nonprofits must also take into consideration the need for additional internal staff resources to support the evaluation. We learned that this can include everything from hiring and training new staff to making small investments in improved documentation systems. We also found it necessary to work out agreements with all of the principals of the schools in which we run our programs. The increased investment in time, energy, and planning is worth it. Today, we are able to better understand and communicate the value and positive outcomes associated with BAM. Obtaining evidence that our program has a significant impact has been instrumental in our efforts to generate more resources and scale the program. We have now expanded to over 80 public schools and anticipate a 32 percent increase in BAM participation over last year. Youth Guidance is now nationally recognized, and our external validation enabled us to obtain more funding to run a second RCT.[41]

When a nonprofit participates in an external evaluation, it should make sure that external evaluators do not report their results to the organization's program heads. Taking that approach will help ensure that the external evaluators' findings are independent. Such independence is especially important if program teams are conducting their own evaluations as well. BRAC's approach to evaluation, for instance, includes not only internal program monitoring and evaluation but also external auditing of programs, and its external auditors report not to program heads but to BRAC's audit department. Conclusions about program results are more likely to be accurate and unbiased when they draw from multiple sources. This independence is critical to effective impact evaluation, but unfortunately many nonprofits fail to protect it.

Share and Share Alike

Rigorous evaluation enables an organization to earn the right to exert influence across the nonprofit sector and in some cases to generate momentum for a particular type of intervention. Randomized evaluations are especially valuable in this regard because, in addition to providing the most rigorous and reliable methodology for assessing impact, they underscore the central importance of asking, "What would have happened if we hadn't done this intervention?"

Paul Niehaus, cofounder and president of GiveDirectly, noted that randomized evaluations have helped organizations to think about both costs and benefits. "Previously, with $1 of spending, the sector didn't know how much benefit gets delivered to the poor," he explained. "GiveDirectly's rigorous RCTs have demonstrated, for example, that cash transfers can be an effective intervention to alleviate poverty."[42] Ultimately, GiveDirectly aspires to use its randomized evaluations to establish its intervention as a model for others. "GiveDirectly wants to help governments and other NGOs use cash transfers as the 'standard of comparison' for aid programs—and ultimately shift resources from less cost-effective programs to cash transfers," wrote Cari Tuna, president of Good Ventures, in a post about her organization's $25 million donation to GiveDirectly.[43]

HKI also treats the evaluation process partly as a way to shape the work of others. In 2015, for example, HKI programs were the subject of twenty-four evaluations, many of them conducted by external evaluators.[44] "Whether the data demonstrates success or highlights challenges, we share lessons learned directly with our partners," Spahn explained. "We also publish our results in peer-reviewed journals and other publications."[45]

Leaders at BRAC have made a similar commitment to sharing lessons that emerge from its evaluation efforts. After an impact evaluation revealed that a BRAC microfinance program was not reaching the poorest people in its target population, the organization launched a new program called Targeting the Ultra-Poor in 2002.[46] BRAC has approached evaluation of this program with the goal of sharing lessons with the nonprofit sector as a whole. To showcase program results, it participates in a broad community of practice that includes the Consultative Group to Assist the Poor (CGAP), the Ford Foundation, IPA, and others.[47] "BRAC has compelling evidence that not only guides our own work but also influences others to invest in what works to eradicate extreme poverty," Abed says.[48] In 2006, CGAP and the Ford Foundation launched an initiative to test and adapt BRAC's model in eight countries. IPA and J-PAL conducted research on six of these pilot efforts—pilots that reached more than twenty-one thousand people—and found "large and lasting impacts on their standard of living across a diverse set of contexts and implementing partners."[49] Those partners, with input from BRAC, have shared their findings broadly; they developed a guide to replicating the model, for example. CGAP has adopted a variation of BRAC's approach as one of its focus areas and is working to support large-scale implementation and testing of the approach, especially by governments.[50]

An organization can contribute to the sector and enable others to learn even if its evaluation fails to generate positive results. The whole sector must fight publication bias, whereby evaluations that reveal statistically significant results for a program are more likely to get published than those that do not. To this end, J-PAL led the American Economic Association to launch the RCT Registry in

2013.[51] This registry, which to date includes more than 1,160 studies conducted in 106 countries,[52] is still nascent (so far it contains more study plans than results), but we are enthusiastic about its potential. There is precedent for this concept in the medical field, which in 1997 saw the creation of ClinicalTrials.gov, an online public repository of all medical trials.[53] Today, most medical journals no longer accept submissions that involve trials that are not registered at Clinical Trials.gov.[54] In that spirit, we offer this advice to nonprofits: announce your intention to evaluate your impact and explain the outcomes that you plan to measure. When you get the results, be transparent about both successes and failures so that others in the sector can learn from your experiences.

GiveDirectly provides a compelling example of such transparency. In 2013, it announced a randomized evaluation to the public *before* the results came in, thereby obligating itself to share those results even if they proved negative. The evaluation examined the effect of giving cash transfers (worth US$404 or more) to more than five hundred poor households in rural Kenya.[55] Some observers speculated that recipients would spend this money on alcohol or tobacco rather than food or medicine. If that proved true, GiveDirectly would have to disclose this undesirable result. However, in the end, "the results did not reveal spending on alcohol and tobacco but rather demonstrated significant increases in food security, consumption and well-being," Niehaus explained.[56]

GiveDirectly's commitment to transparency is also evident on its website, which posts real-time data on whether it is achieving its goals. Cofounder Michael Faye explained, "Everyone—including our donors, our staff, our allies, and our critics—can find out about our mistakes and challenges at the same time that we do. No chance of us hiding negative data; no lags so we can spin the messaging."[57]

In 2014, GiveDirectly chose to proactively disclose bad news after it uncovered fraud in its operation in Uganda. Roughly 2 percent of one month's round of cash-transfer payments was stolen as part of a scam orchestrated by a GiveDirectly director.[58] Niehaus later noted: "Of course it wasn't easy to talk about discovering fraud—we viewed this as our own organizational failure—but we were committed to building a brand of transparency, and so talking about it was imperative. It turned out that people were very receptive and supportive of us being public about it. For example, one of our major donors, Google.org, [recommitted to funding] us and even said 'Thank you for letting us know!'"[59]

Funders who are focused on evaluation can play an important role in sharing and collaborating with one another. The education reform community in the United States provides an example of funders that have worked together to focus on impact and evidence. A specific set of donors operates according to shared principles, takes evidence seriously, and brings a great deal of resources to bear on a problem.[60] Alexander Berger, program officer at the Open Philanthropy Project, explained:

Research by Jeffrey W. Snyder has shown that the big new education reform funders have a tight and interconnected set of grantees, including some high-performing charter school networks, alternative teacher prep providers, and advocacy groups. These funders have also supported a number of expensive, high-quality evaluations of the schools they've funded (for instance, numerous Mathematica evaluations of KIPP [Knowledge Is Power Program] schools), which has contributed to the development of an evaluation ecosystem that newer funders and programs can tap into. They've also generated enough business to sustain a network of consultants that focus on developing business plans and providing other advice to help reforms, especially charter networks, scale.[61]

The Edna McConnell Clark Foundation's (EMCF) Growth Capital Aggregation Pilot offers another example of a group of funders working together to prioritize measurement and promote programs that are evidence based. Leading this effort is Blue Meridian Partners, a consortium founded by twelve philanthropic organizations and incubated at EMCF by Chuck Harris (who also cofounded SeaChange Capital Partners after a career at Goldman Sachs). Blue Meridian plans to invest at least $1 billion in the most promising programs shown empirically to lift the life prospects of disadvantaged children and youth in the United States.[62]

We also see promise in enabling small, everyday donors to consult impact evaluations and encouraging them to focus their generosity on nonprofits that conduct such efforts. Before donating to a nonprofit, for example, donors can search its website to determine whether it has carried out robust evaluations. Sure, this is something of a pie-in-the-sky scenario; it takes work, knowledge, and skill to conduct this type of due diligence, and most small-scale donors are not prepared to invest such resources in their giving. Fortunately, they can draw on work by information intermediaries such as GiveWell, GuideStar, ImpactMatters, and Philanthropedia, which play increasingly important roles in helping small donors to perform due diligence.

To summarize, we "analytics who love Yeats" strongly support efforts to make impact evaluation standard practice in the nonprofit sector and an essential element of decision making for nonprofit leaders and funders. Yes, of course, Einstein was right: some important interventions will be difficult, perhaps impossible to measure. But the best—indeed, the only—way to discover what can be counted and what counts is to try. The alternative—withdrawing into a philosophical cocoon where quantification is viewed as inevitably reductionist and intuition reigns smugly unchallenged—is really no alternative at all.

CHAPTER 4

Insight and Courage

While strategy and science, mind and matter, are fundamental to success, it is heart and soul that are often the essential starting points on the road to building paradigm-shifting, high-impact nonprofits. In this chapter we therefore eschew the kind of analysis we have thus far used in our discussion of strategic thinking. Instead, we explore the heart and soul of our subject by concentrating on the stories of individual nonprofit leaders who have displayed exemplary insight and courage.

Insight

Insight is often portrayed in our culture as understanding that comes suddenly and unexpectedly: the epiphanies of James Joyce or the aha moments of Oprah Winfrey. This tradition has given us St. Paul on the road to Damascus, struck down by a bolt from the heavens that caused him to forever change his ways, and Sir Isaac Newton, relaxing under a tree when an apple fell on his head—and led him to discover the universal law of gravitation! While this version of insight makes for great storytelling, it offers little in the way of pedagogical tools—after all, how many of us can count on literally getting hit on the head and then having a life-changing conversion or paradigm-shifting idea?

Fortunately, our culture also offers examples of those who gain insight through years of persistence and determination, hard work and deep thought, exploration of the new and reconsideration of the old—those who know, in the oft-quoted words of Woody Allen, that "80 percent of success is showing up," or, in words attributed to Thomas Edison, "Genius is 1 percent inspiration and 99 percent perspiration."

It is in this spirit that we consider the experiences of some of the most inspiring social entrepreneurs and strategic leaders in the non-profit world.

Great nonprofits invariably start with a profound insight, that is, a distinct and compelling viewpoint about how social change can come about, including a sense of one's personal role in that change. Often, there is a creation story that includes a founder's epiphany as to how a nonprofit might attack the root cause of a challenge or take advantage of an opportunity to maximum effect. Bill Drayton, for example, borrowed the concept of entrepreneurship from business and asked how it could be applied to the social sector. Then, in 1980, he launched Ashoka, an organization that helped spawn the groundbreaking global movement we know as social entrepreneurship.

Drayton's insights were sparked back in 1962, when he was a nineteen-year-old Harvard undergraduate traveling around India in a beat-up, red-and-white Volkswagen minibus. Accompanied by three friends, Drayton had driven overland from Munich, passing through Syria, Jordan, Lebanon, and Iraq. The trip was much more than an adventurous lark—Drayton's goal was to meet with leading Gandhians and to learn about village-level efforts to organize people democratically. Drayton was struck by the massive inequality and poverty he witnessed. "The hundred-to-one difference in average per capita income between America and India at the time was a stark reality for the people who became my friends there," he later told *Forbes* magazine.[1] But he was also impressed by the many exciting social initiatives in India that were led by deeply committed individuals.

Drayton's enduring insight was that society had reached a point at which "social entrepreneurs" with deep commitment to an idea could be identified and then enabled—with relatively small infusions of funding—to generate massive social change. "We could see it," Drayton recalled. "The system was beginning to change. It was like hearing the ice breaking up at the end of winter in a lake. Creak, creak, groan, crash! The need was so big, the gap so huge, the opportunity to learn right before people's eyes. When do systems begin to change? When entrepreneurs decide it's time."[2]

The insights that led to Roy Prosterman's understanding that a tenant farmer obtaining clear ownership of land is often the first step out of extreme poverty—and Prosterman's subsequent decision to create the Rural Development Institute, which was later renamed Landesa—simmered for several years. He began the process of formulating those insights in the 1960s while working as an attorney at a prestigious law firm and doing client work in Puerto Rico and Liberia. Both of those places were very poor, and Liberia did not even have a functioning currency, road system, or telephone service. "This violated my sense of justice and fairness," Prosterman later explained. "This just should not be."[3] Prosterman left his law-firm job to teach property, antitrust, and international investment law at the University of Washington—and it was there that he had a key insight. "The sudden 'spark' happened," Prosterman said, "when one of my law students asked me what I thought of a recent law review article that argued that land reform for the landless poor in Latin America could be carried out cheaply, by using various legal theories to trace land rights back through lengthy periods of intervening time, and take land away from present holders without paying for it."[4]

Prosterman immediately comprehended the connection between poverty and landlessness. But, as he recalled, he believed that by approaching it in the way suggested by the law review article, "you would likely end up with civil war instead of land reform." To resolve the problem, he later explained, "those countries' governments and international aid donors would have to come up with the necessary resources to acquire the needed land at a fair price, and then redistribute it."[5] Prosterman laid out his arguments in a law review article called "Land Reform in Latin America: How to Have a Revolution Without a Revolution."[6] The article—published in 1966, in the midst of the Vietnam War—came to the attention of the United States Agency for International Development (USAID) and the Stanford Research Institute, which then commissioned Prosterman to collaborate with a team from the Stanford Research Institute on a study of the land tenure situation in South Vietnam.

Thus did Prosterman, a young American law professor wearing khaki trousers and a white short-sleeved shirt, find himself stepping down from a clattering helicopter and entering the lush jungle terrain deep in the Mekong delta. The air was dense and humid, peppered only by occasional sounds of artillery fire, unsettling reminders of the raging war. But Prosterman had a job to accomplish, so he set out for the emerald green paddy fields and spent most of the next eight weeks interviewing peasant farmers. He wore a hat, sunglasses, and brown hiking shoes that could handle the mud, and he carried a dog-eared notebook that would soon contain some of the far-reaching insights that would lead to the creation of the nonprofit now called Landesa. Over the following five decades, those insights would enable Landesa to transform the lives of four hundred million people across the globe.

"It didn't take much research or fieldwork to see that the Vietcong were drawing their support largely from the tenant farmers who were the great bulk of the rural poor," Prosterman told the *New York Times*.[7] The poor, landless farmers were drawn by the Vietcong's promise to bestow on them genuine property rights if the farmers joined the fight against the United States and the South Vietnamese government.

Prosterman and his colleagues investigated the specific terms of tenant farmer land agreements and learned that these impoverished rice farmers were typically sharecroppers who split the harvest fifty-fifty with farm owners. This system generated a perverse situation in which the farm owners reaped significant benefits while the farmers could barely feed their families and lacked both the security and the incentives that accompanied land ownership. When Prosterman questioned tenant farmers about this arrangement, they expressed vehement discontent. He noted that they also demonstrated this discontent through their willingness to risk their lives and join the Vietcong with the hope of changing the situation.

Prosterman's fieldwork left him convinced that land reform in South Vietnam was imperative and urgent. He believed that land should be redistributed so that those who worked on it could actually own it, and he began to develop a model of democratic land reform that would involve full compensation to landlords at market prices. "I ended up doing the basic formulation of a land-to-the-tiller law, and then advocating for it in the U.S. and South Vietnam," he explained.[8] He laid out his views in a report that became influential and controversial; the *New York Times* noted that it "assail[ed] Saigon on land reform."[9]

In January 1968, the Vietcong launched the Tet Offensive, a massive campaign of surprise attacks that occurred during Tet, the Vietnamese New Year holiday. Prosterman recalled, "I immediately sent a telegram to the Foreign Operations Subcommittee in Congress which stated that 'if the farmers owned their land, we would not be seeing this.'"[10] His views on the importance of land reform were cited in Congress and covered in media reports. The *New York Times* quoted this passage from his land reform report: "The failure to undertake a sweeping and genuine land reform in South Vietnam assuredly is costing, during each year of delay, the lives of large numbers of American soldiers over and above the number that would otherwise be killed. It is significantly prolonging the war."[11] This public advocacy put Prosterman at odds with USAID and led him to operate independently.

In 1969, President Richard M. Nixon called for land reform in South Vietnam and the adoption of the measures that Prosterman had drafted. In a 2012 interview for the *New York Times*, Prosterman explained that South Vietnam's land-to-tiller "law was adopted in 1970, and a million tenant-farmer families became owners of the land they tilled. The original landlords were paid a decent price, though partly in bonds that had not all matured when the communists took over. The twin results of this reform were that rice production went up by 30 percent and indigenous Vietcong recruitment in the South went down from a range of 3,500 to 7,000 men a month to 1,000 a month."[12]

Tellingly, when the United States fully exited Vietnam in 1975, the North didn't enforce the significant collectivization of farms in the South that they had in their own region. "Yield levels in the

South were 30 percent greater than in the North. In the wake of food shortages, the government backed away from its collectivization in the South. The North recognized that the productivity of the family farms in the South was higher and they needed to feed the country!" Prosterman noted.[13]

De-collectivization of farms began in Vietnam in the late 1980s and by 1993 was countrywide. Prosterman was in his Seattle office on a typical rainy day when he picked up the phone and was astonished to hear an official of the Vietnamese government on the other end. Vietnam had just passed a new land law that formally gave all farmers twenty-year rights on land used for annual crops and fifty-year rights on land used for perennial crops. The Vietnamese official invited Prosterman and his Landesa colleagues to do fieldwork in the country. "I thought we had heard the last word regarding land in Vietnam," said Prosterman. "All of a sudden, out of nowhere, I received a call explaining that they had finished breaking up the collective farms and wanted to see if they could get from us an independent assessment of the farmers. They said they would give us free reign throughout the country to conduct our fieldwork!"[14]

As Prosterman boarded a flight to Hanoi in the summer of 1993, again wearing khaki trousers and a white shirt but this time with a brown tweed sports jacket, he remembered the notebook that he had used in Vietnam forty years earlier and was struck by the extent to which a few fundamental insights had changed everything. In the Mekong delta's rice paddies, he had cemented his growing conviction that land reform is a key lever for global poverty alleviation. He had discovered that such reform could be implemented without violence and revolution by compensating landlords at market prices. Furthermore, he had come to appreciate how similar the problem and its solution were in countries other than Vietnam.

Tenant farmers and other nonlandowning cultivators in rural areas constitute the majority of the poor across the world. This vast unmet need, coupled with his insight into a solution, propelled Prosterman to devote his life to working with governments in more than fifty countries to design and implement land reform programs.

Landesa, the nonprofit that Prosterman founded to do this work, has transformed the lives of more than four hundred million people. As a result of land reform programs, household incomes can double, and farmers not only are able to feed their families more easily but also have surplus resources that allow them to invest in their land. Thanks to Landesa-driven programs, people have sufficient quantities of food, and the range of food available to them—and therefore its nutritional content—has also improved because farmers make their own choices about what to plant. Prosterman's dog-eared notebook is long gone. What remains is a legacy of implementation— a record of tangible improvements in the lives of those in extreme poverty.[15]

Vicky Colbert's codevelopment of the Escuela Nueva, or New School, educational model in Colombia ultimately led to the creation of the highly regarded nonprofit known as Fundación Escuela Nueva and offers another intriguing study of how leaders gain, develop, and implement their insights. Colbert was born into a family that cared about education—her mother founded teacher-training colleges—and grew up with an abiding interest in deepening the links between education and society. After graduating from Javeriana University in Colombia, she accepted an invitation from the university to support and provide distance education courses to rural teachers and began to understand the vast divide that separated rural reality from the theoretical concepts she had studied. When she won a Ford Foundation scholarship in the early 1970s, Colbert chose to attend the Stanford Graduate School of Education, where she received master's degrees in sociology of education and comparative education. Colbert returned to Colombia in 1973 and realized that the cutting-edge teaching techniques and pedagogical approaches she had learned at Stanford—which were being used in some of the best schools in America—could also be effectively implemented in low-income schools in Colombia and across Latin America. "There were so many difficulties and problems in education in Colombia at that time," Colbert explained. "Nothing was working." Among the many problems were high dropout rates, a top-down teacher-centered approach to education, weak school-community relationships, an emphasis on rote memorization, and low teacher morale.[16]

Colbert had discovered the remarkable power of moving away from traditional teacher-centered environments to child-centered settings that fully engage students and allow them to learn at their own pace and to participate. But she also realized that even the best and most heavily resourced schools in America were having difficulty implementing this approach and wondered if she could ever systematically implement it in Colombia, where resources were extremely scarce. A typical school in rural Colombia confronted enormous challenges, including isolation from educational planners as well as teachers who lacked adequate training but faced the outsized task of simultaneously teaching multiple grade levels.

Colbert was struck by the extent to which educational systems are among of the slowest institutions to change in society. She explained: "One observation that has resonated with me, that a friend shared with me several years ago, is if you brought a doctor from one hundred years ago to a hospital today, that person would be lost. But if you brought a teacher from one hundred years ago to a school today, that person would be right at home and would find most things the same." Colbert considered what kind of impetus would be needed to expedite massive, rapid change in the Colombian education system. Her first epiphany was that whatever she did had to be simple, cost-effective, and easily replicable. "We needed to take these wonderful ideas and make them simple enough so that a teacher in the middle of a jungle without a PhD could implement them easily," she explained. "My team and I designed a number of different interventions that shared this common theme of simplicity. Today, this process is called something new: 'design thinking.' But we've been doing it for more than thirty years."[17]

Colbert understood that simplicity was crucial to ensuring that teachers would embrace the interventions created by her team. "For example," she said, "we needed to create a high-quality but simple teacher training manual that could be used by any teacher, showing *how* to get children to learn in a participatory way, recognizing that teachers learn in the same way as they expect their students to do."[18] This included such basic things as allowing young children to sit in small groups, so that they could learn through dialogue and inter- action, instead of sitting in rows of desks and just listening to their teacher. Colbert and her team also developed accompanying learn- ing guides for children that incorporated higher-level thinking skills and could be used by any student. These guides served as planning tools for teachers and made the teachers' jobs easier; it also fostered parents' participation in their children's learning process.

Colbert and her team designed teacher-training programs that allowed teachers to experience the model she was urging them to replicate in the classrooms. They created demonstration schools in rural areas so that teachers could see and experience the "child- centered, personalized, and cooperative learning" approach in action. She also engaged teachers as participants in her effort to disseminate the model. "We created teachers' learning circles," she explained. "The teachers can be so isolated, and these circles enabled them to share what they are doing and their strategies for change. This facili- tated horizontal dissemination and enabled us to replicate and scale the model in a cost-effective way because the teachers themselves became the model's greatest fans; they were the actors of change."[19] The Escuela Nueva model was adopted by Colombia's Ministry of Education, which made it a national policy and extended it to more than twenty thousand schools. In 2000, UNESCO ranked Colombia's rural schools as second best among rural schools in Latin American countries; UNESCO also determined that Colombia's rural schools had surpassed its urban schools in quality of education.[20] As of today, the highly regarded Escuela Nueva model has reached more than five million children and has been formally implemented, mainly through governments, in more than sixteen countries in Latin America and beyond.[21]

Critical insights often arise from personal experience. Duncan Campbell, for example, was inspired by his childhood experience to start Friends of the Children (FOTC), a nonprofit that assigns "friends" to serve as mentors to severely at-risk American children.

Each friend assumes an active and regular presence in a child's life, from kindergarten through high school. "I was one of those [at-risk] kids," Campbell explained. "Both of my parents were alcoholics, we were on welfare living in a tough neighborhood in Portland, Oregon, my dad was in prison twice. In the face of chaos at home, I was fortunate to have profound, shaping influences by other caring adults in my life who encouraged and mentored me, and this was transformational. I landed on my feet and went on to have a successful career working in the private sector."[22] Early in his career, Campbell also worked in the detention system of Oregon's juvenile court, and that experience provided insights that informed the FOTC model. Many of the kids he encountered in that system had committed serious crimes, including arson and murder, but became motivated to change their lives when Campbell developed relationships with them.[23] "The relationships that I formed with these kids were astonishingly powerful," he recalled. "I became convinced that a relationship with a consistent, caring adult could have kept these kids out of juvenile detention, even though they had all been neglected at home."[24]

As a result of these insights, FOTC adopted an approach that enables high engagement over a prolonged period. FOTC employs and trains salaried professional mentors, rather than volunteers—a strategy that Campbell believes is key to providing the quality, consistency, and commitment required to succeed. "This target population of children are all neglected and damaged in some way; many have been abused and simply don't believe that an adult cares for them," he said. "Consequently, it takes a tremendous intervening force and a very long time to heal them. Typically [it takes] a minimum of three to six years to establish a deep trusting relationship. We pay the mentors because the turnover in volunteer mentor programs is so high, [and] this particular population of kids needs consistency."[25] The average tenure of friend-mentors is more than seven years, and many have been working with the organization for twenty years or more.

Rather than cherry-picking the least at-risk kids within the pool of potential participants, FOTC reaches out to the most at-risk kids. Its staff members work with public school kindergartens in high-poverty areas to select children who appear overwhelmed by their circumstances (as opposed to others who display natural resilience). "Even though we pick the most challenging cases, our intervention is transformational enough to break the cycle of intergenerational poverty!" said Campbell. He continued:

For example, research has found that in the United States, daughters of teenage mothers are more likely to give birth as a teen. Although 85 percent of Friends participants were born to a teen parent, only 2 percent of Friends participants become teen parents themselves, which is less than the annual teen birthrate in the United States. Moreover, the model pays for itself in the impact it generates for society. The Harvard Business School Association of Oregon conducted an analysis showing that for every $1 invested in Friends of the Children, the community benefits over $7 in saved social costs. Helping one child saves the community $900,000.[26]

Courage

Courage, like insight, is an indispensable aspect of nonprofit strategic leadership. Some nonprofit leaders and organizations have tremendous insight but lack the courage to stand firm against the social sector's many pressures as they execute on that insight. If leaders do not proactively resist them, these pressures may lead to managerial dysfunction and suboptimal long-term impact for beneficiaries. Fortunately, leaders in the social sector do manifest many kinds of courage.

It takes courage for leaders to keep their nonprofit focused on mission despite the many pressures to allow mission creep. The National CASA (Court Appointed Special Advocates) Association and Pratham, for instance, had several opportunities to extend their activities into different environments but declined to pursue those opportunities. It also takes courage for leaders to build and develop long-term funders whose values and practices are aligned with the needs of their organization. Ashoka, for instance, refused institutional support from many foundations for fear that the foundations' bureaucratic approach would interfere with social entrepreneurs' need for agile, creative funding. Similarly, courage is evident in organizations that resist the temptation to create a rubber-stamp board and instead cultivate board members who will proactively engage with an organization's strategy and even disagree with its leaders. Nonprofits also show courage when they decide to undergo rigorous external evaluations of programmatic impact so that they can face problems head-on and thereby maximize future impact.

So, how does one get courage? Some argue that it is an inborn character trait—that you either have it or you don't. Others say it is a virtue that can be acquired. The American writer Mark Twain proclaimed that courage was not an absence of fear but resistance to it and mastery of it. As a young statesman, John F. Kennedy was so intrigued by the subject of courage that he wrote a book about it, *Profiles in Courage*, which won a Pulitzer Prize in 1957. In it, he suggested that stories about the courage of others "can teach, they can offer hope, they can provide inspiration. But they cannot supply courage itself. For this each man must look into his own soul."[27] Like Kennedy, we cannot supply you with courage, but we can offer you examples that might help you find it.

Courageous organizational leadership is often a by-product of individual courage born of personal experience. Dr. Sakena Yacoobi's experience of growing up in Afghanistan and later returning to found and lead the Afghan Institute of Learning (AIL) is an illustrative example. Yacoobi recounted:

Growing up in Afghanistan, my father did not raise me like a traditional girl. He encouraged me to study and sought out opportunities for me to develop my intellect. After completing twelfth grade in Afghanistan, I had the opportunity to go to university in the U.S. It was an extraordinary but difficult experience. My English was weak, which made the studies very challenging, and I had to do odd jobs at night to pay for my studies. Consequently, I could never sleep more than four hours per night. Many times I considered giving up. But my father taught me to never give up. And my education ultimately changed my life.[28]

In 1992, Yacoobi left a comfortable, successful career as a professor and consultant in the United States to work with the 7.5 million Afghans in Pakistan refugee camps. Afghanistan had been devastated by years of warfare following the Soviet invasion of the country in 1979, with millions of its civilians killed, displaced, or made refugees. The withdrawal of Soviet forces was followed by civil war and, in the 1990s, the rise and subsequent reign of the Taliban. "When [the] Taliban took over, . . . they banned education completely for women," Yacoobi explained. "Women couldn't walk on the street without a man. . . . There is not one single family that didn't lose somebody in their house [during] this war. This has [created] the environment that we [have] today: people don't trust, people don't feel comfortable, people don't feel safe anymore. That's Afghanistan."[29] Yacoobi was so deeply affected by the suffering and privation she saw in her country and among the refugees that she had to act. "I knew that the only way that I could lift these people and help was through education, and that was it—I went after education," she said.[30]

In the early days of AIL, during the 1990s, Yacoobi courageously led its operations from Peshawar, Pakistan, opening schools and health clinics and training teachers. Representatives from communities in Afghanistan came and asked her to support underground schools because education for girls was strictly prohibited under the Taliban regime. At enormous risk to her safety, Yacoobi oversaw eighty underground schools that educated three thousand girls during the period before the fall of the Taliban in 2001. "At any moment, the Taliban could come after me," she said. "I knew I could be killed, and that they would torture me before they killed me. . . . But I continued, quite simply, because I believe in education. It had changed my own life. And I believe that education has the power to help change the lives of the people of Afghanistan."[31] Because of security threats, Yacoobi couldn't establish a home but instead traveled constantly among AIL sites—even when, after the fall of the Taliban, she and her staff began to work openly in Afghanistan. "No one could know my whereabouts, and fear was always there with me," Yacoobi recalled. "I had to summon courage on a daily basis. I did so by allowing my passion for the cause to prevail."[32]

One clear autumn day in 2002, Yacoobi found herself forced to muster every ounce of courage she possessed. She and a female AIL staffer had left Kabul in the backseat of a dilapidated Land Cruiser that was heading to an AIL women's learning center in northern Afghanistan. As the car jostled and swerved on the pothole-filled road, the pair enthusiastically discussed AIL's recent progress. Suddenly the car lurched to a stop, causing Yacoobi to look up. In an instant, searing fear erased her enthusiasm. A group of nineteen young men in tattered clothes and chest-length beards, each with a rifle held to his shoulder, blocked the road. When Yacoobi looked at their eyes, she saw clear bad intent.[33]

The driver of Yacoobi's car asked the men what they wanted. There was a pause—and then they pointed to Yacoobi, said her full name, and demanded to talk to her. Yacoobi's heart raced. It raced even faster when the men insisted she get out of the car.[34] Yacoobi was trembling from fear, but she summoned the lessons of courage she had learned from her fellow Afghans. "First," she explained:

I supplanted my fear by shifting my mind-set to others. I took personal responsibility for the others in my car. I knew that if I didn't do what the young men asked, then my staff and driver could very well be killed. So I focused on my staff and driver and what they needed me to do. I got out of the car. I did not act like I was afraid, even though I was terrified. That is always very important. Never, ever act like you are afraid. As I stood in front of the men, I held on to the car door so that they wouldn't see me shaking and I wouldn't collapse. I looked them directly in the eye. I took deep breaths, which helped me to muster a strong voice so they wouldn't hear my fear. And then I began to negotiate with them.[35]

Yacoobi asked the men what they wanted of her and received an utterly unexpected reply. "Every day we watch your car come and visit your centers for women and girls," the leader of the men said. "They are learning to read. What about us? We have been fighting and living in caves since we were little boys. Now we are too old for school, but we want to study. What can you do for us?"[36]

At the time, AIL had enough funding only to teach girls and women; Yacoobi had no idea if she could quickly find funding for male education. "Give me a week," she said. "We will be waiting," came the reply.[37] And the men unblocked the road.

Yacoobi spent the next few days wrestling with how to proceed—and chose forgiveness as the best option. "I have learned over the years that forgiveness helps to set fears aside," Yacoobi explained. Then she quickly—and miraculously—found enough funding for a boys' education center. She returned to the site of the incident the following week and invited the men to come and learn. She also said to them, "I will help you on the condition that you change your clothes, wash your face, shave, learn manners, be dedicated to your studies, and get a job when you finish!"[38]

And so, Yacoobi explained, the men "went to school, studied hard, and also learned about human rights, cleanliness, manners, and ethics. Their parents were so happy! Soon they were able to transition into regular school. All graduated from high school. Many went on to university or to study computers. Then and now, they have made sure that AIL has no security concerns in their communities. Today their daughters are going to school."[39] Many of these men now work for AIL and have joined Yacoobi's effort to educate others in Afghanistan.[40] (To date, AIL has taught 50,000 women and girls to read, trained 6,000 teachers, and provided health care and health education to 780,000 people.[41])

Yacoobi's personal experiences and the courage she has demonstrated throughout her life are undoubtedly extreme. Most of us are fortunate to grow up in far more peaceful situations and to have little need for that sort of bravery. But Yacoobi's example of putting passion for her cause above all else, her determination to focus on others, her refusal to let her fear show, and her insistence on allowing forgiveness to fuel acts of love and kindness are relevant to all of us.

Most nonprofit leaders will never have to face down armed gunmen, but all nonprofit leaders must develop the courage required to implement their insights—and to accept the sacrifices that come with doing so. The insights that led Sal Khan to found the Khan Academy came somewhat prosaically, starting in 2004 when Khan, who was in Boston, began tutoring his cousin, Nadia, in Louisiana, as she struggled with mathematics. "Then the rest of the family heard there was free tutoring," he recalled, and other relatives started taking advantage of his services.[42] Khan found that he was unable to accommodate all the tutoring requests—until a friend suggested he film the tutorials, post them on YouTube, and let family members view them at leisure. This would enable Khan to preserve his time while still helping others. He was initially somewhat dismissive of the idea. "I thought YouTube was for people to post videos of their cats playing the piano, not for serious academic tutorials," he explained. "But I eventually did it."[43]

For Khan, one rather surprising insight came when his cousins told him that they liked him better on YouTube than in person! In a 2011 TED Talk, he noted that the video format gave his cousins some control—they could pause, repeat, skip ahead, and watch at their own pace. He explained, "Probably the least-appreciated aspect of this is the notion that the very first time that you're trying to get your brain around a new concept, the very last thing you need is another human being saying, 'Do you understand this?'"[44]

At the time of this insight, Khan was working in finance, but his path within that field had been challenging. Khan had earned a master's degree in electrical engineering and computer science and then an MBA. He recalled: "When I graduated from Harvard Business School in 2003, I struggled to find a job in finance. I went to business school to make a career change, to transition from technology to finance. But as I came on the job market looking for a job in finance, I was rejected [by] about forty different places."[45] He persevered and ultimately obtained a position as an analyst for, and sole employee of, Daniel Wohl, who ran Wohl Capital Management.[46] Khan began making and posting video tutorials in 2006. Over time they attracted millions of viewers, and he came to understand their potential as a global educational resource. He reflected, "When I first saw the thank-you letters from people who had benefited from the video tutorials—from so many people around the world beyond my cousins—it was very inspiring."[47] He incorporated Khan Academy as a 501(c)(3) nonprofit organization in 2008 and continued to work on it during nights and weekends. But he was unwilling to relinquish the financial-industry job he had worked so hard to obtain.

In the fall of 2009, Khan summoned the courage to leave his lucrative career and pursue Khan Academy full time. At the time, Khan Academy had no office space, no funding, and no funding prospects. But Khan had made his choice. He lived off his savings and worked out of a desk in his closet for nine months. Then Khan Academy received its first significant donation—$10,000, from Ann Doerr, who provided a second donation of $100,000 after she realized that Khan was working without pay.[48] In September 2010, Khan Academy received large grants from Google ($2 million) and the Bill & Melinda Gates Foundation ($1.5 million) and began to build out its organization.[49]

Khan has since established himself as a successful Silicon Valley technology entrepreneur. Although his salary is high in comparison with many nonprofit sector benchmarks, he could command significantly more in the private sector. But Khan does not dwell on this. "I love what I'm doing now," he said. "I get to wake up and pursue this amazing mission every day, and I must confess that I love making videos!"[50] Khan has also displayed the courage of his conviction by resisting the temptation to make Khan Academy a for-profit company. He explained: "I envisioned Khan Academy as a nonprofit from day one. I registered our domain name as khanacademy.org, not 'dot com.' From the outset, I saw enormous potential for social impact, and I want people to view our tutorials as fully for them, not designed to make a profit."[51]

Courageous nonprofit leaders will often need to make unpopular decisions to maximize their organization's long-term impact on beneficiaries. This can mean having hard conversations with a founder who needs to move out of an executive role, or saying no to a funder or board member whose agenda might cause mission creep. The most extraordinary and effective nonprofit leaders come to grips with unpopularity very early in their careers.

Insight and courage are difficult to quantify and measure, but their importance to a nonprofit cannot be underestimated—and people in the social sector generally recognize how valuable these qualities are. In our 2016 Stanford survey, we asked nonprofit executives and staff to consider how important it was for top leaders to display insight and courage. Notably, 74 percent of respondents indicated that the presence of those qualities in their founder was "essential to the organization's impact," and 86 percent of them indicated that it was "essential to the organization's impact" for their nonfounder executive director or CEO to demonstrate those qualities.[52]

In fact, we believe that insight and courage are so important that they should be included as criteria when foundations and major donors are engaged in grant-making decisions. Experienced (and even inexperienced) funders can recognize insight and courage, and we hope that people in the social sector will learn to reward and fully value those qualities. Insight and courage are the sine qua non of nonprofit strategic leadership—without them, there is nothing.

PART II

Strategic Management
Fuel Your Engine of Impact

CHAPTER 5

Your Team of Teams

Building and Sustaining a
High-Performing Organization

"We are only as good as our people," goes the oft-quoted bromide. True enough—your organization is only as good as those people within it who embody your mission and tirelessly strive to achieve it. But we would amend the old saying to read, "You are only as good as your people . . . and how you organize and lead them." Because your people, however good, will thrive only in a strong organization with wise and responsive leadership.

When it comes to organizational thinking, we take our cue from the immortal words of the song from *Casablanca*: "The fundamental things apply / as time goes by."[1] In this chapter, therefore, we have distilled six principles of high-performing nonprofit organizations that reflect our experiences and the insights of several astute observers of organizations. These principles, we believe, will provide part of the fuel needed to sustain your engine of impact.

But first, we want to present an emerging model that we believe has the potential to reinvent the way that nonprofits build and develop their organizations. It's called team of teams, and it reflects fundamental changes in the world on which nonprofits hope to have an impact.

Team of Teams: An Emerging Organizational Model
There are three approaches to designing organizational structures: functional, business unit, and what has variously been called matrix or network.

We are all familiar with functional organizations. Designed for companies with one business, or nonprofits with a single major focus, such organizations are built around key functions—finance, sales, marketing, operations, and so on—that all report to a general manager. Business unit organizations, which developed as companies diversified into more than one business or into multiple countries, are, in simple terms, a collection of functional organizations (often with some contextual adaptation). Such organizations include General Electric, Citicorp, or, for that matter, the International Federation of Red Cross and Red Crescent Societies.[2]

Starting in the 1980s, businesses experimented with a matrix structure. The matrix organization was an attempt to have each function report to two bosses, one for a business unit and another for a function such as sales. Then, as technology provided the architecture to support greater organizational flexibility, many businesses adopted a network structure. Behind this shift lay the observation that any important role or decision required multiple inputs from parts of an organization that extended beyond one function or one business unit.

Ashoka, which played a critical role in defining, growing, and proselytizing the social entrepreneurship movement, recently adopted an organizational model—the team-of-teams model—that takes the network structure in a promising new direction.[3] In our view, the principles that underlie this model are so strong that more and more high-performing organizations will begin to follow it. Ashoka's transition to this model reflects its shift to a strategy that it calls "Everyone a Changemaker": according to Ashoka, we are entering a world in which all individuals, and not just pathbreaking social entrepreneurs, will become agents of change.[4]

The team-of-teams model emphasizes decentralized autonomy, meritocracy, and a sense of partnership. Teams come together around specific goals, with a single coordinating executive team at the center, and the composition of each team shifts as needed over time. Teams and team members work together in constantly changing, fluid ways. Ashoka founder and CEO Bill Drayton developed the vision for this model in response to a major paradigm shift that is being driven in part by technology and globalization. As the Ashoka website explains: "We are living in a time of rapid change. We are moving from a world of silos and hierarchy to one of fluidity and many leaders. Only institutions that organize differently and individuals who develop different skills will be ready for the world that awaits them."[5] Since the Industrial Revolution, Drayton explained, efficiency and repetition have been driving forces within most organizations: "People specialized and repeated one skill," he said. "This happens to be very efficient in a world of repetition, but it is a complete failure in the world that we are now in." Today's world is one of change rather than repetition. "More and more, everyone is bumping into everyone else," Drayton said. "Forget all the old walls and sectors. The boundaries are being torn down!" Organizational structures, he added, are "morphing and interconnected and [certain to] be different in the future."[6]

Drayton believes that project- and team-based work is critical to navigating this new environment, as are entrepreneurial skills—and empathy. As the Ashoka website explains: "In this new world, empathy is one of the most important skills. Empathy is foundational to the ability to resolve conflict, collaborate in teams, align interests, listen effectively, and make decisions where there are no rules or precedents—to solve problems and drive change."[7]

In a world where everyone is a changemaker, hierarchies need to be broken down and new forms of organization are needed to promote collaboration at the individual level and at scale. As Drayton explained:

Everyone needs to be aware of the changes and help others adapt. People must see opportunities and seize them with other people in new teams of teams. If you see big new opportunities, you have to build a whole new team of teams, and that team of teams is going to have a lot of pieces, and they interconnect and overlap. . . . They morph, and they change all the time. And you can't assume everything else is stable because it isn't. It's just the opposite of the old system. People have to have different skills. They have to organize and lead in different ways. And so the form of organization we're talking about . . . it's not just something sort of efficient or nice, it's necessary![8]

"The challenge with [the] organizational model," Drayton explained further, "is 'How do we develop the architecture that facilitates that?'"[9] At Ashoka, the solution has been to create a leadership team that includes three to six people. Currently, this team consists of Drayton; Diana Wells, president of Ashoka; and Anamaria Schindler, co–president emeritus. Drayton elaborated on other elements of Ashoka's evolving structure: "We have an architects group that focuses on systems. In addition, there are ninety to one hundred leadership group members, five continental hubs (which are mini teams), and then a set of people who step in to provide overall leadership. We do not do one another's jobs. But we have worked together very closely."[10]

Three kinds of people are needed to execute a team-of-teams model: administrative staff, content experts, and area leaders who are on a track in which they need to be promoted or they will leave. Meritocracy is a critical element of this new organizational model. Wells explained:

At Ashoka, we have 115 people in our DC office and 405 worldwide, and there is indeed a meritocracy. We base promotions on how much change making happens based on somebody's contributions, and it does not correlate to age or education. So titles aren't "director" but "senior change leader," "senior change manager," "entrepreneur," "intrapreneur." It's not a promotion after two or three years; it is when they are ready. Managers make recommendations, senior leaders evaluate teams, [and] a group comes together to make final decisions.[11]

The team-of-teams model provides exciting on-the-job leadership development opportunities for Ashoka's staff. Drayton noted, "Two-thirds of people's time is going to be in temporary teams—a partnership team, a goal team. In that world, there are so many more opportunities for people's career paths than were possible previously."[12]

Adoption of this new model has led Ashoka to radically shift its hiring practices. Instead of hiring for specific positions, it hires for fit with its value system and culture. Ashoka employees—who are chosen for characteristics such as entrepreneurial quality, belief in Ashoka's "everyone a changemaker" vision, and social and emotional intelligence—are part of teams that extend beyond the organization. Drayton commented, "As the wall that separates inside and outside goes away, we don't think about teams anymore as solely Ashoka employees—that's ridiculous. We often don't have enough people at a senior level to staff a particular team, so we include experts from outside Ashoka."[13] Wells added, "We also include those who were previously involved with Ashoka but have gone on to do other things. People leave and come back and still feel part of the family and network. This is highly valuable."[14]

The team-of-teams model requires effective back-end processes to maintain a robust organizational structure. In its transition to a team-of-teams culture, the Ashoka team in charge of talent found that the previous system for managing human capital—consisting largely of Excel spreadsheets, physical files, and emails—was hampering employee productivity and collaboration across Ashoka's global offices. Consequently, moving to a more technologically sophisticated solution was critical to facilitating team-of-teams organizing. This led Ashoka to adopt cloud-based software for human resource management.[15] The executive team is now able to manage four hundred employees in less time than it previously took to manage twenty. Ashoka also shifted its financial systems to a cloud-computing environment. As a result, local offices can now upload their monthly reports to a central system instead of sending spreadsheets to global headquarters. According to CFO Mary Andre, this "real-time reporting" has made possible "a tremendous amount of trend analysis and future growth projections not available before."[16]

Ashoka's new organizational model has exciting potential, not least because it provides an elegant way to incorporate all the attributes of high-performing nonprofit organizations. It is an especially powerful model for knowledge-oriented organizations, including foundations. The prevailing organizational model for foundations leads to large, slow bureaucracies that take a long time to make grants that are both small in number and small in scale. We assert that most foundations could achieve better performance, and do so with fewer staff, if they followed a team-of-teams model.

Within a decade, we believe, this model will become the new standard for nonprofits, foundations, and even for-profit global businesses. Many organizations of various types are already migrating to a team-of-teams model (although often without specific acknowledgment), driven by the simple fact that work is increasingly being done in cross-organizational project teams. Indeed, most global professional services firms—management consulting firms, for example—in effect follow a team-of-teams model.

Consider the case of Pratham. While Pratham overall is not organized with a team-of-teams model, it has effectively adopted elements of this model to implement an annual project. Every year since 2005, Pratham's Annual Status of Education Report (ASER) Centre has conducted an annual survey called ASER (*aser* means "impact" in Hindi and Urdu) that provides reliable estimates of children's learning outcomes in every state and rural district of India. ASER is the only source of such data in India, and its findings are used to propel action and create a demand for better education services at the ground level.

ASER surveys six hundred thousand children each year in three hundred thousand sampled households.[17] Collecting this vast array of data is no easy task, especially on a limited budget. That is where Pratham's variation on a team-of-teams model comes into play. The ASER Centre, based in New Delhi, functions as a core team that designs survey tools and procedures. It also oversees teams of volunteers (thirty thousand volunteers per year!) who go door-to-door to assess the educational status of children across the country.[18]

One set of volunteers includes Pratham staff members who work in other areas of the organization. According to Rukmini Banerji, CEO of Pratham, one goal of starting ASER was to build capacity among Pratham staff "with respect to the nuts and bolts of measurement, evidence, and analysis." Banerji elaborated:

The first year, we recruited volunteers from different parts of Pratham. In the second year, we noticed that those units sent different people from the year before. We realized that a time-based project like ASER teaches people a lot in a very short time. No wonder we got a new set of people to train in the second year. ASER is an excellent short boot camp in which you either perform well or perish. The survey is run like a course in which participants acquire skills that are applicable in other parts of Pratham as well. In fact, the skill acquisition is so strong that . . . within Pratham the next generation of leaders often come from ASER.[19]

Another source of volunteers is the more than two thousand organizations that have partnered with ASER to date; they range from universities and colleges to nongovernmental organizations, self-help groups, youth clubs, government departments, and private-sector companies. The ASER Centre manages relationships with these partner organizations, and volunteers from those organizations spread out across the country to conduct the survey and disseminate the results. After a two-to-three-day training, volunteers spend two days in each village talking to stakeholders such as the *sarpanch* (elected head of local village government), headmasters, teachers, and locals. Volunteers seek to understand and map the village layout so that they can select sample households. Next they record basic household information and assess the reading and arithmetic skills of children in each household. Banerji reflected: "Over time, the survey has evolved into a 'See India' program that appeals to a sense of adventure in the volunteers. ASER takes surveyors to far-off villages that they otherwise would never go to. In fact, the harder it is to get to a village, the more excited our volunteers are about it!"[20]

Volunteers are trained in basic sampling, survey methodology, and statistics, and the ASER Centre ensures strict quality control through a framework that consists of three parts: training, monitoring, and "recheck." Training takes place at the national, state, and district levels, and monitoring is equally sophisticated: While volunteers conduct the survey, ASER master trainers review their work, and in turn the master trainers' work is monitored through call centers. This dual approach to monitoring helps ASER to identify areas that require corrective action. Finally, ASER rechecks data through multiple processes, including a field recheck and an external process audit.[21] This form of centrally facilitated quality control resembles the way that a core team operates in a team-of-teams structure.

*Six Enduring Principles of High-Performing
Nonprofit Organizations*

Many nonprofits of every scale and scope—as well as businesses—are gradually moving to a team-of-teams organizational model. Indeed, many millennials have never worked in any other way. But even as this model spreads and becomes an acknowledged norm, great nonprofits must continue to heed certain enduring principles of high-performing organizations. Here, adapted from the work of management thinkers who we admire and reinforced by our own experience, are six such principles.

"MISSION COMES FIRST" (FROM PETER DRUCKER)

Yes, we will take every opportunity to reinforce the primacy of mission—and with good reason. Mission is a critical aspect of nonprofit organizational leadership, culture, and performance. It is what drives a world-class professional to forgo personal wealth to lead a nonprofit dedicated to improving some vital aspect of the human condition. It is the common ground for everyone associated with a nonprofit—the wealthy donor, the busy board member, the talented and driven social entrepreneur, and the staff member who shows up for work, rain or shine. Mission is what helps a nonprofit to motivate, develop, and retain talent when financial incentives are modest, and it remains front and center in a high-performing organization.

By insisting on the primacy of mission, we align ourselves with the founder of modern organizational leadership and management, Peter F. Drucker. We do so partly in the hope of benefiting from credibility through association. Drucker studied leaders and organizations deeply but with little or no reliance on quantitative analysis—and his wisdom continues to resonate. In *Managing the Nonprofit Organization: Principles and Practices,* the first section of which is titled "Mission Comes First: And Your Role as a Leader," Drucker writes, "What matters is not the leader's charisma. What matters is the leader's mission."[22]

"Mission comes first." For this primus inter pares observation, you don't have to believe us—but believe Peter Drucker, who wrote those words in 1990. Your reward for agreeing with us is that we will refrain from presenting more case examples to demonstrate this point!

ENERGIZED BY AN EXTRAORDINARILY INTENSE PERFORMANCE-DRIVEN ENVIRONMENT (FROM MCKINSEY, MICHAEL MURRAY, AND GUILLERMO MARMOL)

High-performing businesses and high-performing nonprofits have certain attributes in common. None is more important, or harder to describe, than an extraordinarily intense performance-driven environment. (We borrow this concept from a classic article by two onetime executives at McKinsey & Company, R. Michael Murray Jr. and Guillermo G. Marmol.[23]) We can walk into any organization and determine within minutes whether it has the kind of intensity that high-performing organizations generate. It is like a pulse, and it says: "We are on a mission. We have an important noble purpose that we all understand. We will not fail. But if we do fail, we will get up again and again and keep going—because we are completely committed to our mission."

Organizations that are less performance driven lack this level of intensity. Certainly, they have people who care about their work and who work hard. But their organizational environment is neutral—or worse: it discourages them from working harder, from collaborating effectively, from sharing common goals, from celebrating successes, and from deciding that failure is not an option.

Similarly, one organizational principle that we rarely observe in nonprofit organizations is meritocracy. Meritocracy fosters the intense, performance-driven environment required to succeed, and it should be a core value of most, if not all, nonprofits. Building such an environment requires leaders to recognize and reward excellence, to develop the skills that contribute to it, and, most difficult, to ease out (or fire, if necessary) individuals whose performance falls short. But, with noteworthy exceptions—such as elite universities and arts organizations—nonprofit organizations seem reluctant to take the leap required to build and sustain a high-performing, meritocratic organization. They need to overcome this reluctance.

FOLLOW THE "FIRST WHO . . . THEN WHAT" PRINCIPLE—
GETTING THE RIGHT PEOPLE ON THE BUS WITHIN SOCIAL
SECTOR CONSTRAINTS (FROM JIM COLLINS)

In his bestselling book *Good to Great*, Jim Collins emphasizes "the sheer rigor needed in people decisions."[24] In a subsequent book aimed at social sector leaders, he expands on that point: "Those who build great organizations make sure they have the right people on the bus, the wrong people off the bus, and the right people in the key seats before they figure out where to drive the bus. They always think *first* about who and *then* about what."[25] This "first who . . . then what" principle, Collins argues, is essential to every nonprofit's success.[26]

For most organizations, actually getting the right people on the proverbial bus remains a persistent challenge. In recruiting top talent, nonprofits cannot use many of the carrots that businesses employ, such as competitive base compensation, profit sharing, or other financial incentives. In a 2008 study of nonprofit retention challenges titled *Ready to Lead?*, 69 percent of survey respondents said that they were underpaid in their current positions and 64 percent said that they had "financial concerns about committing to a career in the nonprofit sector."[27] But Collins's research reveals that high-performing organizations maintain an unwavering focus on finding the best people even when financial incentives are not available. Collins explains:

Business executives . . . can use money to buy talent. Most social sector leaders, on the other hand, must rely on people underpaid relative to the private sector or, in the case of volunteers, paid not at all. Yet a finding from our research is instructive: the key variable is not how (or how much) you pay, but *who* you have on the bus. The comparison companies in our research—those that failed to become great—placed greater emphasis on using incentives to "motivate" otherwise unmotivated or undisciplined people. The great companies, in contrast, focused on getting and hanging on to the right people in the first place—those who are productively neurotic, those who are *self*-motivated and *self*-disciplined, those who wake up every day, compulsively driven to do the best they can because it is simply part of their DNA. In the social sectors, when big incentives (or compensation at all, in the case of volunteers) are simply not possible, the First Who principle becomes even more important. Lack of resources is no excuse for lack of rigor—it makes selectivity all the more vital.[28]

When a nonprofit has the right leader and that individual is high performing, its board must recognize the leader's critical role and compensate that leader well. Nonprofits, of course, can rarely pay salaries commensurate with those in the private sector. But in this case, compensation does need to reflect the board's confidence and its commitment to retaining that leader.

Once an organization has the right leader, it must make sure that the bus he or she is driving has the right people in the right seats. Getting the wrong people off the bus is as important as getting the right people on the bus.[29] Nonprofits often are more reluctant to fire people than businesses are. In our 2016 Stanford survey, only 53 percent of nonprofit executives and staff concurred with the statement "When employees are underperforming consistently according to clear expectations for performance, they do not stay for long in my organization."[30] Keeping those who consistently underperform on the payroll leads an organization to become bloated and ineffective. It also does a disservice to the underperforming employees, who might fit better in other organizations. Letting people go, when appropriate, will not only improve the efficiency of an organization; it also sends a powerful signal about the values of that organization. "When you know you need to make a people change," Collins writes, you need to confront that fact and act right away instead of waiting for things to turn around magically on their own.[31]

Performance reviews provide a critical way for an organization to identify those who should stay on the bus. As in the private sector, the performance review process at a nonprofit must reflect the right goals, it must be managerially useful, and it must begin soon after an individual comes on board. Setting clear, measurable goals and expectations from the outset is essential. Indeed, early assessment is especially important in the social sector. Collins explains, "In the social sectors, where getting the wrong people off the bus can be more difficult than in a business, early assessment mechanisms turn out to be more important than hiring mechanisms. There is no perfect interviewing technique, no ideal hiring method; even the best executives make hiring mistakes. You can only know for certain about a person by working with that person."[32]

COMMIT TO FACT-BASED DECISION MAKING
(FROM JEFFREY PFEFFER AND ROBERT SUTTON)

Transformative leaps in the availability of information have reshaped the environment in which most organizations operate. Yet Jeffrey Pfeffer and Robert I. Sutton—two of our colleagues at the Stanford Graduate School of Business (Stanford GSB)—make a strong case that many leaders still eschew "evidence-based management" in favor of "casual benchmarking," "doing what (seems to have) worked in the past," and "following deeply held yet unexamined ideologies."[33] We agree, and our experience has taught us that nonprofit leaders struggle in this area even more than business leaders do.

GiveDirectly, a nonprofit that provides unconditional cash transfers to people living in extreme poverty, was founded on a bedrock commitment to evidence-based management. Cofounder Michael Faye explained that commitment as follows: "Perhaps the first RCT [randomized controlled trial] is the best example. We asked the big question: does the program work[?] . . . And then [we asked] specific questions around the design: Are there meaningful differences between giving to men and [giving to] women? How much does size of transfer matter? How does frequency matter (lump sum vs. monthly)? GiveDirectly's entire existence is an outcome of evidence-based decision-making. For too long, the sector assumed that providing capital directly to the poor didn't work; well, the evidence proved otherwise, and led us to found GiveDirectly."[34]

One common nonprofit management practice that too often supports a fact-free decision-making environment is the offsite retreat. We have all attended such retreats, whether as executives, staff members, board members, consultants, or facilitators. Each year, in Bill's Stanford GSB course on the strategic leadership of nonprofit organizations and social ventures, the class does a role-playing exercise that resembles a typical nonprofit strategy offsite. In recent years, students have assessed the Tipping Point Community, a relatively new organization that enables up-and-coming philanthropists to support poverty alleviation in the San Francisco Bay Area. Students begin by applying the oft-used SWOT (strengths, weaknesses, opportunities, and threats) framework to that organization, and then they brainstorm over various ideas and initiatives that Tipping Point should consider. Finally, as is standard practice at many offsites, everyone gets to vote on which proposed ideas or initiatives are most valuable. After the exercise, students discuss the benefits of the offsite process, and every year they identify the same ones: It's good for creativity, for inclusion, and so on. But then Bill asks, "What is the exercise missing?" There is a long pause before a student finally raises a hand and shouts, "Facts!"

Yes, facts—without which we have only a collection of untested hypotheses, or just "I had an idea last night." The best idea wins, but only if it is supported by a strong argument that rests on solid evidence.

"SIMULTANEOUS LOOSE-TIGHT PROPERTIES" (FROM PETERS AND WATERMAN)

The 1982 book *In Search of Excellence: Lessons from America's Best-Run Companies* was the first business blockbuster. Written by Tom Peters and Bob Waterman, it popularized important organizational principles in clear and often memorable prose, such as "close to the customer" and "stick to the knitting." Another principle explained in the book that we have found to be equally essential, albeit less pithy and a bit harder to remember, is "simultaneous loose-tight properties."[35]

Yes, it's a mouthful—but it conveys a critical idea. As Peters and Waterman explain, "Organizations that live by the loose-tight principle are on the one hand rigidly controlled, yet at the same time allow (indeed, insist on) autonomy, entrepreneurship, and innovation."[36] In other words, companies must tightly manage things in a few areas even as they enable creativity and flexibility in other areas.

Every organization has a long list of processes that are important—strategy development, talent management, financial reporting, and the like. The principle of simultaneous loose-tight properties simply invites an organization's leaders to decide which three or four processes are critical to success and encourages them to control those processes tightly from the top of the organization. Other processes will thus receive less attention from top management and be subject to looser forms of control.

Processes that should be managed tightly versus loosely will naturally vary with each nonprofit. For many organizations, it is imperative that impact evaluation be tight. For organizations heavily reliant on philanthropy, major donor management should be tight, and for those with large endowments, investment management must be tight. Nonprofits staffed and run by professionals like physicians, social workers, opera singers, or professors will, in contrast, have loose processes in areas requiring individual judgment and autonomy.

All nonprofits, however, should manage their talent processes tightly. Yet relatively few of them do so. Nonprofit HR's *2015 Nonprofit Employment Practices Survey Results* revealed that 52 percent of nonprofits lacked a formal talent recruitment strategy and 67 percent did not have a formal annual recruitment budget.[37] Some nonprofits even fall short in implementing inexpensive but highly valuable practices like providing regular feedback. In our 2016 Stanford survey, only 15 percent of nonprofit executives and staff indicated that they "strongly agree" with the statement "I receive enough positive feedback and recognition for my contribution to keep me feeling highly motivated." Likewise, in a survey undertaken for a 2013 report by the Bridgespan Group, about two-thirds of respondents disagreed with the statement "Our organization is highly effective in developing a strong internal and external pipeline of future leaders."[38]

The inherent challenge of retaining talent within the nonprofit sector undoubtedly contributes to a significant sectorwide attrition problem. According to a 2016 Bridgespan study published in *Stanford Social Innovation Review* (*SSIR*), "In the past two years, one in four C-suite leaders left her position, and nearly as many told us that they planned to do so in the next two years. If these projections turn out to be true, the nonprofit sector will need to replace the equivalent of every C-suite position over the next eight years."[39] Other studies reveal similar trends at lower organizational levels. In one survey, for instance, 45 percent of nonprofit workers with four or more years of experience said they planned to leave their organization and the nonprofit sector entirely.[40]

Staff development through challenging assignments is especially difficult given structural factors in the nonprofit sector. As the *Ready to Lead?* study reports:

Because many nonprofits are small with relatively flat organizational hierarchies, structural impediments to career advancement can limit pathways to executive positions. Internal advancement is difficult where there are no systems in place to guide transition and promotions. A substantial number of respondents view going to another organization as their best chance for career advancement: *55 percent of all survey respondents believe that they need to leave their organizations in order to advance their careers.*[41] (Emphasis in the original.)

In the face of such challenges, all nonprofits—even very small ones—must have tightly focused processes to ensure that they attract and retain great people. These include the following:

- A process for defining desired attributes and skills in prospective employees
- A hiring process that identifies high-potential sources of talent
- A candidate assessment process that not only reflects desired skills and attributes but also promotes a commitment to the success of potential new employees
- A regular feedback process that allows employees to gain perspective on their colleagues' view of their performance
- An annual performance evaluation process that involves rewarding an organization's best performers and adding to their responsibilities
- A process that identifies and removes low performers and that assesses the professional development needs of other employees

There are many off-the-shelf approaches to implementing these processes and many consultants who will help to implement them. On balance, however, we believe that nonprofit leaders will benefit from engaging deeply in the design and implementation of people processes, since these provide an opportunity to reinforce an organization's mission, values, and high-performance ethos. Wendy Kopp, founder of Teach for America (TFA) and Teach for All, reflected, "There's nothing more important in generating social impact than taking great care in selecting and developing the people engaged in the work."[42] TFA, for example, developed a compelling human capital development strategy called the Leadership Development System (LDS).[43] LDS delineates a number of competency areas that hiring managers use when defining the qualifications for new roles. According to the TFA website, this approach allows TFA to "match qualified staff with appropriate roles during the hiring process" and to evaluate staff members in annual performance reviews.[44] LDS also lays out core values that TFA expects each staff member and each member of its teaching corps to uphold, and job applicant interviews include questions related to values fit with the organization.

Or take the example of Global Health Corps (GHC), which places fellows in health organizations in East Africa and Southern Africa, as well as the United States. According to the GHC website, the organization has developed a set of six "leadership practices" that it has identified "as key to achieving progress in global health and social change."[45] "We've always said that great ideas don't change the world, great people do," said Barbara Bush, cofounder and CEO of GHC. "So that's what we're focused on—competitively recruiting, developing, and seeding bright young talent into the field of global health."[46] GHC selects its fellows for their potential in all six leadership practices and then nurtures these practices through a robust curriculum designed to foster resilience, empathy, and systems thinking, among other qualities.[47] Because values and cultural fit are critically important, it is best to address them as early as the hiring phase. In a 2009 Bridgespan report, *Finding Leaders for America's Nonprofits*,

75 percent of respondents placed cultural fit at the same level of priority as "functional experience."[48]

Tightly managed talent processes are especially important given the resource constraints that nonprofits must overcome. Unsurprisingly, compensation plays a key role in nonprofit talent attrition. In the Nonprofit Employment Practices Survey, 27 percent of respondents reported that the greatest retention challenge they faced was the inability to pay people competitively.[49] In the 2016 Bridgespan survey, meanwhile, 57 percent of employees identified low compensation as the root cause of high turnover.[50] While they will never match private-sector standards, nonprofits must increase compensation levels for their top talent. This requires support from board members and funders—and a willingness to avoid the ridiculous idea that maintaining low overhead matters more than anything else.

Nonprofits must also make better use of critical but underused nonfinancial incentives to motivate and retain talent and reward performance. Considerable evidence suggests that nonfinancial incentives may matter more than compensation for both private and nonprofit sector employees. More than 60 percent of respondents to a *McKinsey Quarterly* survey of financial and nonfinancial motivators in the private sector reported that "praise and commendation from one's immediate manager," "attention from leaders," and "opportunities to lead projects" were effective or extremely effective in motivating them.[51] Respondents, in fact, ranked each of those factors higher than the most highly ranked financial incentives, which included performance-based cash bonuses, increase in base pay, and stock or stock options. Such nonfinancial incentives are also effective in motivating nonprofit-sector employees, as we have seen time and again. Additional key nonfinancial incentives include a positive work culture and interesting work (both cited as top priorities among college-educated professionals in Net Impact's *Talent Report: What Workers Want in 2012*),[52] growth and development opportunities, and recognition from teammates and managers. (Incentives of this kind are also emphasized in the Gallup's *Q12 Meta-Analysis*, which finds a strong correlation between retention and day-to-day "employee engagement.")[53]

A number of studies have demonstrated that nonfinancial incentives affect performance. A study undertaken by Innovations for Poverty Action in Lusaka, Zambia, for example, found that a nonfinancial reward scheme was more effective than financial schemes in motivating hair stylists to sell female condoms to their clients. The nonfinancial scheme was called the "star treatment"—stylists received a star for each condom pack sold and displayed such stars on a large thermometer diagram. Stylists who sold more than 216 packs in one year were invited to a special ceremony. Intriguingly, these stylists sold twice as many condom packs as stylists in the control group or in an alternative treatment group that involved small or large financial incentives. The study authors posited two reasons for this significant difference. First, the authors wrote, nonfinancial incentives "seemed to leverage intrinsic motivation for the cause"—the cause, in this case, of reducing HIV transmission. (This mechanism seems to be at play in a number of studies that evaluate the value of implicit, intrinsic motivation over explicit, financial performance contracts.) Second, the authors noted, nonfinancial incentives "appear to have facilitated social comparison among stylists," because the impact of the incentives "increased with the number of neighboring salons that received the same treatment."[54]

In particular, as nonprofits scale geographically, they need to identify their secret sauce, that is, the essence of what they do that needs to be tightly managed and controlled, usually by an organization's hub or center. Consider the experience of the Nurse-Family Partnership (NFP), which has scaled across forty-three states and nearly six hundred counties in the United States and to six countries abroad.[55] NFP maintains tight control over its highly specific and proprietary programmatic approach, and it works to ensure programmatic fidelity by its implementing partners. Its approach relies on registered nurses (versus other types of paraprofessionals, caregivers, coaches, and so on); these nurses conduct home visits (versus other types of interventions); and the visits are made prenatally to

first-time mothers (versus beginning later in a pregnancy or serving second- or third-time mothers). As the organization has scaled,
NFP has remained committed to this approach and has refused to
compromise key aspects of its program design. Woody McCutchen
of the Edna McConnell Clark Foundation (EMCF), a lead funder
of NFP since 2002, recalled, "When EMCF originally approached
NFP to provide funding to scale the program, founder David Olds
said, 'I'm absolutely excited that you think we're worthy of scaling
up across this country. But if the program dissemination at scale ever
compromises the integrity of the program, I will pull the plug.'"[56] In
Germany, for example Olds withdrew NFP's license from its partner
in that country because the partner strayed from requirements that
involved sending skilled nurses to home visits.[57]

Maintaining strong central control over its brand and over key
elements of its programmatic approach has borne fruit for NFP. The
nonprofit landscape in which NFP operates has grown increasingly
vast, crowded, and fragmented in recent years, but the NFP board's
steadfast commitment to NFP's programmatic approach and to its
mission has enabled the organization to stand out as one of the stron-
gest players within that landscape. McCutchen noted, "When we
first started looking at NFP, . . . we went through the process of due
diligence, and we found out that NFP is one of the most effective,
scientifically proven poverty alleviation interventions in the U.S."[58]
Numerous research centers have produced evaluations that compare
organizations in the home-visiting sector, and these studies have identified NFP as having strong impact data and high net benefits to society
(when considering benefits minus costs over time).[59] For example, a
2011 analysis of eight home-visiting programs by the Coalition for
Evidence-Based Policy concluded that NFP offered the only program
deserving a "strong" level of confidence that it would "produce important life improvements in the lives of at-risk children and parents."[60]

PLANNING FOR SUCCESSION: DO OR DIE!
Succession planning is immensely important but inherently difficult.
It is, of course, imperative in organizations whose leader is nearing

retirement age, but it is equally essential in organizations led by the middle aged, or even the young. Many organizations founded by dynamic and visionary young entrepreneurs require a founder transition to a more professionalized second generation of leadership far sooner than any founder is inclined to accept. Such transitions are almost always rife with primal emotional challenges and are what kills most entrepreneurial ventures, be they social or commercial. Great social organizations are often founded and built by visionaries who see through constraints and beyond the boundaries of time. These visionaries talk about their organization's past, present, and future all at once and in the present tense. They do not see their approaching professional mortality as something to plan for.

Succession within nonprofits can therefore be particularly challenging. A board might have to encourage—or insist—that a visionary and dedicated social entrepreneur founder step aside or take on a different role. A wounded psyche cannot be salved with a huge financial package, and an honest and direct conversation may do more harm than good. But if the choice is between an organization's impact and effectiveness, on one hand, and a founder's understandably fragile ego, on the other hand, the decision must favor the organization's future.

Given these challenges, it is unsurprising that succession planning is not prevalent in the nonprofit sector. In the 2015 Survey on Board of Directors of Nonprofit Organizations, conducted by the Rock Center for Corporate Governance at Stanford, 69 percent of respondents indicated that their organization does not have a succession plan in place for their executive director or CEO.[61] Similarly, in our 2016 Stanford survey, 53 percent of nonprofit executives and staff disagreed (to varying degrees) with the statement "My organization conducts thorough and proactive succession planning for the executive director and top executives." And 31 percent did not believe that "the founder/executive director of my organization has a realistic sense of when and how succession should occur."[62]

To improve succession planning, nonprofit stakeholders should first determine whether their founder or executive director has a realistic sense of when and how succession should occur. Sir Fazle Hasan Abed, founder of BRAC, is one visionary leader who was able to develop realistic expectations in this area.[63] Abed served as executive director of BRAC from 1972 until 2000, but he began identifying potential successors as early as 1990. Since 2000, BRAC has had three executive directors, as has BRAC International (which oversees programs in eleven countries outside Bangladesh). Abed now serves as chair of the organization. "I have tried to ensure succession at BRAC without thinking about myself," he said. "I wanted to address succession from the inside by gradually taking steps backwards and seeing how things worked out. I believe an organization can have more than one leader; in fact, leadership roles should be well dispersed throughout an organization."[64]

Helen Keller International (HKI) established a track record of smooth leadership transitions as far back as 1920.[65] Its founder, George Kessler, was a New York wine merchant who began to develop what would become HKI after he survived the sinking of the *Lusitania* by a German U-boat in 1915. While recovering in London, Kessler resolved to devote his remaining years to helping soldiers who had been blinded in combat. He and his wife began to raise funds for that purpose and asked for support from Helen Keller, the deaf and blind woman who had become an advocate for those who were disadvantaged. She enthusiastically agreed, and the Permanent Blind Relief War Fund for Soldiers and Sailors of the Allies was incorporated in 1919. (The organization later changed its name to Helen Keller International, and its mission evolved to encompass the prevention and treatment of blindness and malnutrition in other populations.) The following year, Kessler died. The organization avoided a succession crisis because early on Kessler had brought in "centers of influence" to help the organization pursue its mission. In addition to involving Keller, he had enlisted support from the Wall Street lawyer William Nelson Cromwell, who, in 1920, succeeded Kessler as president. "Cromwell was already highly involved in the organization when Kessler died. Consequently, the succession happened very naturally and very smoothly," noted Kathy Spahn, the current president and CEO of HKI.[66] To this day, Cromwell's law firm, Sullivan and Cromwell, remains a force that provides leadership continuity to HKI: attorneys from the firm have served on the board of the organization for nearly one hundred years.

At Landesa, leaders identified Tim Hanstad as the future replacement for founder and chief executive Roy Prosterman in 1992—but Hanstad didn't officially become president and CEO until 2005. During this period, Hanstad served as executive director, honing his skills and developing credibility among various Landesa stakeholders. "We had done so much succession planning for so long that by the time Tim took over as CEO, the transition was incredibly smooth," said Prosterman.[67] The Landesa approach, we believe, sets the best-practice standard in this area. In 2005, after stepping down from his executive position, Prosterman took a seat on the Landesa board but wisely announced that he would never become its chair. We generally believe that the former founder who has served as chief executive or executive director should not become the board chair, and should even consider stepping away from the board altogether. An effective board must have a safe environment in which to think critically, to reconsider what was done in the past, to challenge sacred cows. Yet most founders, consciously or not, will want to protect their legacy. That said, we recognize that there are exceptions to every rule. At BRAC, as we noted, Abed stepped down as executive director but continues to serves as its chairman, an arrangement that by all accounts is working.

Succession planning is also important for other key positions on the senior management team of an organization. Focusing only on the founder "does an organization a disservice," Abed argues. "BRAC now conducts succession planning at every level. We learned that we must pay attention to the pipeline." Abed cited an occasion on which that lesson was brought home for him: "We were taken by surprise when a critical member of the senior management team passed away unexpectedly in 2010. He had been my right-hand person since 1976. Fortunately, we had some bench strength. But we learned firsthand the importance of succession planning."[68]

Board members must understand that one of their primary responsibilities is hiring, evaluating, and (when necessary) replacing the chief executive of their organization. The task of replacement becomes especially difficult when there is a respected founder at the helm. Long friendships can be put at risk, tight-knit boards can unravel, and organizations can lose their focus—all because a board is unwilling or unable to ensure a strong transition to the next generation of leadership. The board (usually through its chair) must initiate a conversation about succession in situations that involve a founder or a long-standing executive director. In doing so, board members should understand that they are entering complex psychological territory and should expect both active and passive resistance.

We close with what we might call the paradox of people: once your strategic thinking is sound, nothing will shape your impact more than your people, how they are led, and how they are organized. But while we can offer you encouragement, insight, and a few ideas—like the team-of-teams model—your success in the selection, evaluation, and motivation of people will largely be a function of your personal wisdom and judgment. And the wisdom comes from the oft-quoted words of Tony Robbins, Rita Mae Brown, Will Rogers, and others: "Good judgment comes from experience. And experience comes from bad judgment."

CHAPTER 6

Money Matters

Funding as Essential Fuel

Incongruous as it seems, nonprofit executives and board members spend more time and effort on money matters than their counterparts in business. Many of them, in fact, will admit to spending half their time or more on making appeals to past, present, or prospective donors: "Would you consider making a leadership gift? A significant gift during our Campaign for Excellence? Would you chair our Capital Campaign? Increase your gift from last year?"

Yet despite all of the time-consuming effort expended, most nonprofits struggle to meet their fund-raising goals. In a survey conducted by Bill and several colleagues at Stanford's Rock Center for Corporate Governance, 40 percent of nonprofit directors admitted that their organizations had been unable to meet fund-raising targets and 29 percent said that they had experienced serious financial difficulty.[1] We focus in this chapter on money matters because funding is essential fuel for any nonprofit. A well-built, finely tuned engine of impact simply cannot function without it. Nonprofit leaders who want to increase their impact must redouble their commitment to fund raising. Those who succeed in this effort generally do so by adhering, whether knowingly or not, to a number of tried-and-true principles.

View Your Revenue Model as a Strategic Choice

Obtaining the funding needed for a nonprofit organization to achieve the impact to which it aspires often requires intentional, strategic choices. As William Landes Foster, Peter Kim, and Barbara Christiansen explain: "When a for-profit business finds a way to create value for a customer, it has generally found its source of revenue; the customer pays for the value. With rare exceptions, that is not true in the nonprofit sector."[2] In other words, when a nonprofit finds a way to create value for a beneficiary (for example, integrating a prisoner back into society), it has not identified its revenue source; that is a separate step.

Many nonprofits remain small because they adopt revenue models that simply do not enable them to fulfill their mission. In this section, we explore two distinct models of nonprofit funding—earned income and donations—and delve into the nuances of each. Note, of course, that many nonprofits combine the two.

In determining the optimal funding model for your nonprofit, start by asking whether any core program components or by-products— program content, goods produced by participants, or data generated—can be fully or partially monetized, including through sales to third parties. BRAC, for example, generates most of the funding for its anti-poverty work in Bangladesh through earned revenues. From 2011 to 2015, it spent an average of $682 million per year in that country, and earned revenue from its diverse social enterprises— including dairies, printing companies, and microfinance operations, as well as socially responsible investments—accounted for 76 percent of that spending.[3]

BRAC's social enterprises are a key part of its impact model and thus serve the dual purpose of helping people become self-sufficient and generating revenue for the organization. To ensure that BRAC does not succumb to mission creep, or begin cherry-picking entrepreneurs simply for their moneymaking potential, the organization engages in cross-subsidization. Some BRAC enterprises are designed merely to cover their own costs, whereas others generate net income to support other BRAC projects. This is important because an earned revenue stream should not depart substantially from an organization's mission, nor should revenue considerations distort its choice of a target population. Impact, rather than revenues, should drive programmatic decisions.

Notably, BRAC developed its earned revenue stream slowly over time. While BRAC now funds a large percentage of its budget from earned income, its transition away from relying primarily on donations was very gradual. BRAC has succeeded by honing the fundamentals of social enterprise: build a strong organization first, choose businesses wisely, know when to let go of struggling businesses, and listen closely to stakeholders.[4]

Most nonprofits are not in a position to attract earned income to cover their entire budget and must therefore seek donations. The Positive Coaching Alliance (PCA), for example, originally hoped to derive 80 percent to 90 percent of revenues from earned income through sales of workshops, training, and materials to schools and youth-serving organizations. However, explained founder and CEO Jim Thompson, "We came to realize that it was unrealistic to expect these organizations to pay the high prices that would be needed for us to be fully funded by earned revenues. The money just isn't there in youth sports. These organizations have money, but not that kind of money." PCA did not want to focus on serving only organizations that could pay high prices. "A business might take this approach," Thompson continued, "but we are a nonprofit, and our mission is oriented around influencing the culture of youth sports. To do this effectively, we need to sell way below our costs." In order to scale, PCA has funded its work largely through donations. By 2015, according to Thompson, donations accounted for more than half of its revenues, while earned income generated less than one-third of revenues (and corporate sponsorships generated roughly 10 percent).[5]

The vast majority of nonprofits are not in a position to attract earned revenue to cover their entire budget. Organizations generally fare best when they approach their funding model, and especially the specifics of how they will raise donations, as a fundamental strategic choice. In their article "Ten Nonprofit Funding Models," William Landes Foster, Peter Kim, and Barbara Christiansen lay out funding approaches that are commonly used by large US nonprofits.[6] The process of choosing and clearly articulating which model is the best fit for an organization in the long term—while continuing to prioritize the organization's mission—is highly valuable.

Because most nonprofits cannot rely entirely on earned revenue and must depend on donations, we focus in the rest of this chapter on ways to improve your organization's fund raising through donations. In working with donors, we strongly urge them to make funding decisions in a strategic and analytical way that puts a premium on achieving real impact. But when it comes to fund raising, we are profound realists. Most donors give in response to an "ask" from a peer or a development staffer. We also know that recognition in some form remains the predominant motivation of most donors. For that reason, our emphasis here is on discussing the fundamentals of building a successful development culture.

Start with Your Board

A cardinal principle of fund raising is to start with your board, the best resource you have. Every board member has a responsibility to give money and participate in fund-raising activities, but many are falling short. In our 2016 Stanford survey, less than half of nonprofit executives and staff members concurred with the statement "The financial giving to my nonprofit by its board members is currently very strong."[7] Similarly, in a survey conducted for a 2015 Board-Source report, 60 percent of CEOs and 58 percent of board chairs identified fund raising as one of the most important areas for board improvement.[8]

Once you set out to improve your board's giving and leadership in fund-raising activities, you will likely find low-hanging fruit. You might start by developing an accurate picture of what your board has done in this area to date. Our clients have found it useful to conduct sanitized (meaning: all names removed!) aggregated analyses that draw on both qualitative assessments and quantitative data and to discuss those analyses with their board. (We provide examples of such analyses on the website for this book.[9])

When analyses reveal room for improvement, address this by discussing shortcomings and clarifying expectations with the full board. Conversations of this sort are not easy, so it might behoove you to work with board leaders who will help you develop and hone expectations before you present them to the full board. You should also consider creating a development committee, if you don't yet have one. And, if your initial board discussions cause you to conclude that few of your board members are willing to accept their fund-raising responsibilities, you might need to change the composition of your board. To be sure, this is a heart-wrenching remedy, but if it is the only way to raise the funds needed to achieve your mission, you must do it—and do it before you initiate any major new fund-raising initiative.

While there is no magic number for board giving, and expectations vary by organization, as a general rule board members should give at a personal stretch level and should prioritize your organization within their charitable giving. "We view our board members as family members," explained Daniel Lurie, founder and CEO of Tipping Point, a nonprofit that funds poverty alleviation organizations in the San Francisco Bay Area. "Our organization needs to be a priority in their life. We do not invite an individual onto our board if they are already on ten boards; generally they need to be on no more than three nonprofit boards for us to feel confident that Tipping Point would be a priority for them."[10]

Some organizations have had success by implementing minimum contribution requirements. In a study of nonprofit boards in New York City, the fund-raising consulting firm Marts & Lundy found that when boards set minimum expectations for giving, actual giving exceeds those minimums.[11] That said, a nonprofit board needs to be diverse, and not all members will be able to give significant amounts. This is as it should be—but all members should give something, and their giving should be as generous as their resources will allow.

The expectation that board members will help to identify and approach other potential donors should also be explicit. Each board member should point your organization toward at least a handful of new potential donors every year. If these expectations are clear but your board members ignore them, then your organization is in urgent need of help.

The organizational culture of Right to Play, which uses sports and games to educate and empower children and youth in disadvantaged communities, reflects these principles. "Expectations of board members regarding development are very explicit," explained its founder, Johann Olav Koss. "Every board member is expected to make Right to Play one of their top three priorities for charitable giving, and also is expected to help us raise money from others. Every year, the board chair and I have a conversation with each board member about what they've given, what they've raised from others, and plans for next year."[12]

Go Where the Money Is

According to an oft-told story, the American bank robber Willie Sutton was once asked why he robbed banks. "Because that's where the money is," he replied.[13] Nonprofit leaders should seek out donations in much the same spirit, and they should start by recognizing that most of the money in US philanthropy comes from individuals—not from foundations or corporations.

A mere 5 percent of the $373 billion of philanthropic giving in 2015 came from corporations, and only 15 percent came from foundations, whereas 71 percent of the total came from living individuals—a sum that would be even higher if it included giving by foundations whose founders are living. (The remaining 9 percent came in the form of bequests from individuals; see Figure 6.)[14]

Unfortunately, the nonprofit sector still largely fails to appreciate the importance of individual giving, and this is reflected in fund-raising strategies. A survey of participants in our 2015 *Stanford Social Innovation Review* webinar "The Fundamentals of Fundraising" validated our belief that nonprofits are not yet going where the money is.[15] First, among our sample—which primarily included leaders and staff at nonprofit organizations—individual giving appeared to be only slightly more important than funding from foundations: respondents indicated that on average their organizations relied on donations from individuals for 34 percent of their revenues and on foundation giving for 27 percent of their revenues. Second, the survey suggested that many leaders view their fund-raising future in a way that does not accord with the reality of where they can tap additional funds: 49 percent of respondents said that they expected the share of their

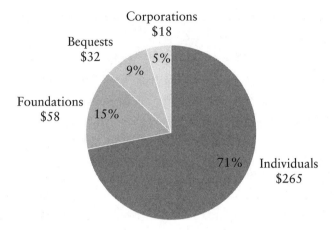

FIGURE 6 Charitable contributions in the United States by donor type, 2015 (in billions)

SOURCE: *Giving USA 2016: The Annual Report on Philanthropy for the Year 2015* (Chicago: Giving USA Foundation, 2016), 27, 238. Data used with permission.

funding from foundations to increase over the next five years, while only 52 percent said that they expected the share of their funding from individuals to increase over the same period. Third, the survey showed that most nonprofits do not yet excel at raising funds from individuals: only 3 percent of respondents said that their current efforts to raise funds from individuals were "very effective," and only 28 percent said that those efforts were "effective."

This reliance on foundation support can have adverse consequences for nonprofits. "Foundation grants are usually for short-term projects and typically fund little, if any, of the types of expenses that lead to stronger organizations—things like evaluation, leadership, and additional fund raising," said Melissa S. Brown, a fund-raising consultant who manages the Nonprofit Research Collaborative.[16] Support from individuals can be less burdensome, and more likely to grow over time, than foundation giving. In many cases, it also comes with additional benefits such as expertise, leadership, and access to networks. This multidimensional value puts donations from individuals at a premium, and targeting such donations is therefore worthy of strategic focus.

Learn from Partners in "Plutophilanthropy"

In most cases, the prioritization of major donors and major gifts from individuals is the key driver of sustained large-scale fund-raising success by nonprofits. The Growth in Giving Initiative, a data platform organized by the Urban Institute and the Association of Fundraising Professionals, has analyzed millions of gift records from thousands of organizations and has consistently found that 80 percent of funding comes from 20 percent of donors.[17] The majority of nonprofits, however, find it challenging to raise major gifts. In our 2016 Stanford survey, only 40 percent of nonprofit executives and staff indicated affirmatively, "My organization's current efforts to raise major gifts from individuals (according to my organization's definition of major gifts) are very effective."

There are four types of nonprofits that typically excel at raising major gifts: colleges and universities, medical centers, high-end performing arts organizations, and museums. In the 1980s, Tom Wolfe used the term *plutography* to describe the graphic depiction of the acts of the rich.[18] In the same spirit, we have coined the term *plutophilanthropy* to refer to philanthropy of the ultrawealthy, and we call institutions that draw on this source for financial support partners in plutophilanthropy (PIPs).

Nonprofits in other sectors, especially those in human services, poverty alleviation, and education, tend to assume that they will be unable to raise major gifts, and this can become a self-fulfilling prophecy. While the four PIPs have some inherent advantages—alums, patients, attendees—there is no necessary reason that nonprofits that serve the needy can't build major gift or major donor functions. As the PIPs have learned, seeking major gifts from individuals has numerous benefits. A study of higher education capital campaigns revealed that in 2013, 78 percent of funds received came from 1 percent of donors.[19] Experts at the Fund Raising School at the Indiana University Lilly Family School of Philanthropy and similar training programs advise nonprofits to build a fund-raising pyramid in which roughly 30 percent of their donors account for about 80 percent of the money raised (see Figure 7).[20] For many organizations,

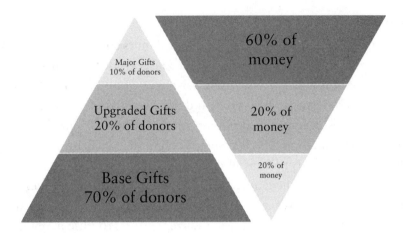

FIGURE 7 Giving trends (based on field experience)
SOURCE: The Fund Raising School, Lilly Family School of Philanthropy, Indiana University, *Developing Annual Sustainability Study Guide*. Used with permission.

the pyramid will be even steeper, and an even smaller percentage of donors will bring in an even greater percentage of funds.

There is ample evidence to demonstrate that a small number of donors provide an outsized share of donations. In 2014, just 4 percent of tax returns—those filed by tax filers with incomes of $200,000 or more—accounted for 51 percent ($108 billion) of all individual itemized charitable contributions.[21] Targeting a small number of individual donors—especially those with whom you have a strong relationship—has the additional advantage of giving your organization an opportunity to raise funds without needing to meet the often cumbersome requirements that foundations impose. It also provides a measure of protection from economic and political risks: individual donors are often able to continue giving even during economic downturns or amid shifting political winds that might lead to cuts in government and institutional funding.

"Most social service organizations tend to assume that there are no wealthy people in their midst, but when they take a deep dive into their base—looking carefully at individuals, who these individuals are married to, who they are connected to—the vast majority of social service organizations can see that in some way they *are* connected to wealthy people. *Every* donor base has rich people in it," said Nancy L. Raybin, senior consultant and principal of Marts & Lundy and former chair of the Giving Institute. "Understanding this makes it easier for organizations in human services, poverty alleviation, and education to focus on developing a major gifts program."[22]

Nonprofits that don't prioritize major gifts have much to learn from those that do. For starters, they will learn to identify top prospects who might be able and willing to make such gifts and to actively cultivate those prospects over time. Bob Lasher, senior vice president for advancement at Dartmouth College, who previously led fundraising campaigns that generated more than one billion dollars in philanthropic investment for the San Francisco Museum of Modern Art, the San Francisco Symphony, and other Bay Area cultural arts organizations, gave this advice:

If you don't know where to start, consider the power of networks. Your existing donors can help you identify additional possible contributors, and they will be your champions. . . . In your effort to identify top prospects, it can be helpful to research other nonprofits [that] aren't necessarily in your niche but whose mission might resonate with yours—because of regional pride, a shared peer group, or parallel mission-based interests—to see who their top donors are. Then go to your board or other champions of your organization and ask if anyone knows [those donors] and might be willing to facilitate an introduction for your organization. You'd be surprised at how productive this conversation can be and [at] the amount of detailed information you will learn, not only about your new prospects but also [about] your board members.[23]

It is also important to remember that philanthropic decisions are now often made within families. "The world is changing," noted Lasher. "There was a time when development professionals conducted the majority of their meetings with top prospects in downtown office buildings with the man [from a household]. Today, we also meet with other members of the family and rarely [meet with] the man by himself. It is important to always bear in mind that giving decisions today are typically made jointly by spouses, with children often included for input. My earliest questions to a new supporter often are

'How do you make your philanthropic decisions?' and 'Who is part of that conversation with you?'"[24]

Once you identify top prospects, you must create individualized plans to cultivate them. "Cultivation is tremendously important and requires thoughtful planning," said Ernie Iseminger, vice president of advancement at Claremont Graduate University. Previously, as vice president for development and external relations at Claremont McKenna College, he spearheaded a $635 million campaign that was one of the largest successful fund-raising efforts ever for a US liberal arts college. Iseminger continued:

> You need to make a plan for each of your top prospects, and the plan should include a detailed survey of their interests, their passions, and the sequence of steps that you will take to cultivate them. It's a game of chess, not checkers: you need to think three, four, or five moves ahead, and that means planning your fundraising activity 12 months, 24 months, or even 36 months in advance of when you hope to make a formal "ask." Once you have your list of top potential donors, you need to make sure that they hear from you and your organization once a month. It's not necessarily a visit, or even a phone call. It can be an email. But ideally there needs to be some sort of contact once a month. Out of sight, out of mind.[25]

It is crucial that you don't let your enthusiasm for identifying and cultivating new donors distract you from engaging with your existing donors. After an individual makes a donation, stewardship is key; you must properly thank your donors and let them know how important their gift is to your organization. Too often, nonprofits neglect this responsibility: in a study by the Nonprofit Research Collaborative, fewer than six in ten surveyed organizations indicated that they took the very basic step of sending information about their ongoing activities to all of their donors.[26] Many organizations today have unnecessarily high donor churn levels. Research by the Fundraising Effectiveness Project shows that for the median nonprofit in a set of more than eight thousand organizations, just 43 percent of donors from 2013 renewed a gift to the same organization in 2014.[27] In the private sector, sales and marketing professionals understand that losing customers is especially problematic because acquiring new customers is so costly. Similarly, in the nonprofit sector, there is much data to show that an organization is most likely to find its next donor among its past donors—and to do so at a much smaller cost per dollar raised.

Nonprofits must earn the right to look for new donors by properly stewarding existing donors. Iseminger recounted: "Over the past twenty-five years, I have advised countless social service nonprofits that approach me because they want my advice about how to find new donors. But when I sit down and look at their data, I invariably find that these organizations are not doing a good job at taking care of their existing donors. I see churn rates as high as 40 percent to 50 percent, which is, in my view, egregious and unacceptable. Invariably, my first piece of advice to these organizations is to stop looking for new donors and first figure out how to keep the ones you have!"[28] Lasher also emphasized the importance of stewardship: "As gift amounts get larger, a donor's expectations and even apprehensions also grow. So there are high stakes for any organization to prove that it can put those funds to work quickly and personably, demonstrate impact, and execute exquisitely and with consistency. It is wise to put the effort in; often that same donor has additional resources and might be inspired to build on the first investment if it is successful."[29]

Indeed, for most organizations, major gifts tend to come after a period of steadily cultivating donors who started with small gifts. Martin Shell, vice president for development at Stanford University, explained:

It is very rare to find a major gift donor whose first gift is [in the] high six or seven figures. In fact, donor gift decisions to most organizations often start with small contributions. More than a decade ago, we participated with twenty-five leading colleges and universities in a study examining the characteristics of donations of $1 million and above. The researchers found that approximately 80 percent of those who had made a donation of $1 million or more made their first gift within three years of graduating, and their average gift was about $50! This cohort also made an average of sixteen additional gifts along the way before making their $1 million commitments. Imagine this as a journey or pathway where getting to make that next gift requires appropriate and meaningful stewardship on the part of the organization. It is why we emphasize that all gifts matter at every gift level.[30]

Meet Donors Where They Are

The best fund raisers meet donors on their terms and enable them to give in the manner that makes them most comfortable. Using the Internet, fund-raising professionals can assemble an amazingly comprehensive file on prospective donors that includes their personal details; their philanthropic history; information on their network of friends, colleagues, and acquaintances; and an overview of their personal and philanthropic interests. Then, having gained such insight, fund raisers can ensure that discussions with prospective donors will involve a board member or another representative of the nonprofit who is their peer, or hoped-for peer.

In Bill's course at the Stanford Graduate School of Business, he conducts a role-playing exercise during which students—some of whom were nonprofit leaders prior to business school—have an opportunity to ask for a contribution from a prominent person who has agreed to play the role of prospective donor. Amateurs and professionals alike usually make the same mistakes. Instead of working to understand the donor's interests and how the donor might connect with a given organization, they launch into a passionate discussion of how compelling that organization is. And they usually ask for much less money than the donor is capable of giving. The best practice, in this scenario, is to ask authentic and curious questions to understand the motivation of donors. Is the environment or poverty alleviation important to them, for example? What issues do they consider to be most crucial? At some point in the discussion, you need to identify something that clearly connects your organization with the donor's interests. In general, you need to have a clear roadmap for this discussion and a good sense about how big a gift to request. While many fund raisers fear asking for too much, the more common mistake is to ask for too little.

An example of meeting donors where they are was the creation in the early 2000s of the Chinese New Year Concert & Celebration by the San Francisco Symphony, in response to relatively low engagement by the Chinese American community. Christopher Hest, who has held development roles at the San Francisco Symphony, the Nature Conservancy, and other nonprofits, reflected: "Michael Tilson Thomas helped us identify a music director for the concert who really [understood] what we were trying to do—build relationships through music and participation. Overnight it became the signature cultural event of its kind and led to much higher participation at the symphony among leading . . . Asian American philanthropists and arts patrons."[31]

Once someone is likely to make a gift, it is imperative that you carefully consider how the donor would like to be recognized. Some donors prefer to give anonymously—and development professionals should always encourage this practice. Anonymous giving has a long tradition, rooted in many religious faiths. For example, Maimonides, the great Jewish philosopher of the medieval period, developed a list of eight levels of giving in which the second-highest level is giving anonymously. Similarly, the Bible instructs in the book of Matthew, "But when you give to the needy, do not let your left hand know what your right hand is doing, so that your giving may be in secret." One philanthropist who gives anonymously described the benefits of this practice: "Keeping the specifics of my gifts as 'happy little secrets' has given me some of the greatest joy and pleasure of my life. It makes my heart sing in ways that I never could have imagined. It also helps keep my motivations laser-focused on the need at hand, so that I can make decisions focused entirely on which organization can do the most good for the most people."[32]

Anonymity is a wonderful practice, but few donors are likely to adopt it. While the word *philanthropy* is derived from a Greek term meaning, in essence, "love of humanity," in practice philanthropy often springs from a donor's desire for recognition—from the public, from hoped-for social peers—or at least from a desire to leave a publicly recognized legacy. Universities, hospitals, and museums have had considerable success with major gifts in part because they are able to offer so many opportunities to name important assets—buildings, wings of buildings, professorships, scholarship programs, collections, galleries, and more—after donors.

The offering of naming opportunities is a fund-raising method that has a clear upside: it works. Lasher reflected, "The true power of naming opportunities is that they help the donor to envision a place or role in the history of the institution—in the inception of a groundbreaking new program, or [in] the physical expression of its mission via the facility. These [opportunities] are incredibly powerful in motivating donors to think about gifts at uncommon levels and in ways that drive projects to successful achievement."[33] Indeed, many nonprofits would do well to emulate PIPs' adept use of naming opportunities. No rule prevents international development or social service organizations, for example, from offering such opportunities. While they may lack obvious assets such as buildings to name after donors, a great deal of untapped potential exists to be creative in finding naming opportunities.

There are potential drawbacks to the use of naming rights. Hest explained: "The main drawback with naming is that other donors can feel neglected. There can [also] be inflation over time that erodes the value of the named entity. And it can send the wrong message; ideally, philanthropy ought not be contingent on a reward or be perceived as a quid pro quo."[34] Creating explicit tiers with labels for donors can be helpful. "The Nature Conservancy successfully created tiers for giving levels, with a label attached to each tier," Hest noted.[35]

Another approach taken by nonprofits that excel at raising major gifts is to provide top donors with exclusive benefits, including access to certain experiences, people, or venues. A study by the Nonprofit Research Collaborative found that organizations that offered such benefits to "donors above a certain level"—including special gifts and meetings with top leaders to discuss an organization's future—had more success in reaching fund-raising goals than those that did not follow this practice.[36] "The Nature Conservancy is very thoughtful about giving major donors access to lands that are not open to the public, through walking tours led by scientists and initiative leaders who are subject matter experts," explained Hest.[37]

Designing exclusive benefits in a way that takes a donor's passion to the next level can be especially helpful. Lasher explained:

The experience of getting to know an artist or an academic is intellectually rewarding. When a donor has already signaled their interest in a subject through philanthropic support, the benefiting organization is wise to continue [that donor's] education and take [the donor's] passion to the next level. At the San Francisco Symphony, guests to the hall want to fully appreciate a piece of music or the craft of performance—to become better audience members—and so educational events are compelling. Similarly, at Dartmouth we provided a donor with a developed interest in contemporary geo-politics with an introduction to a faculty expert on the Middle East. [The donor] enjoyed [a] "front-row seat" to that scholar's emerging insights and they have developed an ongoing dialogue that has included contributions toward further research.[38]

In addition to appreciating recognition and access to exclusive benefits, donors also value the social prestige that comes through their association with certain groups. Nonprofits in social services, international development, and the like often look at colleges, universities, and museums and say, "That's where all the wealthy, elite people are, so it's easy for those organizations to cultivate major gifts." Fair enough—but it is possible to emulate this approach through the manner in which you cultivate your board and other supporters. Indeed, there are many nonprofits that have no inherent connection to potential donors (such as an alumni affiliation) but still develop a reputation as a socially desirable place.

Tipping Point has been highly successful at mobilizing significant resources to support its mission. Part of its effectiveness springs from its creative outreach to the next generations of donors—Gen X and Gen Y—among whom it has fostered a strong sense of community.[39] Members of Gen X (usually defined as individuals born between the mid-1960s and late 1970s) approach philanthropy differently than their predecessors. They conduct more extensive research on charitable causes before making a gift, for example, and are more likely to choose volunteer activities that offer challenges and social connections.[40] Tipping Point's annual fund-raising events provide donors with a chance to learn about poverty alleviation, the nonprofit organizations that Tipping Point funds, and the individuals these nonprofits help. However, while these events include donor education and acknowledgment, they are also known as one of the best social events in town. "Our events create a feeling of community," reflected Lurie. "Our generation is so hungry for community; you see it with the success of social platforms like Facebook. . . . We host events where we have thirteen hundred people stuffed in a room, many of whom are under thirty-five. That just doesn't happen with most groups."[41]

In addition to its annual gala, Lurie explained, Tipping Point organizes educational events, such as the Tipping Point Talks series: "We invite fifteen to twenty donors and potential donors to attend a breakfast in which they can engage with one another as well as two executive directors of nonprofits that alleviate poverty."[42]

If people think of your board or annual meeting as "the place to be and be seen"—as well as a place through which they can do good for others and learn something—then you have created a sense of social affiliation that can benefit your fund-raising efforts. Many nonprofits eschew this approach because they equate it with elitism and are uncomfortable with it. But, as a wise person once said, "You shouldn't marry someone because they're wealthy, but you shouldn't hold it against them either." Being viewed as a cool nonprofit in the world of elite donors can be advantageous when it comes to attracting major gifts.

Donor recognition events can also be helpful, especially to the extent that they give donors a chance to learn. Penelope Burk, a fund-raising researcher, has found that donors place a high value on receiving education about issues and on learning firsthand about what their gifts are achieving. In a survey that she conducted, 87 percent of donors who had attended a donor recognition event reported that the event positively influenced their decision to give again.[43] Likewise, fund raisers who excel at major gifts tend to remember that, as Lasher put it, "eagles flock," meaning that well-respected, high-profile people may be more inclined to give when they hear that their peers have done so. "Knowing that others you respect have come to the table and given makes a difference," said Lasher. "Hospitals, universities, and arts institutions all thrive because there are *groups* of leaders who are giving major gifts. It is a flock in almost every case." Lasher cited an example from 2003, when he and his colleagues at the San Francisco Symphony sought to increase annual giving: "So we went to ten people—great San Franciscans and respected community and business leaders—and got them on board. . . . We then had many others wanting to step up and join them, doubling the membership within two years. The notion was that 'if these people are doing it, and they are people of impact, I want to [give] as well.' Eagles flock."[44]

In summary, we embrace donor recognition, but only in the service of impact. In the absence of impact, it is empty, even corrupting. That said, we strongly encourage high-impact nonprofits—particularly those that provide basic human services— to enlist the power of donor recognition in service of growing their impact.

It Takes Money to Raise Money

Any nonprofit can raise more money from individuals to fuel its growth, but this often requires up-front investment. According to a benchmarking report by the Association of Fundraising Professionals, the median nonprofit raises $3 to $5 for every $1 that it spends in a noncampaign year.[45] During a fund-raising campaign, moreover this figure can jump to as much as $20 raised per $1 invested.[46] Organizations with paid development staff are far more likely to meet their fund-raising goals. The Nonprofit Research Collaborative found that while 39 percent of organizations with no paid staff met their fund-raising goals, this figure rose to 60 percent for organizations with at least one full-time employee (FTE) devoted to development and to roughly 70 percent for those with more than one FTE.[47] Putting in place a best-in-class development function clearly brings tremendous payoffs—even the smallest nonprofits should consider hiring at least one development officer to build out development functions. If strong development is essential for nonprofits, however, it is also challenging.

Many social entrepreneurs can't imagine reaching the point at which they have the resources to justify asking somebody for a lot of money. Roy Prosterman, founder of Landesa, explained how his organization struggled with this challenge: "We spent more than twenty years working out of a small apartment on an annual budget of less than [$1 million]. In fact, for much of that time, our budget was less than $200,000. We were so accustomed to our shoestring budget—on which we still managed to achieve significant impact—that it was difficult to imagine a major step-up."[48] But in 2006, Landesa won the Henry R. Kravis Prize in Nonprofit Leadership, and that milestone provided the impetus to change course. "Our credibility and profile increased, and we invested in development functions. All of this led to various sources of new funding that fueled big efforts to scale," Prosterman said.[49] By 2016, Landesa had increased its annual budget to approximately $12 million.[50]

To replicate a successful model like Landesa's on a large scale requires resources. So once a leader like Prosterman demonstrates that a model has impact, he or she often must assume the role of salesperson and sell the model to donors. To manage this transition and raise money successfully over the long run requires hiring fund-raising professionals and spending money on development functions. Making this transition is sometimes unpalatable to nonprofit leaders, who often feel great pressure, from internal and external stakeholders alike, to spend all of an organization's money on programs that will directly benefit its mission. But there is no way around it—you simply must hire fund-raising professionals and spend money on development functions. A typical nonprofit should have three or four development officers, each with a portfolio that involves handling relationships with 50 to 250 donors and prospective donors at different stages of cultivation, solicitation, and stewardship. To achieve a significant return on an investment in development typically requires a twelve- to eighteen-month process—and a fair amount of patience. But given the payback that an organization is likely to reap within two years, making that investment is a no-brainer.[51]

In addition to hiring paid fund-raising staff, it is also important to engage a core group of volunteers (in addition to board members) who can play an active leadership role in the organization's fund-raising efforts. These volunteers typically have a strong commitment to the nonprofit's mission, and many organizations find it helpful to give them explicit roles. For example, Eastside College Preparatory School created an "ambassador program," whose members meet every other month and organize events intended to introduce new groups of people to Eastside Prep. "All of the members of our ambassador program have been volunteers at the school in other capacities such as tutoring and teaching extra-curricular classes, and so they are passionate and highly motivated to organize events and tell others about our mission and impact," explained cofounder and principal Chris Bischof.[52]

Giving from board members often takes the form of unrestricted funding and is therefore available to support fund-raising or other operational costs. Because board members are highly informed about what it takes to run an organization, they are willing to support it. Tipping Point can proudly state that 100 percent of the funds that it raises externally go to programs because its board underwrites all of its overhead costs.[53]

Investing in fund-raising capacity often demands spending ahead of receiving donations and entails a genuine risk of failure. But it is a risk that must be taken.

Master the Ask

The ask, of course, is the process of asking for money to support your nonprofit. It involves art and science, luck and skill, passion and persistence—and it can take years.

"The first step to improving the way you are making 'the ask' is to conquer your fear," explained Iseminger. "Even the boldest of nonprofit leaders often feel fear or discomfort when they talk about money and ask for a gift. To overcome this discomfort, start by changing your mind-set. If you really believe in your organization's mission, then think of it this way: You are doing potential donors a favor by inviting them to support your work."[54] Koss elaborated on point: "Of course, every nonprofit leader is uncomfortable asking for money. By definition, our passion is making change in the world, not asking for money. The best way to deal with this is by talking mostly about the passion: Bring the donors along on the journey."[55] Another way to set aside your fear is to focus on why the request makes sense for the donor, or on what he or she has done for your organization, rather than on how self-conscious or nervous you might feel. Lasher suggested: "It helps to go into a meeting with a clear plan for the funds, and then you can speak to the mission value and impact. The 'ask' is then almost secondary, a means to accomplish an end."[56]

Of course, you have to ask people to make a donation; it won't just happen automatically as a result of cultivating a relationship with them. Be specific and concrete, and ask for the actual amount you hope to receive. Some fund raisers ask for twice as much as they want with the hope of receiving half of the ask, but we advocate a more authentic and straightforward approach.

If the circumstances are right, ask for a matching gift that will help you raise additional funds from others. Make sure that the terms of the match are reasonable and not too restrictive, and that the match reflects the priorities of your organization. Sometimes a donor will urge you to accept a matching gift that suits the donor's priorities, and not yours. In that case, we advise you to say no. In structuring a matching gift, remember: "The easier it is to explain, the better off you are," noted Iseminger. "A one-to-one match ratio, for example, is always the best way to go."[57]

It is also important to make an ask that is realistic and enables your organization to cover its full costs. Much of the blame for the "nonprofit starvation cycle," as discussed in an important article by Ann Goggins Gregory and Don Howard,[58] lies with funders who do not want to pay for overhead costs. In a 2015 survey conducted by the Nonprofit Finance Fund, 19 percent of nonprofit respondents indicated that raising funds that cover their full costs is one of their greatest challenges.[59] In fact, 47 percent of nonprofits indicated that foundations never or rarely cover the full costs of the programs they intend to support, and 48 percent indicated that individual donors never or rarely cover those costs.[60]

In this environment, many proactive nonprofits are learning to represent their full true costs and, in some instances, they are successfully bundling fund-raising requests in a way that covers those costs. Raybin reflected, "Over the past five years, the sector has made tremendous progress in fund raising for operating expenses and learning how to package [or] bundle them in a compelling way to donors."[61] Brown echoed that observation: "Effective programs achieve results because staff members have what they need to provide services. And I have seen many organizations successfully explain their true costs to donors. For example, the Homeless Initiative Program in Indianapolis calculates [a return on investment] that incorporates full costs but appeals to donors."[62]

An important element of making the ask is connecting your organization's needs with an opportunity for donors to make a significant difference. Shell explained: "I often twist the famous quote of Tip O'Neill [speaker of the US House of Representatives during the 1970s and 1980s], 'All politics is local,' into 'All philanthropy is personal.' In the realm of major gift support, donors have to see themselves in those large gift commitments that they are considering and believe that through their gift they are making a difference—'changing lives and changing the world,' as we all like to say. . . . Making a positive difference in the world remains one of humankind's greatest desires. Connecting prospective donors' hopes, dreams, and aspirations with the needs of your organization can be amazingly rewarding for both donor and organization. It is oftentimes where the magic occurs."[63]

Practicing good stewardship is essential to sustaining the relationship with the donor between "asks." Thank your donors for their gift, and take care to be a good steward. Remember that, properly done, a thank-you also sets the stage for the next gift. In a survey conducted by Burk, 93 percent of donors said they would be likely to give again if they (1) were thanked promptly and in a personal way for their gift and (2) received meaningful information about the program they funded.[64] The best fund raisers always assume that the first gift is never the last gift.

We end this discussion with a call to action to nonprofits that have avoided building a major donor fund-raising effort—especially those that focus on the poor, ill, old, abused, and needy. We urge all nonprofits that have mastered the fundamentals of strategic thinking and built a finely tuned engine of impact to build robust development functions. Yes, you will have to "invest money to make money." Yes, you might have to alter the composition of your board to include people of means and people who are willing to ask others for money. And, yes, you might have to emulate the practices of plutophilanthropic organizations like elite universities, hospitals, performing arts groups, and museums. But even if your mission is worthwhile, your theory of change is well conceived, and your strategy is effective, you cannot escape the wisdom of Willie Sutton: You must go where the money is. And you must embrace the human desire for recognition.

CHAPTER 7

Board Governance
Do What Works

A nonprofit cannot thrive long without strong board governance. Yet governance is one of the most challenging areas for nonprofits to get right. Many people in the sector seem to assume that ineffective nonprofit boards are an inescapable fact of life—like government inefficiency, technological change, or failed diets. But exceptional nonprofit boards do exist. And any organization can improve its board's performance if its board members are willing to confront the people, process, and behavioral challenges that drag competent, well-intentioned people into an abyss of ineffectiveness.

In conducting due diligence on a wide range of nonprofit organizations, first for the Henry R. Kravis Prize in Nonprofit Leadership and now at King Philanthropies, we have always taken special care to scrutinize the board governance of those organizations. We ask about the composition of each board and about how it operates. Sad to say, in the majority of cases, we receive unsatisfactory answers. To take an egregious example, we once learned about an international poverty alleviation organization that had developed a compelling mission. Then we discovered that for nearly a decade, the board of this organization consisted only of a handful of the founders' childhood friends, all of whom were based in the United States and none of whom had any substantive experience or relevant professional expertise in international poverty alleviation. How could such a board operate as anything other than a rubber stamp for the decisions of the organization's executives?

Our belief that many boards today suffer from ineffectiveness is confirmed by empirical data from many sources. In a survey of nonprofit chief executives and board chairs conducted for a 2015

BoardSource report titled *Leading with Intent,* respondents on average gave nonprofit boards a grade of B minus (on a scale of A to F).[1] And the 2015 Survey on Board of Directors of Nonprofit Organizations, an effort conducted by Bill and several colleagues at Stanford's Rock Center for Corporate Governance, likewise offers extensive data on the serious challenges confronting most nonprofit boards.[2] More than two-thirds of nonprofit directors said their organization had faced one or more serious governance-related problems in the previous ten years. The same study suggests that the skills, resources, and experience of many directors do not meet the needs of their nonprofit organizations. A majority of respondents indicated that they did not believe that their fellow board members were very experienced or very engaged in their work.[3]

How can you increase the effectiveness of the board on which you sit? To start, we offer a "stake through the heart" suggestion for nonprofit board members, especially those who might feel underinformed or unsure about the organization's performance: Ask stupid questions, until you figure out what the smart questions are. Then demand answers to the smart ones. If you don't get good answers to your smart questions, or if you don't get support from your fellow board members when you ask them, resign. While this approach might seem harsh, it reflects our many years of experience in advising and serving on numerous nonprofit boards. Much of board dysfunction results from board members' reluctance to contribute actively to board discussions for fear that they will appear uninformed or out of sync. You are a talented and scarce resource. Dive in—the water is fine! Or, to echo one of Stephen R. Covey's "habits of highly effective people": "Be proactive!"[4]

As with so many organizational topics, the context of a specific situation often shapes, or even determines, one's appropriate actions, making hard-and-fast rules unhelpful and even destructive. Instead, we offer six principles of effective nonprofit governance. We have applied them countless times in our own work. If you have the courage to apply them to your nonprofit board, and if you apply them persistently, they will work for you as well.

*Make sure that your organization has a clear mission that is fo-
cused where the organization has the necessary skills/resources and
embraced by the board, management, and other key stakeholders.*
Nonprofit board members play a critical role in ensuring that their
organization's mission is sufficiently clear. Too often, board members
just accept, often without much thought, that a nonprofit's mission
"is what it is"—and forget that it is, in fact, subject to discussion or
review. Assuming an organization's mission statement is effective to
begin with (a too-rare situation), we believe that a board and senior
staff should openly discuss it every three to five years. We hope that
the result will be greater understanding of, and commitment to, the
mission, but with few changes to it since great missions are, in our
considered view, timeless, or close to it. Often we are asked, "What
if we achieve our mission?" This is such an extremely rare event that
our answer is simple: call us when and if it happens!

The effective nonprofit board needs to make sure that the mission
is not just clear but also focused on strategies for which the organization has the necessary skills. Nonprofit leaders must regularly ask,
"Does our organization have the core competency or skill required
to achieve our mission?" It is imperative that every nonprofit organization narrows the scope of its mission so that the mission covers
only the skills and resources the organization actually has or will
likely acquire in the foreseeable future. Why would an organization
have a mission but not the skills to execute it? Happens often, sadly.

By contrast, consider GuideStar, whose mission is to revolutionize
philanthropy by providing information that advances transparency,
enables users to make better decisions, and encourages charitable giving.[5] Its core competency lies in collecting, organizing, and presenting
information about every single IRS-registered nonprofit. GuideStar
has acquired tremendous resources with which to pursue its mission;
indeed, it currently has more than 2.2 billion pieces of data, including
information on more than 2 million organizations. And GuideStar
forecasts that by 2018, its data will be used one hundred million
times by at least twenty million people.[6] Jacob Harold, GuideStar's
president and CEO, reflected:

If strategy is the art of deciding what not to do, I think GuideStar has some victories to point to. For example, we decided not to focus on gathering data on grants. We've also had to be willing to acknowledge that if we are going to organize the data, we have to be comfortable with others analyzing and interpreting that data. In all of these cases, we've had to rely on partnerships. For instance, [the] Foundation Center has strong data on grants, so we're working to cross-reference our data with theirs. Recently, SeaChange Capital Partners used our data to analyze the financial performance of nonprofits in [New York City]. So, interestingly, not only does our focus require letting go, but it requires a willingness for us to share data and thus to share credit.[7]

The mission of the Center for Global Development (CGD) is focused where the organization has specific skills in conducting rigorous research and engaging with the policy community. As its mission states, "The Center for Global Development works to reduce global poverty and inequality through rigorous research and active engagement with the policy community to make the world a more prosperous, just, and safe place for us all."[8] A study by Arabella Advisors asserted, "The Center for Global Development has carved itself a niche by linking rigorous research and cutting-edge communications to the non-partisan pursuit of policy change."[9] This focus on core skills has enabled CGD to perform at a high level. According to the CGD website, a review by the Redstone Strategy Group concluded that "CGD is one of the preeminent think tanks working on development" and that "the consensus among interviewees was that CGD 'punches above its weight.'"[10] Cari Tuna, the visionary and insightful president of Good Ventures and the Open Philanthropy Project, commented, "The Center for Global Development stands out as the premier analytical voice in Washington for low-income people globally. It's always hard to attribute impact in advocacy, but we've seen multiple cases in which CGD's research has influenced the allocation of billions of dollars. We think CGD has yielded returns for the global poor [that are] many times [as high as] its historical spending."[11]

When it comes to underperforming nonprofit organizations, we invariably find that their mission is poorly understood even by board members; in the worst cases, the mission statement is so poorly conceived and so poorly written that it is simply impossible to understand. In fact, when BoardSource (for its *Leading with Intent* report) asked nonprofit board members and CEOs to "grade your board's performance in understanding your organization's mission," only 50 percent gave their board an A.[12] The 2015 Survey on Board of Directors found that 27 percent of nonprofit directors do not believe that their fellow board members have a strong understanding of the mission and strategy of their organization.[13] How can a board oversee efforts by a nonprofit to execute its mission when board members are not clear on what that mission actually is? This situation is far too common, and it often stems from the mission statement itself being unclear. Among registered participants in our *Stanford Social Innovation Review* webinar "Making Mission Matter," 59 percent said their organization's mission was unclear and 87 percent said their organization's mission statement was not memorable or sticky.[14]

Board members of top-performing nonprofits are deeply engaged with the mission of their organization—they understand it, remember it, and believe in it. Consider the example of After School Matters, which provides teens in Chicago Public Schools with high-quality after-school and summer opportunities that develop their talents and skills. Chief executive officer Mary Ellen Caron commented, "Our board really believes in our mission, and [it] provide[s] leadership to help us stay focused on teens even when we are pulled in other directions. The board wants us to grow in the areas in which we already work. Our board chair, Mellody Hobson, knows how to steer the boat. She is very passionate about the lives of teenagers in Chicago and uses our mission as an impetus to encourage the leadership team and staff to stretch."[15]

Helen Keller International (HKI) provides another example. According to its mission statement, HKI "saves and improves the sight and lives of the world's most vulnerable by combating the causes and consequences of blindness, poor health and malnutrition."[16] HKI has become an example of highly effective governance in large part because its board members have such a solid grasp of that core purpose.

"HKI has in its organizational DNA a deep sense of mission and focus," president and CEO Kathy Spahn explained.[17] She continued:

The board takes the initiative to periodically review our mission as part of strategic planning. HKI is somewhat unusual in that we *require* our board members to visit our programs in Africa and Asia at least once every three years. They come back not only inspired and passionate about our mission, but also with a deep understanding of what is involved in executing on that mission. For example, they learn that dispensing a vitamin A capsule or a deworming pill is not as easy as it sounds.[18]

Hire, fire, and evaluate your executive director on the basis of a sound, objective, ongoing process. Many nonprofit board members shy away from engaging personally in the work of supervising an executive director (ED)—hiring, firing, setting goals, evaluating performance, and setting compensation—even though this is a board's primary responsibility. This reluctance is especially pronounced when an ED happens to be the founder of an organization. Founders often tend to believe that they personally embody the mission of their organization ("The mission? C'est moi!"), and that attitude can undermine their desire to be as transparent as possible.

A rigorous evaluation process is necessary in and of itself but also as a basis for thoughtful succession planning. It does not have to be complicated—in fact, we recommend a relatively simple one. At the end of the year, the board chair and the ED should agree on the goals for the organization and for the ED in the coming year. Then, at the end of the coming year, two steps should be taken. First, there should be an open and transparent discussion with the chair and the ED about which goals have been achieved; which have not and why; and in light of the results, what the goals for the next year should be. Second, these goal-setting efforts and progress against the goals should be tied to compensation and performance evaluation.

Johann Olav Koss, founder of Right to Play, underwent an especially rigorous ongoing evaluation process when he served as CEO

of the organization.[19] This process unfolded on a quarterly sched-
ule, and the Right to Play board led the effort. In the first quarter of
each year, the board would conduct a performance appraisal. In the
second quarter, Koss worked with the board to develop and refine a
talent management plan that covered contingencies (an "if I get hit
by a bus" scenario, for instance) as well as provisions for long-term
succession. In the third quarter, Koss received a 360-degree review
in which he got feedback from a group of stakeholders that included
not only board members but also his ten direct reports. In the fourth
quarter, Koss and the board worked collaboratively to create goals
for the following year. Koss, speaking during his tenure as CEO, explained the value of this approach: "Some CEOs or executive directors
might view such an intensive and time-consuming process as burdensome, but because the resulting content is substantive and honest, it
is extremely helpful to me and ultimately to our whole organization.
Our process gives me tremendous clarity about how to leverage my
strengths and how to address my weaknesses. Consequently, I can
lead more effectively."[20]

In cases of leadership transition, boards should begin conversations about performance evaluation before a new ED even begins the job. As Spahn explained: "In advance of my start date, the
board and I developed and agreed upon not only a clear and specific job description, but also mutually agreed objectives and deliv-
erables for my first three, six, and twelve months. Consequently,
there were no surprises or speed bumps, and I was able to hit the
ground running and partner effectively with the board from the very
beginning."[21]

There are few more contentious situations for a nonprofit than
when its executive director plans to continue serving forever but
that ED's effectiveness is such that a leadership transition becomes
necessary. Such situations require wisdom, a balance of toughness
and compassion, and deft interpersonal skills. An ED whose effectiveness is less than acceptable, or declining, should be dealt with
sooner rather than later. Addressing these situations usually requires
difficult conversations and often involves board members who will

resist the need to be tough-minded. Our advice in such cases is simply to persevere; as Bill's late mother used to say, "You will get your reward in heaven."

Ensure that management has in place explicit goals, strategies, and impact measurement and evaluation directly tied to your organization's mission. One of the primary tasks of management is to develop goals and strategies for making meaningful progress toward achieving the organization's mission. The management team must translate the mission into concrete plans, and the board in turn needs to ensure that those plans are sound and achievable. The board has the responsibility to review and respond to management's proposals, beginning with the most fundamental questions: How are you planning to achieve our mission? What theory of change ties our strategies to achievement of our mission? Is there empirical evidence that makes you think these strategies will work? What measures of impact and performance will you use?

But many nonprofit boards aren't even aware of their overall roles and responsibilities. In the survey undertaken by BoardSource for its *Leading with Intent* report, 35 percent of chief executives and board chairs gave their board a grade of C, D, or F on making sure that the roles and responsibilities of their board were understood. Although 80 percent of respondents said that their board "actively participated in developing the strategic plan by setting priorities and goals," only 20 percent said they would give an A to their board's ability to adopt and follow a strategic plan. Indeed, 35 percent gave their board a C or below in that category. (The remaining 45 percent gave their board a B.)[22]

Rigorous impact evaluation is the bedrock of good governance, but it is also a primary area in which boards fall short. Indeed, there is a sectorwide virus of too little evaluation, and boards are largely to blame because they allow nonprofits to operate without conducting impact evaluations. We have witnessed this repeatedly in our decades of work as consultants, and empirical evidence confirms that it is a pervasive problem. In the *Leading with Intent* survey, only 13

percent of respondents gave their board an A for monitoring organizational performance and impact, and 38 percent gave their board
a C or worse. (The remaining 49 percent gave their board a B.)[23]

Similarly, the 2015 Survey on Board of Directors found that
20 percent of nonprofit directors were either "moderately" or "very"
dissatisfied with their board's ability to evaluate the performance of
their organization. While almost all respondents (92 percent) said that
their board reviewed data to evaluate organizational performance,
many were uncomfortable with the quality of that data. Indeed,
46 percent of directors expressed little or no confidence that such
data fully and accurately measured the success of their organization
in achieving its mission.[24] How can a board claim to know whether
the initiatives of its organization are successful if it does not ensure
that the organization is accurately measuring its impact?

Boards must insist that their organization conduct impact evaluations, and funders must be more willing to pay for them. We regularly hear from nonprofits, "Our funders ask us to demonstrate that
we are having impact, but they won't fund evaluations." Nonprofits
that do not conduct evaluations also tell us that their boards have
never asked them to make evaluation a priority. Leadership at the
board level must demand rigorous impact evaluation.

In addition to too little evaluation of an organization's impact
over time, there is also far too little benchmarking of performance
against similar organizations. According to the 2015 Survey on Board
of Directors, more than half (57 percent) of nonprofit boards do not
benchmark their performance against a peer group.[25]

*Compose and structure your board using transparent structures and
processes that support effective decision making.* The most common
nonprofit governance question we are asked is, "How large should
our nonprofit board be?" Well, it depends. Boards of organizations
that have significant responsibilities to raise money and represent diverse stakeholders (e.g., major cultural organizations) can be quite
large—often they include dozens of members—if managed effectively.
A nonprofit that strives to have all board members involved deeply

in all major decisions (i.e., no committees, or no active committees) has a practical limit of around a dozen, given the dynamics of small-group discussion.

All strong boards need a small group of committed, serious, informed, and aligned leaders. For a board of twelve to fifteen, that might be three or four; for a board of fifty or more, perhaps a dozen. Beyond that small, highly engaged group, effective nonprofit boards also need a diverse array of individuals with the skills, resources, and dedication to address the needs of their nonprofit. The authors of the *Leading with Intent* report note that "if a board isn't thoughtfully composed as it relates to skill sets, leadership styles, and diversity of thought and background, it is less likely to excel in other areas of board performance. But unfortunately, . . . only [one in five] chief executives [of nonprofits] strongly agree that they have the right board members [and] 58 [percent] of chief executives say it is difficult to find people to serve on the board."[26]

In determining the appropriate composition of a nonprofit board, you are unlikely to go wrong if you remember the venerable idea of the three Ws: work, wisdom, and wealth. Your goal, in other words, should be to attract board members who bring one or more of those valuable assets to the table. Excellent board composition is not a conceptual challenge—it is about the good, hard work of finding and adding one strong board member after another.

Every nonprofit board needs a significant number of board members who are going to focus on contributing their *work*—their time, effort, energy, advice, and devotion. There are fund-raising dinners to lead, potential board members or donors to cultivate, management advice to offer, audits to review.

In addition, effective boards also typically require at least a few members who contribute their *wisdom*—a special talent or expertise that helps an organization achieve its mission. For example, the board of INJAZ Al-Arab is populated by business leaders because that organization's model depends on leveraging corporate volunteers who can provide education, training, and mentorship to help inspire a culture of entrepreneurialism among Arab youth who might otherwise face unemployment.[27] Most boards benefit from cultivating different kinds of wisdom. Dr. Tommy Clark, founder and CEO of Grassroot Soccer, recalled, "Our early board was doctors and researchers only . . . because that was my world when I founded the organization as an MD. But, fortunately, Anne Marie Burgoyne, who was then at the Draper Richards Kaplan Foundation before her current role at Emerson Collective, joined our board. Her expertise in social entrepreneurship was invaluable, and she helped us to professionalize our board and recruit others with different kinds of relevant experience."[28]

Another example comes from a performing arts organization in a major US city that was frequently obliged to interact with the municipal government over issues related to taxes, real estate, and the like. Its board included a high-profile lawyer who was not particularly devoted to the art form. However, a phone call to this board member could provide helpful connections to, and even influence with, the local government. Nonprofit boards need to be open to the fact that they may need access to one or two special kinds of wisdom or professional expertise, although this should be the exception and not the rule. Board composition is often more a matter of pragmatism than principle.

We all know that well-functioning nonprofit boards bring *wealth* through the fulfillment of fund-raising responsibilities. Some board members should be in a position to give generously or to solicit generous donations from others. All members of the board of Eastside College Preparatory School in East Palo Alto, California, treat that organization as a top priority in their financial giving, and board members play a lead role in raising money from outside donors. To ensure a high level of commitment to fund raising, leaders at Right to Play involve board members heavily in discussions of the organization's budget. "Our budget discussion is central because our board members need to take ownership," Koss shared. "We start the budget discussion for the following year in May [or] June, and then seven hours of our ten-hour November board meeting is devoted to the budget—how to raise funds, and what the consequences are if we don't."[29] At HKI, meanwhile, the expectation is that board members will not only support the organization with an annual gift, but also include the nonprofit in their will. "Fueled by their site visits," members of the HKI board have become "passionate fund raisers," noted Spahn. "They can speak firsthand about what they've seen and our impact on lives."[30]

We believe that 100 percent board participation in giving is always an appropriate goal. That said, not everyone on a board needs to be a major donor. Nonprofit boards, after all, need to reflect the diversity of the societies in which they operate, and that often means including members who are not affluent.

The second most frequent question we receive regarding nonprofit board governance is "What committees do we need?" All boards need certain committees—or, in the case of small boards, certain board members—to take the lead in particular areas. Every board needs both a finance committee and an audit committee. (To represent best practice, the audit committee should report to the board chair, not to the finance committee, in order to ensure that any financial issues receive scrutiny from another set of eyes.) The board of every nonprofit that raises money through donations also needs a development committee. And every board also needs a governance or trustee committee that nominates and evaluates board members. Beyond these committees, best practice varies.

Boards can have a marketing committee, a program or operations committee, and a committee on any issue that is of ongoing importance to the organization. Museums and performing arts organizations may have artistic committees, and colleges and universities may have academic committees; in both cases, such committees often exercise gentle guidance on core management decisions. Temporary task forces for strategic planning, capital campaigns, or any other time-limited effort can also be very useful.

Executive committees are imperative for boards that are larger than fifteen to twenty people. Although executive committees must do their best to avoid making other board members feel like second-class citizens, they serve an essential function by shaping the board's working agenda and, if needed, being available to handle an emergency. In the 2015 Survey on Board of Directors, 52 percent of nonprofit directors said their organization had a "board within a board," meaning a subset of directors that exercised an outsized influence on board decisions. In two-thirds of these cases, these boards within boards were in fact formal executive committees, but in one-third of these cases, they reflected an informal dynamic that had evolved over time. Among respondents who said their organization had a board within a board, 74 percent said this feature improved board functionality and decision making.[31]

The Stanford University Board of Trustees has thirty-three members, and it includes an agenda committee that serves the board planning functions of an executive committee.[32] But the agenda committee operates without the formal powers of an executive committee, so as to avoid the sense that there are "two boards" and two hierarchies of board member. Isaac Stein, a former Stanford University trustee and a past chair of the board of trustees, explained: "Because the agenda committee's members [include] the chairs of the other committees and a rotating group of trustees selected by the board chair, there is no sense of a secretive small group making all of the decisions, which can be a common problem of executive committees. Its focus on planning topics for future board meetings creates synergies among the other committees but also allows [for] a 'focus group' of trustees where the president [of Stanford] can test ideas before advancing them to the full board."[33]

Evaluate and sustain your board. The best nonprofit boards periodically review and assess the performance of each board member, typically through their governance committee. Some boards utilize anonymous online questionnaires, outside consultants, face-to-face discussions, or a range of other approaches. Our preference is for each governance committee member to have responsibilities for a group of board members. As a board member's term (usually of two to three years) nears completion, they should write a summary of their contributions to the board, their goals, and any other interests they may have, as well as listing a few other board members who have a perspective on their performance. The designated governance committee member should then have a face-to-face discussion with the board member whose term is nearing completion and should interview other board members about their performance. In the governance committee meeting, the designated member reviews the board member's performance and makes a recommendation about future service and possible committee or other roles. Then, after a full discussion, the committee votes on whether to renew their service for another term.

Unfortunately, such frank discussions and self-assessments happen only rarely. In our 2016 Stanford survey, only 51 percent of board members indicated that they receive regular and specific feedback on their participation and involvement that helps them improve.[34] In the 2015 Survey on Board of Directors, 36 percent of respondents said that their board never evaluates its own performance.[35] The *Leading with Intent* survey similarly found that 43 percent of boards have not recently undertaken a self-assessment. Further, 23 percent of nonprofit CEOs and 20 percent of board chairs said that self-assessment of board performance was one of the top three areas in which they hoped to see improvement at their organization.[36]

A governance committee must be ready and willing to hold candid conversations with noncontributing or disruptive board members. To be sure, it's difficult and uncomfortable to ask a fellow board member to step aside. Nobody really wants to sit down with Mr. Jones or Ms. Smith and bring up the fact that he or she doesn't attend board meetings and is very generous to many organizations—but not to this one—or to say that although his or her time and commitment are appreciated, it's time to move on. Because of the social peer aspects of many boards, there is a real reluctance to hold such difficult conversations, but this is exactly what a governance committee is supposed to do.

In part to avoid uncomfortable conversations with nonperforming board members, some organizations choose to implement formal term limits. The problem with term limits is straightforward: they oblige an organization to throw the baby out with the bath water—to force out board members who are contributing at a high level alongside those who aren't. This is a significant loss, because many of the best nonprofits have a few extremely valuable board members who maintain their passion for the organization and its work for decades. Term limits also can decrease board giving. A study of nonprofit organizations in New York City found that average board giving among boards with term limits was $5.5 million, compared with $16.3 million among boards without such limits.[37]

As Chris Bischof, cofounder and principal of Eastside Prep, explained: "We have no term limits for a reason. There are a number of important key players who are tremendously dedicated to Eastside and have been actively engaged on our board for twenty years. . . . Why would we want to lose them?"[38] Fuller Theological Seminary is another organization that has chosen to have terms but no term limits. As its president, Mark Labberton, explained: "There are forty-one people on the Fuller board, of which fifteen have been on the board for multiple decades. In fact, some people have been on the board for thirty years, and they are amazing champions! Because they have such a long history with the organization, they have incredible perspective. One might argue that they might be inclined to feel overly nostalgic about the past, but that has not been our experience. In fact, our long-standing board members are most embracing of risk."[39]

For those who favor term limits, we offer what seems to be the most common compromise: allow each board member to serve two three-year terms, followed by a year off and then (for those worthy of returning to the board) two more three-year terms. If this is your policy, be sure to engage your best year-off board members during their time away.

Last but not least, strong boards identify, cultivate, and attract new members largely on their own, with support from, but not by delegating to, the executive director. A quick diagnostic to check a nonprofit board's effectiveness is just to ask who sources new members. If it is solely the executive director and perhaps the development director, that is a sure sign the board is not as proactive as it should be. Put that together with short board terms and term limits and a long-standing executive director, and you have a nonprofit that has delegated its governance responsibilities to management.

One other responsibility for a governance committee is to commission or conduct a review of the board's overall effectiveness roughly once per decade. Many nonprofits seem to take this step in preparation for a capital campaign, while others do so in less busy times. Lucile Packard Children's Hospital Stanford (LPCH) provides a case in point. LPCH successfully undertook such a review in 2004, even though it already had an extremely high-performing board. Conducting interviews with forty-seven people (including current and former board members, members of the management team, top donors, and other stakeholders), the LPCH governance task force addressed the roles and responsibilities of the board and its individual members, along with a host of other topics, such as the size and structure of the board, board processes and conduct, relationship with other boards, board composition and evaluation, and term structure. As a result of this process, LPCH further clarified and communicated the roles and responsibilities of both the board as a whole and individual board members, and it reviewed and revised the charter of all current committees. Susan Packard Orr, who served as chair of the LPCH governance task force, reflected: "The LPCH board was already quite well functioning. But we initiated a governance review in 2004 because we wanted to engage our board and its members more fully and ensure we were prepared for the increasing demands we were confident we would be facing over the next decade. LPCH has continued to expand over the past twelve years, providing world-class clinical care and achieving extraordinary outcomes for even more children and expectant mothers. The board remains highly engaged at all levels, with very high satisfaction scores year after year on our annual board evaluation survey."[40]

Engage board members seriously. Board members need to be engaged deeply in the issues facing the organization—but, alas, many are not. In the *Leading with Intent* survey, only 19 percent of nonprofit CEOs indicated that they strongly agree that the majority of board members are actively engaged in overseeing and governing their organization.[41]

The agenda of a typical nonprofit board meeting consists of pre-baked committee reporting that is designed to preclude discussion— and, truth be told, nonprofit staff often like it that way because it keeps board members from suggesting ideas that might be unrealistic or generate unnecessary work. But a board meeting that doesn't give board members a chance to engage is not as effective as it could be. As a result, issues are typically brought to the board too late, leaving members with the option of either politely nodding or causing an embarrassing ruckus. The right time for the executive director and staff to bring up issues is early in the process, when board members can give real input and have a dynamic discussion. One of our board practice quips is "I have no objection to a good discussion breaking out in the middle of a board meeting."

It is essential that nonprofit board members be engaged in discussion of the important strategic questions faced by the organization. If board members don't engage directly and deeply in the substantive work of an organization, then board meetings will degenerate into a staff-driven, prebaked exercise. Labberton, referring to his work at Fuller Theological Seminary, reflected: "We have intentionally fostered a board culture at Fuller in which it is assumed that board members will engage and ask questions. The board members at Fuller are critical thinkers in the best sense, and their critical thinking is very constructive and useful. They analyze and discuss in a way that is invigorating to the board members while also being extremely helpful to the institution and to me as the president. This creates a self-reinforcing culture that causes our board meetings to be well attended: being at a board meeting is an experience that our board members do not want to miss."[42] The board meetings of Proximity Designs, a social enterprise in Myanmar, follow a similar pattern. Cofounder Debbie Aung Din commented: "Our board is extremely active and engaged in the substance of Proximity's work, and this is an impetus to strong attendance. The board meets four to five times per year, and we've only had one meeting in which [any member] was absent."[43]

To ensure that its board members remain engaged during meetings, HKI leaders build their agenda around high-level strategy discussions. "We had an important discussion in a recent board meeting about whether we should enter Kenya—the pros, the cons, the trade-offs—and the board members gave HKI their best strategic guidance," Spahn explained.[44] A crucial part of that approach, she noted, involved keeping details related to committee work off the agenda: "Committee reporting is done beforehand within the committees and also provided in written form [committee meeting minutes are included in the board books], so that in board meetings we can discuss and engage [around strategic issues]."[45] Spahn emphasized the value of such discussions:

In the past we have discussed questions such as, "We are known as an innovator in our work to combat malnutrition, but we are losing our edge in eye health. How do we continue to innovate within blindness prevention, and how do we resource this? Or, most recently, do we need—and can we afford—a unified accounting system [with] full-fledged ERP [enterprise resource planning]? Can we afford not to have one?" Such discussions require advance education—and time! Which is why the minutiae of committee work stays off the agenda. We have worked to instill a culture that is transparent, self-reflective, and open to criticizing ourselves, and that frees us up to speak freely—in very blunt terms—about HKI's challenges and to think together about how best to address them.[46]

Most board members, of course, are bright people who have a wealth of experience. But they often lack expertise in the day-to-day work of the organization on whose board they sit. So how can they engage with that work? Board members should start by taking a page from the HKI playbook and make field visits to see program activity firsthand. In addition, as we noted earlier, board members must be willing to ask "stupid" questions at board meetings, and they need to keep asking so-called stupid questions until they figure out what the "smart" questions are. Then board members need to make sure that staff members answer the questions!

In addition to discussion, board members need to engage in what could be called "the thing itself." For example, the San Francisco Symphony board on occasion has musicians perform during their meeting, and afterward the musicians answer questions from board members. Similarly, a homeless shelter should occasionally invite clients who have been helped by its work to attend part of a meeting to discuss their experiences. Board members are almost always involved with a nonprofit because they care about its mission; they want to be engaged in the substance of the organization. "At Eastside Prep, at least half of the board members are on campus daily or weekly, tutoring or teaching after-school classes to kids or engaging in other ways. This involvement causes the board to really have their pulse on the school," noted Bischof.[47] HKI board members are required to travel to the field regularly to engage in the organization's work. Spahn explained:

Those trips to the field to see our programs are really key in engaging our board. How can you go to Burkina Faso and see eye surgery that saves a family breadwinner or a mother from a life of blindness and not leave changed—and engaged? I don't mean to sound corny, but these visits provide a visceral connection to the work.[48]

Part of engaging board members is to make sure that board members view their time as well spent. As board members walk to their cars after the board meeting, do they say, "That was a waste of my time"? Or do they say, "That was a productive meeting"? Unfortunately, nonprofit leaders sometimes forget that board members are choosing to spend time with their organization. Smart nonprofit executive directors therefore ensure that their board members' time is respected, valued, and wisely used.

CHAPTER 8

Scaling

Leveraging the Seven Essentials
to Magnify Your Impact

Scaling is perhaps the most researched, surveyed, discussed, and written-about topic in the nonprofit sector in recent years. Much of the substance of the discussion is of high quality, but most of it focuses on *how* to scale. *Stanford Social Innovation Review* (*SSIR*), for instance, has published worthy articles with titles like "Demystifying Scaling," described as a "five-part series on developing a common framework for nonprofits to scale for impact," and "Scaling Impact" which asks "How to get 100x the results with 2x the organization."[1] So has *Harvard Business Review* (*HBR*), which has carried articles titled "Why Don't the Best Nonprofits Grow?" and "How to Take a Social Venture to Scale."[2] The topic is so hot that every few weeks, we seem to receive another invitation to a conference focused at least in part on how to scale.

This fervor for scaling accompanies an all-too-common, and often misguided, assumption. "I had an idea last night," says a smart, compelling millennial. "I think I have a way to . . ." And what follows is the germ of an insight about reducing extreme poverty in East Africa, empowering struggling students in US public K–12 education, or building the "ready to work" skills of the disenfranchised in Appalachia. We both spend about a day a week meeting with such budding social entrepreneurs. We try to strike the right balance between encouraging them, teaching them, and focusing their attention on what works and what doesn't, the basics of nonprofit business models, and the demanding lives of the best social entrepreneurs. There is now a whole ecosystem of funders, conferences, incubators, and university-based programs in place to encourage these often inspiring, well-intentioned young adults in their hopes to address one of society's intractable problems. "Every idea is a good idea," they are told. There's an ecosystem for scaling too, and it sends an equally misleading metamessage to young social entrepreneurs: "Start up, then scale up."

Our perspectives on scaling are informed by our experiences over numerous decades with Bill Drayton and Roy Prosterman. Bill Meehan developed a working relationship and friendship with Bill Drayton, founder of Ashoka, and Drayton established a lifelong benchmark for Bill for what it takes to achieve broad social impact at scale. It takes, among other things, an unwavering focus on what drives impact (and not just size), a patient search for talent that is truly aligned with sources of capital, and a default mind-set that puts growing the impact of a movement ahead of boosting public recognition for a charismatic leader. Kim first encountered Roy Prosterman twelve years ago during the selection process for the inaugural recipient of the Henry R. Kravis Prize in Nonprofit Leadership, and he has since become the guiding light for her conviction that impact at scale is possible, even on a limited budget. Other Kravis Prize recipients that have scaled significantly—including BRAC, Pratham, Helen Keller International, and Endeavor—have reinforced that conviction. Through our encounters with leaders like Drayton and Prosterman, we have come to appreciate that scaling for impact is best achieved through an intentional and well-guided process that centers on honing the fundamentals of strategic leadership.

It is no accident that Drayton and Prosterman share three common attributes. First, both founded organizations that played a highly leveraged role in launching global social movements: social entrepreneurship, in Drayton's case, and rural land reform, in Prosterman's. Second, both focused from the beginning on scaling for impact rather than size. Each devoted considerable attention to refining his organization's mission, strategy, and impact evaluation. Third, each took the time needed to ensure that his organization's engine of impact was ready and working before expanding the size of that organization. In 1990, ten years after its founding, Ashoka's budget was still only $1.4 million; roughly twenty-five years later, it had reached $41.5 million, and the organization had offices in more than thirty-six countries.[3] For most of its first twenty years, Landesa's budget was less than $1 million; indeed, for much of that time it was less than $200,000.[4] By 2016, Landesa had a budget of approximately $12 million, and it employed 146 people in ten countries.[5]

Importantly, Drayton and Prosterman both resisted the temptation to accumulate "fuel" prematurely. Both were picky about types of funding. Because they did not consider it consistent with their organizations' models, Drayton did not seek foundation funding and Prosterman did not seek government funding. Prosterman, for two decades, ran Landesa out of the living room of a modest one-bedroom apartment near the University of Washington. A handful of staff members came to work each day and sat at desks and small tables arranged in the living room; some of the files were kept in the bathtub! Yet, lacking even a proper office, Prosterman and his small team continuously refined Landesa's model and created significant impact: as a direct result of their efforts, hundreds of millions of tenant farmers obtained property rights.

Scaling is an important topic and, for certain nonprofits under certain conditions, a powerful way to increase impact. But the critical yet oft-neglected first step in scaling is to dispassionately assess readiness to scale. Consequently, in this chapter, we start by considering how an organization can gauge that readiness. Then we shift to synthesizing important lessons in how to scale.

Readiness to Scale

Assessing readiness is the essential first step for any social entrepreneur or nonprofit organization that seeks to scale. However, it is also often the elephant in the living room when social entrepreneurs and nonprofit leaders discuss their grand plans to scale. We have seen it many times. Ardent and ambitious, these leaders have read all of the excellent *SSIR* and *HBR* articles on the subject and have formulated exciting plans detailing how they will scale rapidly and successfully. Their teams have starry eyes, their funders have bought in and committed some of the necessary resources, and everybody is ready to go. Except—there's that elephant.

Many of these organizations simply are not ready or able to scale their impact any time soon. To earn the right to scale, they must ensure that their engine of impact has a theory of change that has demonstrated and meaningful evidence of working. The engine must also have a complete, feasible strategy that takes into account product or service, sales, and distribution. And the engine must feature a commitment to impact evaluation. (Far too many organizations lack that last component—a 2013 study by Veris Consulting found that only 39 percent of nonprofits that are scaling had measured the impact of their work; only 12 percent had undergone a third-party study; and only 2 percent had done a randomized controlled trial.[6])

How to assess an organization's readiness to scale? As recovering management consultants, we often try to clarify our thinking about a complex question by identifying the key dimensions that frame the potential answers to that question. Sometimes, that process of simplifying can best be enabled by creating a matrix. Don't laugh. The field of corporate strategy was launched in 1970 with the now-famous growth-share four-box matrix created by Bruce Henderson of Boston Consulting Group. Anyone who has used the phrase "cash cow" has had his or her strategic thinking influenced by this nearly fifty-year-old model.[7]

We have designed a readiness-to-scale matrix (shown in Figure 8) that we believe will not only assist nonprofit leaders in their high-level thinking but also serve as a robust managerial tool. The matrix includes five boxes—five categories that indicate how ready an organization is to scale—and we have designed visual and verbal metaphors to make these categories richly memorable. On our website, we provide a straightforward tool that you can use to evaluate your nonprofit organization (or any other) in terms of the four dimensions of strategic thinking (mission, strategy, impact evaluation, and insight and courage) and the three dimensions of strategic management (organization and talent, funding, and board governance).[8] But here we focus on high-level definitions of the five categories.

Strong

The Waterfall
"Reality or illusion..."

Promised Land
"...I have been to the mountaintop..."

Finding the Fuel
(Organization and Talent, Funding, Board Governance)

Small Is Beautiful
"...when you are in front of someone suffering"

Scale Jail
"Do not pass go. Do not collect $200."

Field of Dreams
"Build it, and they will come..."

Weak

Weak   Strong

Building and Tuning Your Engine of Impact
(Mission, Strategy, Impact Evaluation, Insight and Courage)

FIGURE 8   Readiness-to-scale matrix

SCALE JAIL

According to the IRS, there are more than one million 501(c)(3)s in the United States. What do they all do? Sadly, some do not do very much. A small local social service nonprofit or cultural organization with the resources to pay an executive director and little else, for example, is not in a position to think through issues like theory of change or impact measurement, or even to raise much money. Organizations in this category are trapped in Scale Jail. (We are not students of whatever corruption exists in the sector. But those individuals who manipulate nonprofit status for personal gain belong in a real jail.) These nonprofits in Scale Jail do not have a well-built engine of impact, and they have little or no fuel. They are neither ready nor able to scale their impact any time soon. Let's leave them be, assuming they are drawing no resources from more impactful organizations. Our advice to them (with apologies to the game of Monopoly): "Do not pass Go. Do not collect $200."

FIELD OF DREAMS

Organizations in the Field of Dreams have built a proven engine of impact but still need to develop a solid plan for finding the necessary fuel to scale. These organizations wonder whether they should scale: Can we find sufficient funding? Can we develop the right talent? Is our board capable of leading our growth strategy? Patience can be a virtue. Your impact model comes first, and fueling scale should follow. We say (in a nod to the movie *Field of Dreams*), "If you build it, they will come."[9]

SMALL IS BEAUTIFUL

Many nonprofits serve a small population and do it well. There is great dignity in helping another person, even if you are not able to help millions of people. Dr. Paul Farmer, cofounder of the renowned nonprofit Partners in Health, once commented, "For me, an area of moral clarity is: you're in front of someone who's suffering and you have the tools at your disposal to alleviate that suffering or even eradicate it, and you act."[10] Let us celebrate the value and importance of organizations—a soup kitchen or theater or community health clinic—that provide a needed service in one locality or to one small target population. May these organizations continue to flourish in the land of Small Is Beautiful.

THE WATERFALL

Organizations stuck in the Waterfall have a weak or poorly built engine of impact, and that weakness often starts with a flawed theory of change. Yet these organizations continue to benefit from significant funding or from other forms of fuel. Like the Penrose triangle in M. C. Escher's *Waterfall*—an impossible object of seemingly perpetual motion—these organizations are more illusion than reality. Impact evaluation for such organizations is typically weak or nonexistent, and in many cases their management team simply lacks the experience or hardheaded knowledge needed to build and tune an engine of impact. Nevertheless, fuel pours in, often because the leaders of these organizations excel at creating the kind of buzz that fills the atmosphere at social sector conferences. Certainly, the temptation to be a hip entrepreneur is strong and the love of the buzz natural for many. But, like the ancient Greek hero Odysseus, any nonprofit leader or funder on the vital journey to genuine impact must resist the enticing call of the Sirens often called fame and recognition and sometimes simply fads.

THE PROMISED LAND

The Promised Land beyond the mountaintops is a place that exists in all our minds thanks to the great Dr. Martin Luther King and the iconic 1968 speech (now known as "I've Been to the Mountaintop") that he delivered the day before his assassination.[11] Organizations that have reached, or at least stood in view of, the Promised Land have earned the right to scale their impact by creating a well-built, proven impact model and by finding the fuel that they need to sustain growth. Most of these organizations have moved from being a regional force to launching a global movement. We draw on this powerful metaphor from the part of our hearts and souls touched by

Ashoka and Landesa, as well as a select few others such as Partners in Health, Pratham, and BRAC.

Applying the Readiness-to-Scale Matrix as a Managerial Tool

We think this matrix can help any nonprofit assess its readiness to scale. In addition, it can serve as a tool for a range of stakeholders—executive staff, board members, and funders—to use in assessing their organization's overall strategic position.

We have developed and placed on our book website an assessment tool that will enable your organization to figure out where it falls on the matrix.[12] There are several applications for this tool. For example, executives, board members, and other stakeholders can place their nonprofit on the matrix and use that choice of placement as a discussion starter. Or, if you are tired of SWOTs for offsite retreats (and who isn't?), then members of your executive staff and board can use the assessment tool to initiate a strategic discussion with a breakdown showing where different stakeholders believe your organization currently is on the matrix. There will be a range of assessment results among stakeholders, which will provide a helpful basis for discussion: you can explore why there is variation in viewpoint and determine what should be done to achieve clarity, consensus, and a plan of action to enable your organization to achieve its goals.

What proportion of the organizations in today's nonprofit sector fall into each quadrant of the matrix? To obtain a general sense of the current landscape in the nonprofit sector, we conducted a statistical analysis of the data from our 2016 Stanford survey.[13] This analysis (depicted in Figure 9) revealed that a large proportion (37 percent) of respondents' organizations are currently stuck in Scale Jail, while a much smaller number (11 percent) have made it to the Promised Land. Also, 10 percent are in Small Is Beautiful territory. And 27 percent are in the Field of Dreams; they have earned the right to more funding by building an effective engine of impact but have yet to find their fuel. Meanwhile, 15 percent are in the Waterfall; these organizations have ample fuel (often in the form of generous funding) but lack a well-built and well-tuned engine of impact.[14]

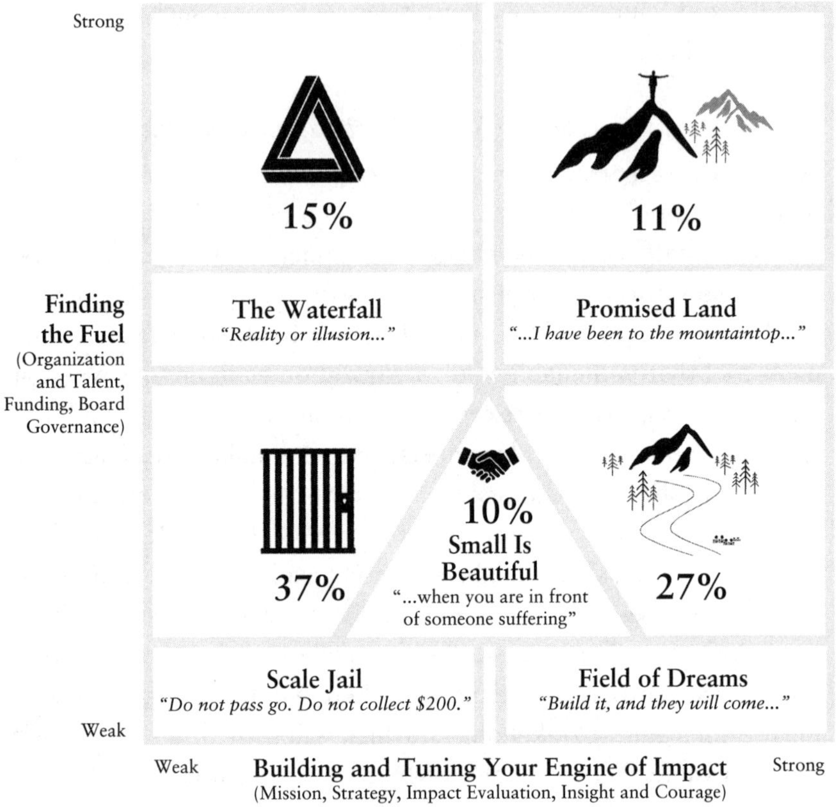

Strong

15%

11%

Finding
the Fuel
(Organization
and Talent,
Funding, Board
Governance)

The Waterfall
"Reality or illusion..."

Promised Land
"...I have been to the mountaintop..."

10%
Small Is
Beautiful
*"...when you are in front
of someone suffering"*

37%

27%

Scale Jail
"Do not pass go. Do not collect $200."

Field of Dreams
"Build it, and they will come..."

Weak

Weak   **Building and Tuning Your Engine of Impact**   Strong
(Mission, Strategy, Impact Evaluation, Insight and Courage)

FIGURE 9 Distribution of today's nonprofits in the readiness-to-scale matrix

SOURCE: Data are drawn from William F. Meehan III and Kim Starkey Jonker, 2016 Stanford Survey on Leadership and Management in the Nonprofit Sector, Stanford Graduate School of Business, 2016, engineofimpact.org/survey.

We aspire to have our matrix, and the thinking that underlies it, influence strategic leadership throughout the nonprofit sector. Over time, we hope to encounter fewer organizations that are stuck in Scale Jail or in the Waterfall—fewer organizations that divert attention and resources from nonprofits that have a real engine of impact. We hope to see greater appreciation of the vibrancy and importance of Small Is Beautiful organizations and ready support for nonprofits that have entered the Field of Dreams. Finally, we anticipate the day when we will see full scaling and resourcing for those nonprofits, in vogue or not, that have reached, or see not far in the distance, the Promised Land beyond the mountaintops.

How to Scale

The primary role of nonprofit leaders is not to grow the size of an organization, or even to reach more people, but to achieve the greatest possible impact. Sometimes that means growth that enables your organization to provide a core service to more people, often in more locations. But that is not the only path to increased impact.

Incisive thinking on how to scale has come from multiple quarters. Major consulting firms such as the Bridgespan Group, FSG, and McKinsey & Company have developed important expertise in the subject. *SSIR*, the major journal in the sector, has published more than one hundred articles on scaling since 2004. Other intermediaries, such as Grantmakers for Effective Organizations and *Nonprofit Quarterly*, also contribute to sectorwide knowledge of the topic. In their excellent 2014 *SSIR* article "Transformative Scale: The Future of Growing What Works," Jeffrey Bradach and Abe Grindle outlined nine approaches that organizations can use to magnify impact while "keeping a lid on the growth of their own organization."[15] Grouped into two categories, these approaches include "organizational pathways" that allow for "building on and expanding what individual organizations can do" (distribute through existing platforms, recruit and train other organizations, unbundle and scale for impact, and leverage technology) and "field-building pathways" that call for "pushing the field and its constellation of actors towards a shared target" (strengthen a field, change public systems, influence policy change, consider for-profit models, and alter attitudes, behaviors, and norms).[16]

Because there is so much strong thinking and writing already in existence on the topic of scaling, we focus on offering a synthesis that reflects the most important lessons we have learned through our own experience and extensive reading.

Always start with your business or economic model (especially if you are going to scale your organization's impact through partnering). Options for scaling a nonprofit are fewer than they may seem. If you need funds and other resources to scale, examine your business or economic model and realize that your partners in scaling are most likely your current partners. So, for example, if you are an organization that delivers social services and a municipal government is your major funder, as is very common, that government—or the governments in other municipalities into which you are considering expansion—is also your most likely partner in scaling.

Kevin Starr and Laura Hattendorf, incisive thought leaders on the topic of impact at scale, wrote an excellent *SSIR* article titled "The Doer and the Payer: A Simple Approach to Scale," in which they emphasize that "growth and scale are not the same" and provide valuable advice on getting to scale.[17] They posit that only two questions truly matter for organizations that aim to achieve real scale: Who's the doer? and Who's the payer? In other words, if you have a proven model, then you need to determine who is going to replicate that model (the doer) and who is going to fund the replication (the payer). When it comes to the doer, Starr and Hattendorf suggest that only four choices exist. Here, in their words, is a summary of those options:

> You: Running an NGO or business that gets impact to scale through growth or leverage
>
> Lots of NGOs: Replicating your model
>
> Lots of businesses: Replicating your model
>
> Governments: Delivering your model through programs and policies[18]

Because these are the only options, Starr and Hattendorf argue, you need to pick the "doer" that "will dominate at a scale of a million and beyond."[19] "Pick one, and pick it early," they write, because "a model will only scale if it is designed with the doer in mind."[20] Ideally, we believe, identifying the doer should be part of the strategy process that is involved with building an engine of impact, and identifying the payer should be part of both the strategy process and the process of finding fuel for the engine of impact.

Starr and Hattendorf helpfully analyze the advantages and disadvantages of each "doer" option. Here, again in their words, is a summary of that analysis:

You: Having full control over replication means that you can deliver a complex model at high quality. Building and growing a really big organization is a pain in the ass, especially in a dysfunctional funding market.

Lots of NGOs: Plenty of bandwidth there, and it shifts fundraising off your back, but [NGOs] are notoriously bad at implementing other [NGOs'] ideas; either they don't want to, because they perceive a need to seem unique in the aforementioned dysfunctional market, or they try to implement on the cheap and fail to get the same impact.

Lots of businesses: We're not interested in one-off businesses—it's industries that solve problems. Obviously, to make use of this doer, a solution needs to come with a profitable business—the more profitable, the more imitators—and that precludes a lot of important solutions. Capital remains a problem: Mainstream investors won't touch most of this stuff, and impact investors are way more risk-averse than the name implies.

Governments: They have big bandwidth, lots of resources, and a mandate to serve—and they're probably the only way a lot of basic service solutions will scale. They are often inefficient, inconsistent, and corrupt. Have fun.[21]

Cost-efficiency and cost-effectiveness are critical for scaling, but impact must remain the top priority. For businesses, the desire to scale is often driven by the availability and achievability of economies of scale, that is, reducing per-unit costs by leveraging a significant fixed-cost basis over a greater number of units produced. In the nonprofit sector, cost-efficiency (cost per unit of service delivered) is often important, especially for organizations that have aspirations to scale. As organizations consider ways to diminish their costs, we refer them to the excellent book *Getting Beyond Better: How Social Entrepreneurship Works*, in which Roger L. Martin and Sally R. Osberg describe major cost-diminution change mechanisms that affect either operating costs or capital costs.[22]

Cost-efficiency is extremely important, but cost-effectiveness (cost per unit of service delivered viewed in light of impact) is also critical. If other organizations like yours are achieving similar outcomes at a lower cost, you should consider revising your approach. That said, although your cost-benefit equation should be attractive, your intervention does not need to be the lowest-cost option. In some instances, having a laserlike focus on achieving deep impact might mean that your organization will have a higher-cost model than some of your peer organizations. If forced to make a trade-off between maximizing impact and minimizing cost, you should prioritize impact.

Scaling a nonprofit organization itself is mostly about the hub versus the spokes. Virtually every organization that chooses to scale by establishing multiple sites, chapters, or programs in the field has a functional hub-and-spoke structure. Its national or international headquarters is the hub, and its regional or country-level operations are the spokes. The relationship between the headquarters and the entities in the field can be structured in a number of different ways, largely depending on the degree of centralization and control maintained by headquarters.

What function, or part of a function, goes where depends on what the nonprofit does and what is most important to it. Nonprofits with strong brands will generally control their brand from the central hub, for example, while nonprofits that deliver social or educational services in many localities will conduct most of their functions in their spokes. Fund raising is often split between the hub and the spokes. The hub may focus on national accounts, or on philanthropists who are helping shape the movement, while the spokes concentrate on active development of donors where the organizations' services are offered and received.

In their seminal article "Managing Multisite Nonprofits," Allen Grossman and V. Kasturi Rangan emphasize that, regardless of where your organization falls on the continuum between central and local control, tensions will inevitably emerge in the relationship between headquarters and the local organizations. Grossman and Rangan point to two key drivers of cohesiveness: "Multisite systems were more or less cohesive, depending upon the nature of two critical sets of forces at play—one determining the degree of autonomy sought by the local units, and the other [determining] the degree of affiliation desired."[23] They caution against the tendency to assume that high levels of autonomy always must be correlated with low affiliation. On the contrary, their research reveals that some of the best multisite systems simultaneously display both a high degree of autonomy and a high degree of affiliation.[24] Headquarters can provide field offices with significant autonomy but still engender a very strong sense of affiliation—for example, by providing a strong brand that helps field offices attract donors and volunteers, by sharing best practices, or by leveraging economies of scale to gain systemwide cost advantages.[25]

Helen Keller International (HKI) provides a compelling example of how an organization can strike this balance. Its president and CEO, Kathy Spahn, reflected:

Field versus headquarters tensions tear apart nearly every international development organization. At HKI, we have been very intentional and proactive in minimizing these tensions. We decentralize whenever possible: we strive to make decision making as close to the action as possible given the skills needed and available. HKI works in twenty-one countries in Africa and Asia, and most of our more than seven hundred staff work in country field offices helping increase in-country buy-in and local expertise; only forty staff are in the US headquarters. At the same time, the field has strong representation at headquarters. Each region elects a country director to sit on the senior management team; 50 percent of the members of the eighteen-person senior management team are from the field. The executive management team is comprised of six people, of which two are from the field. And any candidates for top positions at headquarters must be interviewed extensively by those in the field so that they can provide critical input.[26]

Scaling typically requires proactive action to build necessary skills, resources, and processes. Consider the example of Endeavor, a non-profit that aims to catalyze long-term economic growth by selecting, mentoring, and accelerating high-impact entrepreneurs worldwide (with the support of a global network of business leaders). In 2004, Edgar Bronfman Jr., former CEO of Warner Music Group, became chair of the Endeavor board. He said, "I believe in the model, but . . . if I am going to commit to this organization and get other people involved, it needs to become important."[27] Bronfman's ambition served as a catalyst. In response to it, Endeavor founder and CEO Linda Rottenberg, together with the board, set a goal of working in twenty-five countries by the end of 2015.[28]

This was an aggressive goal, involving a dramatic increase from Endeavor's footprint at the time, and Endeavor set out to prepare for it. In 2008, for example, supported by a $10 million grant from the Omidyar Network, Endeavor made changes to its leadership team and management structure. This included recruiting a management team whose members had experience at companies like AOL, Bloomberg, and Dell; working to improve employee retention; establishing the role of president to complement Rottenberg's CEO role; and executive coaching for Rottenberg.[29] "When Omidyar Network first invested, Endeavor was a founder-led organization with a talented but young and inexperienced team," explained Matt Bannick, managing partner at Omidyar Network. "We helped Linda hire ahead of the curve and secure the executive team she needed to accomplish the inspiring yet daunting goals they had set for themselves. Linda demonstrated incredible personal growth and a commitment to acquiring the skills she needed to delegate effectively and manage a high-powered executive team. Not all founders can step up in this way, and it has been paramount to Endeavor's success."[30]

Endeavor also built processes and systems to support a larger global footprint. It developed a strategic plan, designed a performance measurement system, identified best practices for each affiliate office, restructured its headquarters staff to better serve affiliate offices and entrepreneurs, refined its service offerings and its approach to managing relationships with entrepreneurs, created entrepreneur profile types, and refined its entrepreneur selection methodology.[31] Today, Endeavor works with more than 1,100 entrepreneurs from more than 750 businesses, and those entrepreneurs have created more than half a million high-quality jobs. In addition, the organization operates in twenty-two countries—and has thus nearly reached its ambitious goal of working in twenty-five countries by 2015.[32]

Scaling the size of an organization is much easier with a growth capital plan. Any organization that plans to scale should consider developing a growth capital plan, or at least a general growth plan that specifies capital requirements. This approach enables an organization to raise committed funding to support scaling efforts over a long period (five or more years). Unfortunately, most nonprofits today live off short-term funding; they rely on year-to-year donations and allow donation levels to determine spending levels. Moreover, because funding often comes with restrictions attached to it, organizations and leaders can't invest in building overall capacity. This is totally at odds with what is needed to scale effectively. We applaud sector leaders—including Chuck Harris and his team, first at SeaChange Capital Partners and more recently at the Edna McConnell Clark Foundation (EMCF); Bridgespan; and New Profit—that have made early progress in popularizing the use of growth capital plans. While the F. B. Heron Foundation, whose president, Clara Miller, earlier founded and led the pathbreaking Nonprofit Finance Fund, does not use growth capital plans per se, its use of Enterprise Capital Grants—distinct from revenue—to finance "star organizations that are growing" is similarly exemplary. We hope to see the adoption of such practices become more pervasive, and we hope that more and more funders will embrace multiyear commitments in which reporting centers on progress measured against a plan rather than how funds were spent.

Youth Villages, for example, has successfully developed and executed a growth capital plan. As part of a five-year growth capital aggregation pilot that EMCF launched in 2007, Youth Villages secured more than $40 million in investments from fourteen co-investors.[33] The organization created a business plan that laid out its growth strategy and investment needs, and it prioritized internal capacity-building work that will help it achieve this growth.[34] Following the success of the first round, it launched a new $100 million five-year round of growth capital fund raising as part of a 2013–2017 campaign.[35]

The next frontier involves scaling service delivery through technology. The nonprofit sector, in our view, has done less to leverage technology than any other sector of the US economy. We shared this perception with Sal Khan, founder of Khan Academy, and he replied: "I would agree that the Internet has had much less impact on the nonprofit sector than any other aspect of the economy. What's the reason? Well, if you look at a Venn diagram of people in technology and people in nonprofit [organizations], the overlap is not very big."[36]

Another reason, no doubt, is that much of what nonprofit organizations offer involves human presence (nurses, social workers, artists, ministers) or physical goods (a meal, a bed, a church, a theater)—factors that do not lend themselves to obvious technological solutions. But whatever the explanation, the opportunity to increase social impact by leveraging technology is huge and the challenge of doing so is pressing.

Start-ups—unburdened by the baggage of an existing business model—are often able to make the most progress. The Internet was a prerequisite for the very existence of Khan Academy and also enabled the organization to scale its impact. "I had scale in my mind from early on," Khan acknowledged.[37] But most nonprofits today are more akin to retail banking branches of the 1960s: they might be excited to offer drive-through banking lanes, but they cannot imagine ATMs, computer banking, or data-driven loan underwriting, much less online lending or Bitcoin.

One of our favorite examples of a nonprofit that has shifted from a conventional hands-on model to a more impactful, technology-enabled approach is QuestBridge. QuestBridge works to recruit, develop, and support motivated low-income high school students with the goal of helping them succeed in America's best colleges, graduate schools, and companies.[38] Between 1994 and 2005, the organization (which at that time was called Quest) operated a highly effective five-week summer residential program known as QuestLeadership on the Stanford University campus. By 2003, QuestBridge was receiving more than two thousand applications for twenty spots in the program.[39] Its leaders therefore decided to change course. QuestBridge now provides a technology-enabled service—modeled on the national residency placement system for medical schools—that matches students with programs at multiple higher education institutions. It currently partners with thirty-eight of the most rigorous and selective colleges in the nation, including the Massachusetts Institute of Technology, Stanford, Williams, and Yale.[40] Reid Hoffman, the legendary Silicon Valley entrepreneur and venture capitalist who founded LinkedIn, has chaired the QuestBridge West Coast Advisory Board since September 2008; he maintains that QuestBridge's scalability—achieved largely through its smart use of technology—helped set it apart from other nonprofits.[41]

We are also excited by the early progress that we have seen in efforts to deliver human services, or parts of them, online. For example, the health-care start-up CareMessage is leveraging technology to achieve behavioral change in low-income and underserved patients. Its mobile platform allows health-care providers to send automated and personalized text messages to at-risk patients. By sending patients targeted information at specific times, CareMessage is decreasing no-show rates, improving follow-up care, increasing clinical efficiency, and improving patient outcomes. In less than three years, it reached one million users by working with two hundred partners in thirty-six states across the country.[42] Jacquelline Fuller, president of Google.org and the Google Foundation, commented that CareMessage cofounder and CEO Vineet Singal and his team "have a strong combination of technical expertise and true empathy for the low-income patients that their platform is built to serve. We see huge potential for CareMessage to create real change in the health outcomes of the tens of millions of citizens who are still uninsured."[43]

A core reason that technology has not disintermediated many nonprofit activities is that a lack of clear financial incentives has limited the funding available for upfront investment. Spahn offered an example of challenges that HKI faces in this regard: "Even just the cost of getting PDAs [personal digital assistants] for our community health volunteers really adds up, let alone the cost of designing something, such as we just did in designing an online database for our ChildSight program to facilitate data capture and service delivery. It took us four or five years to find a donor willing to fund this relatively small (less than [$100,000]) investment. It is part of the vicious cycle."[44]

We are occasionally frustrated in our interaction with some of the large nonprofits that have been the backbone of the sector for decades. Most of them built national hub-and-spoke systems with dozens, or even hundreds, of organizations in regions throughout the country (or, in the case of global NGOs, with offices in dozens of countries). They resemble retail banks from fifty years ago, with local and regional organizations that often have separate boards (or at least separate advisory boards) and a headquarters entity that is funded largely by fees from those local and regional organizations. In the absence of competitive forces that would compel them to change, they have adapted to new technology slowly. Consider United Way, which still raises $4 billion a year for US charities.[45] While United Way as a movement has tried to leverage technology, it remains analogous to an old-style business that has yet to adopt a model that fully deploys state-of-the-art digital tools. Think Blockbuster, not Netflix.

When it comes to the nonprofit sector and its leveraging of technology, online philanthropy has long been a source of particular frustration for us. When Buzz Schmidt launched GuideStar in 1994, we shared his vision of a world in which well-informed donors would use the Internet to evaluate nonprofits and to make more optimal donations. Yet progress toward that goal has been slow. In 2015, the online fund-raising platform Network for Good processed only $242 million in donations.[46] That same year, Kickstarter raised more than $692 million, most of it for businesses that could not offer funders a tax deduction for their investment![47] So far, there is only modest evidence that people will use easily available digital technology to donate to nonprofits. Maybe millennials, as they get older, will begin taking full advantage of technology's ability to support fact-based philanthropy and to reduce fund-raising costs.

Paths Toward the Promised Land: Three Nonprofits That Are Scaling for Impact

We have shared our views on scaling, offered an approach for assessing readiness to scale, and highlighted top lessons in how to scale. We close this chapter by describing the scaling journeys of three nonprofit organizations that, knowingly or not, have incorporated the principles described in this chapter. In doing so, they have made their paths toward the Promised Land smoother and straighter, and they have significantly increased the likelihood that they will reach that destination.

THE JOURNEY OF LAST MILE HEALTH TO THE FIELD OF DREAMS

Dr. Raj Panjabi, associate physician at Harvard Medical School, cofounded Last Mile Health (LMH) in 2007, along with a group of Liberian civil war survivors and American health workers. LMH leverages community health workers to bring primary-care services to remote communities in Liberia. Panjabi was born in that country and narrowly escaped it at age nine, after civil war broke out there. When he returned to Liberia as a twenty-four-year-old medical student, he found that there were just fifty doctors serving a population of four million. This discovery inspired him to establish LMH. To provide seed funding for the effort, he relied on $6,000 that he and his wife received for their wedding.[48]

By 2016, LMH had begun to achieve significant impact. "We're poised to scale that impact in the coming years in partnership with the government of Liberia," said Panjabi. "But during our first five years, we faced our fair share of failures. It took our team time to hone our impact model. Our early mission statement was 'Advance health care and the fundamental rights of the poor,' which was far too broad and unfocused. We eventually refined our mission considerably, evolving it to a statement that is much more focused: 'Save lives in the world's most remote communities.'"[49]

LMH benefited early on from the sage advice of funders such as the Draper Richards Kaplan Foundation, Echoing Green, and the Mulago Foundation. This advice proved critical as LMH developed essential components for its engine of impact: a clear mission, an effective strategy, and a solid plan for impact evaluation. Between 2012 and 2015, in partnership with Liberia's Ministry of Health, LMH evaluated its impact in two districts. It was able to demonstrate dramatic, statistically significant increases in the rates at which patients received treatment from a qualified provider for conditions such as childhood diarrhea (from 6.1 percent to 66.3 percent), pneumonia (from 6.6 percent to 57.8 percent), and malaria (from 26.2 percent to 56.8 percent), as well as in the rate at which mothers gave birth in a clinic (from 55.8 percent to 84.0 percent).[50]

LMH's investment in its engine of impact proved fruitful when the Ebola crisis struck. The organization found itself on the front lines of the national response when the disease began to spread in Liberia in 2014. Working with Partners in Health and the Liberia Ministry of Health, LMH trained more than one thousand three hundred health workers and community members in Ebola-specific services, screened more than ten thousand people for the disease, and helped stop an outbreak in a region where people had been infected and died, thereby preventing the spread of Ebola to other regions.[51] These services were critical at a time when other health-care facilities in Liberia had shut their doors to patients. LMH's effective response to the Ebola crisis served as a proof of concept for its model—and in particular for the critical role that community health workers could play in remote, rural areas.

Advice from funders also helped Panjabi consider how he would find the "fuel" that he needed to scale LMH. He shared, "The Draper Richards Kaplan Foundation helped us to think about our board governance and transition our early friends-and-family board to a more professional one. The Mulago Foundation encouraged me to identify . . . what our ultimate path to scale would be—in our case, scaling via government—and so we started partnering with the Liberian government very early on."[52]

LMH's pioneering work has directly affected public policy in Liberia. In 2015, LMH collaborated with the Liberian Ministry of Health and other partners to reform the country's National Community Health Services Policy. Together, they transformed a fragmented array of volunteer-based community health programs into a unified, standard, and professionalized national community health workforce. The reformed system now includes contracts and cash payments for community health workers, targeting of services to remote rural communities, and field-based supervision by nurses. The new policy led to the launch of the National Community Health Assistant Program by Liberian president Ellen Johnson Sirleaf in July 2016. This program aims to train, employ, and equip four thousand community health workers and nurse supervisors to bring primary care to the nearly 30 percent of Liberia's population who live farther than an hour's walk from the nearest health clinic.[53] A randomized evaluation will be part of this national scaling effort. In recognition of its ability to drive large-scale change, Last Mile Health was awarded a Skoll Award for Social Entrepreneurship in 2017.

THE JOURNEY OF THE POSITIVE COACHING ALLIANCE
TO THE FIELD OF DREAMS, HEADING TOWARD THE
PROMISED LAND

The Positive Coaching Alliance (PCA) is an example of an organization that earned the right to scale by establishing a proven impact model and then worked successfully to find the fuel to support its growth.

PCA was founded in 1998 to address the troubling win-at-all-costs mentality that increasingly pervades youth sports in the United States. This mentality contributes to the unfortunate trend in which 70 percent of kids drop out of athletics by age thirteen, and it leads to many missed character-building opportunities.[54] PCA's model of coaching prepares teams to win, but its primary purpose is to prepare athletes to succeed in life. PCA achieves its mission through partnerships with schools and youth sports organizations, and it uses in-person and online workshops and a variety of media to provide tools and advice for youth sports leaders, coaches, parents, and athletes.

PCA spent its first decade establishing a proof of concept and developing its content and curriculum. Then, working from its headquarters in Northern California and collaborating with a few partners elsewhere, it launched a strategic planning process that aimed in part to design an organizational model that would facilitate nationwide scaling. "We felt a mission-driven imperative to scale because we believed that staying small, with one or two locations, would not enable us to change an entire culture," explained founder and CEO Jim Thompson.[55] PCA received a grant of $300,000 from David Weekley, a Houston businessman and philanthropist, to begin its expansion, and it formulated a plan to open one new chapter per year from 2007 to 2012 and two chapters per year from 2012 to 2017.[56]

The most complicated aspect of this plan involved determining how much power PCA's headquarters would have in relation to its chapters. Thompson recounted:

PCA decided to adopt a hub-and-spoke federation model with a national office in Northern California plus chapters in cities across the country. Social entrepreneurs are often control freaks, and not surprisingly one of the main issues for us was control: . . . How much control nationally versus locally? We ultimately decided that we wanted to let go and shun the urge for the headquarters to be overly controlling. We wanted to hire extremely smart, talented people to run the chapters, and we wanted to give them a stake in things so that they would go nuts! This could not happen if we held on too tightly. So while legally our local chapters are advisory groups, we give them considerable power.[57]

PCA's model allows for the strong local presence and local owner-ship necessary to support its workshop-based programs. Its chapters become an integral part of their local community, and as a result they can facilitate deeper engagement with local schools and youth-serving organizations.[58] At the same time, the national office provides a num-ber of benefits to chapters, such as developing content, establishing distribution partnerships with national youth sports organizations (Little League and US Lacrosse, for example), and overseeing infra-structure (e.g., IT, accounting, marketing, human resources, and communications).

In addition to undertaking structural initiatives to foster joint decision making, PCA leaders promote a "we are all in a movement together" attitude and have adopted a policy toward local chapters that has proven to be extremely important in fostering good rela-tionships. Thompson explained: "We assume the best motives from our chapters. Whenever there is a potential conflict between national [headquarters] and a chapter, the policy is to be as generous as pos-sible to the chapter. This gives us credibility when we need it."[59]

This organizational model has positioned PCA well for significant future expansion to achieve its goal of "spark[ing] and fuel[ing] a 'social epidemic' of Positive Coaching."[60] PCA currently operates fif-teen chapters across the United States and has more than 250 chapter board members; in 2015, it reached more than three million youth athletes. It plans to operate a total of twenty-six chapters, and to reach more than twenty million youth athletes, by 2020.

PRATHAM'S JOURNEY TOWARD THE PROMISED LAND

Pratham, the largest nongovernmental organization that operates in the Indian education sector, successfully earned the right to pursue its journey to the Promised Land. By 2015, it had expanded to twenty-one of India's twenty-nine states and had achieved a significant impact on the lives of 7.7 million children.[61] Kim oversaw the selection process that led to Pratham being named 2010 recipient of the Kravis Prize, and since then it has received many other important awards, including the Skoll Award for Social Entrepreneurship in 2011, the WISE Prize for Education in 2012, and the BBVA Foundation Frontiers of Knowledge Award in 2014. In addition, the Asia Society in 2014 bestowed its Asia Game Changer Award on Pratham cofounder Madhav Chavan.

Pratham has adhered tightly to its admirably brief and well-focused mission statement, "Every child in school and learning well,"[62] thereby shunning distractions and staying on its path to the Promised Land. It crafted its strategy thoughtfully and intentionally, grounded that strategy in a proven theory of change, built on the organization's skills to deliver impact, and ensured from the outset that its model would be scalable. Pratham also stands out for its long-standing commitment to rigorous impact evaluation—it has undergone eleven randomized evaluations so far!—and especially for its implementation of a feedback loop.

In addition to creating a proven model that incorporates mission, strategy, and impact evaluation, Pratham has always had a tremendous store of insight and courage—and ambition. Chavan reflected: "Pratham had a mandate to scale at birth. We were a new organization, without any resources, working in Mumbai. The sheer magnitude of the unmet need that we were trying to address simply demanded that we plan for scale from the beginning. Our interventions needed to be inherently spreadable; there were no other options."[63]

Pratham has also been distinctive in its ability to find the fuel to scale its impact. It has, for instance, drawn heavily on the team-of-teams model in its approach to various initiatives. It has also adopted a federation model that facilitates efforts to scale across multiple states by providing for strong local autonomy. Pratham currently has a network of nineteen regional offices and allows for regional variation in its programs.[64] With regard to a program called Read India, for example, Pratham notes the following: "there is a broad similarity in the learning camp models across states but certain implementation details differ . . . based on the regional context."[65]

Decentralization has also been a prominent theme in the international expansion of the ASER (assessment, survey, evaluation, and research) program, an autonomous unit within the Pratham network. To date, the core message of ASER has spread to seven countries outside of India: Kenya, Mali, Mexico, Pakistan, Senegal, Tanzania, and Uganda.[66] Chavan likens this process to the expansion of Chinese restaurants:

Generally, expansion can take a couple different models. One can be seen as the McDonald's model and the other as the Chinese restaurant model. With McDonald's, [all franchises] still need Idaho potatoes from Idaho; there are exactly the same burgers. But the Chinese restaurant—they're not the same thing on every corner. There are typically different menus in different Chinese restaurants, but they are still recognizable as a Chinese restaurant. We've taken the Chinese restaurant model: when you [open a restaurant], you own it, and you make it your own.[67]

Two of the levers that have facilitated Pratham's successful decentralization were hallmarks of private-sector companies that successfully decentralized in the 1960s: performance measurement and getting people together. Rukmini Banerji, CEO of the Pratham Education Foundation, explained, "For us, measurement has been a strong uniting force. And we have to accept certain variations as long as we reach the [desired] outcome."[68] Getting people together is an especially vital skill for large organizations like Pratham, since regular, substantive convenings can lead over time to greater trust and to a sharing of best practices.

Another critical form of fuel for Pratham has been its distinctive approach to fund raising. Pratham created Pratham USA and Pratham UK to mobilize individuals in the United States and the United Kingdom, respectively—members of the Indian diasporas, in particular—to support its operations in India. Pratham USA and Pratham UK organize events such as concerts, road races, and dinners to bring together—and to raise funds from—people who share a dedication to its cause.

Pratham's experience reveals that the Promised Land is reachable. In any event, scaling impact is a long and often incremental process that requires you, your organization, and its stakeholders to make multiple decisions and conduct considerable soul-searching. To paraphrase the great Austrian poet Rainer Maria Rilke, ask yourself in the most silent hour of your night: must we scale? Then, in Rilke's words, "Dig into yourself for a deep answer. And if this answer rings out in assent, if you meet this solemn question with a strong, simple 'I must'"[69]—well, then make sure your organization has earned the right and found the fuel to pursue scaling. Embark on your journey with a deep awareness of the hard work ahead but fully equipped with the guidance that we, along with others, have provided. The Promised Land beyond the mountaintops is in view.

Strategic Leadership
Now Is the Time

We write this conclusion six months after Election Day 2016. The national chatter includes talk of impeachment of an elected president; raw and mean commentary about gender, race, and social status; and expressions of sharp division on nearly every topic of political importance—and indeed within society at large. There are also fundamental challenges to freedom of speech and privacy; and threats to centuries-held beliefs, as science and technology create major philosophical questions we have never before faced. Listening to the 2016 winner of the Nobel Prize in Literature, Bob Dylan, sing "The Times They Are A-Changin'," baby boomers have not felt such shaky societal ground since the 1960s.

We celebrate those of you who pursue direct involvement in the US political system, which of late seems to be amplifying, rather than resolving, the country's many divisions.

We ourselves, however, return to Alexis de Tocqueville, who so eloquently commented on the American way of binding together in common purpose. In the United States, the French philosopher observed, people of all ages, all stations in life, and all types of disposition were forever forming associations. "Americans combine to give fêtes, found seminaries, build churches, distribute books, and send missionaries to the antipodes. Hospitals, prisons, and schools take shape in that way. Finally, if they want to proclaim a truth or propagate some feeling by the encouragement of a great example, they form an association," Tocqueville wrote.[1] In America, he continued, as in other democracies, this "knowledge of how to combine is the mother of all other forms of knowledge; on its progress depends that of all the others."[2]

Since Tocqueville's time, Americans have buttressed the foundation of civil society and paved the way for the current Impact Era. They formalized and expanded traditions of philanthropy and nonprofit organizations during the Industrialist Era, created a strong sense of identity for nonprofits and foundations during the Independence Era, and began to lay the groundwork for fact-based decisions during the Information Era.

In this early stage of the Impact Era, Americans have all the money they will need as a society—and, in fact, enough to share generously with other, less fortunate people. Current and future generations can choose to use the spoils of economic growth—and the highly concentrated wealth that has accumulated over the past twenty-five years—to make truly significant investments in serving and transforming our society.

We wrote our book to topple the Tower of Babel that has existed in the social sector until today and replace it with a common language, a new way of thinking, a clear approach. The basis of this approach is strategic leadership—a vehicle for meeting the urgent needs both of the sector and of the people it serves. We have issued our call to action to ensure that stakeholders in the nonprofit sector, and above all its leaders, can maximize financial and other contributions by bringing strategic leadership to bear on the quest for impact.

And now is the time. On the one hand, we have a nation and a world divided. On the other hand, there is a nonprofit sector poised to bring unprecedented resources and, for the first time ever, a set of robust tools that will support the fact-based decision making that maximizing impact requires. A perfect match.

We have every reason to be confident in the nonprofit sector and its capacity to further the march of progress. Pick your most inspiring example from the distant—or not-so-distant—past to see what can be accomplished by visionary, generous philanthropists and extraordinary nonprofit leaders: the immigrant industrialist Andrew Carnegie, for example, who gave away his entire fortune to build America's public library system.[3] Or John D. Rockefeller Sr., who sponsored a successful five-year public health campaign to eliminate hookworm disease in the American South.[4] Or the Robert Wood Johnson Foundation, which supported the creation of nationwide 911 in the 1970s.[5] Or the Rockefeller Foundation, which initiated the Green Revolution with support from the Ford Foundation, the Kellogg Foundation, and others.[6] Or George Kessler, who joined forces with Helen Keller more than one hundred years ago and established what is now Helen Keller International, an organization that fights blindness and malnutrition and reaches nearly three hundred million people per year. Or Sir Fazle Hasan Abed, who founded BRAC more than four decades ago and turned it into one of the largest nonprofits in the world, with thousands of evaluations to demonstrate its sweeping impact. Or Bill Drayton, who launched Ashoka in the early 1980s and then built a global social entrepreneurship movement. Or Paul Farmer, Jim Kim, Ophelia Dahl, and their colleagues, who established Partners in Health in 1987 and dispelled the widely held conviction that quality health care is impossible to deliver in resource-poor areas. Or Tom White, a donor who quietly fueled Partners in Health through his extraordinary generosity and shunned recognition in favor of impact.

And right here, right now: Bill and Melinda Gates's stunning accomplishments in global health; Rukmini Banerji and Madhav Chavan's proven educational interventions at Pratham, which has a positive impact on millions of children per year in India; Michael Faye and Paul Niehaus's leveraging of randomized evaluations at Give Directly, along with their positioning of cash as a new benchmark for poverty alleviation; Chris Bischof and Helen Kim's founding of Eastside College Preparatory School, a shining Small Is Beautiful organization that serves as a vivid reminder of those who work tirelessly to address unmet needs in their local communities; Cari Tuna and Dustin Moskowitz's integration of altruism and analytics and their efforts to set a standard of seriousness of purpose, which we hope will become the norm for über-wealthy technology millennials. And organizations such as the Skoll Foundation, Omidyar Network, Emerson Collective, ELMA Philanthropies, the Chan Zuckerberg

Initiative—and others that have gone before and will come after—fill us with hope and excitement as the brilliance, creativity, wealth, and empathy of this generation's most successful business entrepreneurs seek distinctive ways to improve the human condition.

Please take a minute and add your own examples of extraordinary, impactful nonprofits and their leaders and donors. Many have journeyed to the Promised Land, and many more are poised to voyage there from the Field of Dreams. Among these, there is certainly at least one nonprofit that matches your values, your experiences, and your ideas on how to improve society: large, robust institutions of higher education whose research and teaching are shaping the future; social service organizations that help your communities' neediest; nongovernmental organizations with proven records of alleviating poverty, improving health outcomes, or serving refugees; amazing organizations that offer culture in every form and media; environmental organizations, inspiring us to take immediate action as climate change becomes real; and places of worship, which offer so many ways to enrich the human spirit.

With the advice and examples, practical and inspirational, presented throughout this book, we have provided a plan of action to help ensure that the nonprofit sector will earn the right to grow and maximize its impact. Our call to action is summed up in two words: *strategic leadership*. Here is what we think that means for each group of stakeholders within the sector.

Philanthropists and Major Donors

In the next few decades, the US economy will unleash more potential philanthropic resources than ever before—but how much of those resources will flow to the nonprofit sector to ensure maximum societal impact is hardly a fait accompli. We urge those of you who are capable of writing very large checks to open your hearts and minds to the possibility of giving at a historically ambitious level. Foundation leaders, consider spending down your endowment (instead of sustaining it in perpetuity) when doing so matches your mission.

Wealthy individuals, consider investing the spoils of your generation while you are still living—by giving away not just 50 percent of your wealth but, say, 90 percent of it. Your kids will be fine.

And along with seeking recognition, embrace strategic leadership and commit to fact-based decision making.

Everyday Donors

For everyday donors, the recipe is the same, albeit in smaller batches. The donations of small and medium-sized givers (those with incomes of less than $200,000 per year) account for nearly half of all charitable contributions to the nonprofit sector.[7] By understanding strategic leadership and what constitutes a high-performing organization, these donors have the power to direct their checks to the most effective organizations. Some will need to rely on information intermediaries to identify high-impact organizations, while others can gather and analyze data on their own—which is no longer so hard to do. Indeed, in the transition from the Information Era to the Impact Era, reams of data have become available at the click of a mouse, yet most individual donors make little use of this valuable information. Instead, they still give largely in response to a friendly schmooze from a development professional, a request by a social peer, or a heart-tugging photo of a starving child. Most have a minimal understanding of how their donations are spent or what impact those donations have. But we hope that situation will soon change.

You, the everyday donors, are integral members of civil society, and your donations matter.

Nonprofit Board Members

Your responsibility is to ensure that the nonprofit you serve will maximize its impact and will do so cost-effectively. We understand that not every nonprofit board member will command the details of strategic leadership. So we offer a useful starting point for conversation. Ask members of your nonprofit team these three questions:

1. What is our organization's mission? Is it clear and focused?

2. What is our organization's theory of change, and what is the resulting strategy? Is the theory of change logically sound? Is it supported by empirical evidence?

3. Does our organization's impact evaluation support the theory of change and the resulting strategy? Does it do so cost-effectively?

In most cases, your incisive and persistent questioning will launch a hugely productive assessment and discussion, and that process often results in a profound shift in how your organization approaches the fundamentals of strategic thinking: mission, strategy, and impact evaluation. Then, once there is clarity in your organization's strategic thinking, you and your fellow board members must embrace the critical role of helping your nonprofit to find its fuel by mastering the essentials of strategic management: organization building, fund raising, and especially excellent governance.

Nonprofit Executives

We exhort you to abide by the time-tested principles presented in this book. Embrace strategic leadership wholeheartedly so that your organization can earn the right to benefit from more philanthropy. Remember this mantra: simplify and focus, don't complicate and "creep." And proactively resist any distractions that take you away from your mission. Every heroic journey going back to the Odyssey features Sirens that tempt its hero to go off course. Such Sirens are alluring and enticing, but they can sink your ship.

We encourage each of you—all nonprofit stakeholders—to individually and collectively heed our call to action by embracing strategic leadership. True transformation in the Impact Era, we believe, will come about only through unity and partnership among all stakeholders. Furthermore, we hold as an essential guiding light a vision of true, deep, and abiding partnership between funders and nonprofit organizations.

It has been our goal in writing this book to strengthen applied knowledge of strategic leadership and thereby to increase dramatically the capacity of the nonprofit sector, upon which so much future progress, both nationally and globally, will depend. We think that we have added tools to the collective toolbox, and we hope that you will hone, share, debate, critique, improve, and, most important, apply these tools. Our forebears have left behind a vibrant sector that facilitates individual and collective action and enables citizens to proactively shape society with a minimum of artificial constraints. The time for strategic leadership is now—so we urge you to make the best possible use of this inheritance of wealth, generosity, and empathy.

Acknowledgments

We choose to begin by thanking each other, with mutual gratitude for the two decades that we have spent together working with, and writing about, nonprofits. It's been an enormously fulfilling partnership and friendship that we expect to continue for years to come.

Bill would particularly like to thank Bill Drayton and Joel Fleishman, two of his many mentors in the nonprofit sector, for setting a standard to which he will always aspire, if never reach. Similarly, he would like to recognize the many social entrepreneurs and nonprofit leaders who provide him with continuing inspiration and undeniable evidence that it is in serving others that we find meaning in our own lives: Chris Bischof, Jane Chen, Lue Douthit, Paul Farmer, Michael Faye, Jacob Harold, Greg Hawkins, John Hennessey, Daniel Lurie, Ana Rowena McCullough, Michael McCullough, Clara Miller, Paul Niehaus, Roy Prosterman, Bill Rauch, Buzz Schmidt, Jim Thompson, Brian Trelstad—and so many others!

In addition, Bill draws continued support and role modeling from the many volunteer leaders and philanthropists who devote their talents and resources to high-impact social sector organizations: Bob and Dottie King, Nancy Bechtle, Bob Fisher, Sakurako Fisher, Isaac Stein—and so many others!

Bill would also like to recognize his incredible colleagues at McKinsey & Company. Among many other things during his thirty-year McKinsey career, Bill learned and practiced an approach to fact-based problem solving that recognizes that rigorous analysis and qualitative judgment work together. The firm supported his career-long interest in organizational performance and helped launch his pro bono avocation as adviser, teacher, mentor, and writer on nonprofits. And great thanks to Jim Collins for his friendship, encouragement, and standard setting, and for providing a foreword to this book.

Bill continues to draw inspiration and challenge from his students at the Stanford Graduate School of Business (Stanford GSB). Over his twenty years of teaching, Stanford GSB students—in particular those pursuing careers focused on social impact—have helped hone the insights he brings to this book. His faculty colleagues Jennifer Aaker, Jesper Sørensen, Laura Arrillaga-Andreessen, Matt Bannick, Paul Brest, Steve Ciesinski, Steve Davis, the late Greg Dees, Laura Hattendorf, Dave Larcher, and Jim Patell set the gold standard for research, thinking, and teaching on the social sector.

Personally, Bill deeply appreciates the joy and encouragement that his daughters, Courtney, Kelly, and Katie, and their families bring to his life. David

Morgenthaler III is a fulfilling and creative stepson. He also wishes to thank the Dennings, Rappaports, and Tinsleys—his Stanford GSB '78 brothers and sisters, Lafayette Partners, and supporters in many ways of his teaching, research, and writing at Stanford GSB. And he thanks his wife, Randi Zeller, who has made all the difference.

Kim would like to thank Marie-Josée and Henry Kravis for the opportunity to spend a decade learning from their incisive thinking about organizational performance and leadership. Working with members of the Selection Committee for the Henry R. Kravis Prize in Nonprofit Leadership provided an unparalleled opportunity to engage with incredible minds on the topic of leadership in the social sector. In addition to Marie-Josée and Henry, that group includes Harry McMahon, Surin Pitsuwan, Josette Sheeran, Amartya Sen, Ratan Tata, Lord Jacob Rothschild, and Jim Wolfensohn. Kim is grateful for their insights.

Kim would like to thank the Stanford Center on Philanthropy and Civil Society (PACS), where her experience as a visiting practitioner shaped her thinking about the social sector and especially about the important role of donors in promoting excellent leadership in civil society. And thanks to Mesa Refuge, where many words in this book were penned on the edge of Tomales Bay, arguably the best place in the world to sit and think and write.

Kim extends special and deep gratitude to Bob and Dottie King, whose extraordinary generosity, vision for alleviating extreme poverty, and deep concern for others create the basis for an incredible working partnership and provide opportunities for Kim to hone her thinking about the social sector. Kim draws daily inspiration from exemplary social sector leaders such as Rukmini Banerji, Madhav Chavan, Tim Hanstad, Roy Prosterman, Kathy Spahn, Debbie Taylor, Jim Taylor, Sakena Yacoobi—and so many others!

Personally, Kim is immensely thankful for her family's love and encouragement, beginning with her parents and including a wonderful extended family. This book would not have been possible without love and unwavering support from Jeff Jonker, who recognized from the earliest days that this was a book that deserved to be written and made significant personal sacrifices to help Kim ensure its fruition. Kim is most grateful to Jeff. Sam Jonker, Ben Jonker, and Grace Jonker also deserve special thanks. These three have blessed Kim beyond measure with their presence in her life, providing tremendous joy, inspiration, and love. Her gratitude runs deep.

Bill and Kim would like to thank their core book team: Melissa Brown, Devin Bruckner, Sonal J. Goyal, Sheila Melvin, and Birgit Zischke. All of these team members contributed their distinctive skills and expertise and also willingly pitched in wherever they were needed. We thank Melissa, Devin, Sonal, and Birgit for their excellent research, attention to detail, and unrelenting commitment. We thank Sheila for her insightful, sharp editing as well as her wise guidance and encouragement. And we thank Marcia Brammer, Shauna Bligh, and Rose Lopez for their tremendous efforts to keep all the trains moving so that we could write and promote our book. We also thank Barbara McCarthy and Stephanie Gliozzo for creating excellent illustrations.

We thank those who were willing to read drafts and provide valuable perspectives, especially Jacob Harold, Rik Kirkland, Marie-Josée Kravis, Mario Marino, Michael Slind, and Brian Trelstad. We are grateful to Ori Brafman for providing a unique mix of encouragement, inspiration, and practical advice as we navigated the book-writing process. We also thank Michael Slind for his expertise and excellent ideas for reaching our audience.

In addition, Bill and Kim acknowledge the support of the Stanford GSB Dean's Office—in particular Dave Brady, Glenn Carroll, David Kreps, Jon Levin, and Garth Saloner—and of the Center for Social Innovation (CSI) at Stanford GSB, led by Bernadette Clavier and Neil Malhotra. PACS executive director Kim Meredith, a role-model nonprofit leader, has been an indispensable source of counsel and support, and PACS faculty directors Paul Brest, Woody Powell, and Rob Reich have provided welcome support as well. Kim and Bill also extend their thanks to their partners in the 2016 Stanford Survey on Leadership and Management in the Nonprofit Sector: BoardSource, CSI, GuideStar, PACS, and *Stanford Social Innovation Review* (*SSIR*). Johanna Mair, Eric Nee, and Michael Slind provided critical vision and encouragement for our initial *SSIR* series, "Fundamentals, Not Fads," which ultimately led to the creation of this book.

And our gratitude to Margo Fleming, our editor at Stanford University Press and to her many colleagues, who led these first-time authors through the rigors of writing and editing with deftness, kindness, and wisdom.

And to all those who serve others.

Notes

Preface

1. Peter F. Drucker, *Concept of the Corporation* (New York: John Day Co., 1946); and Drucker, *Managing the Nonprofit Organization: Principles and Practices* (New York: HarperCollins, 1990).

2. Thomas J. Peters and Robert H. Waterman Jr., *In Search of Excellence: Lessons from America's Best-Run Companies* (New York: Harper & Row, 1982).

3. Jim Collins, *Good to Great: Why Some Companies Make the Leap . . . And Others Don't* (New York: Harper Business, 2001), 1–3.

4. Jim Collins, *Good to Great and the Social Sectors: A Monograph to Accompany* Good to Great *(Why Business Thinking Is Not the Answer).* (Boulder, CO: Jim Collins, 2005).

5. R. Michael Murray Jr. and Guillermo G. Marmol, "Leading from the Front," *McKinsey Quarterly* 3 (Summer 1995): 18–31.

6. Richard N. Foster and Sarah Kaplan, *Creative Destruction: Why Companies That Are Built to Last Underperform the Market—And How to Successfully Transform Them* (New York: Currency/Doubleday, 2001).

7. Jeffrey Pfeffer and Robert I. Sutton, *Hard Facts, Dangerous Half-Truths, and Total Nonsense: Profiting from Evidence-Based Management* (Boston: Harvard Business School Press, 2006).

8. Leslie R. Crutchfield and Heather McLeod Grant, *Forces for Good: The Six Practices of High-Impact Nonprofits* (San Francisco: Jossey-Bass, 2008).

9. Mario Morino, *Leap of Reason: Managing to Outcomes in an Era of Scarcity* (Washington, DC: Venture Philanthropy Partners, 2011).

10. William F. Meehan III and Kim Starkey Jonker, 2016 Stanford Survey on Leadership and Management in the Nonprofit Sector, Stanford Graduate School of Business, 2016, engineofimpact.org/survey.

Introduction

1. On hospital care, see Henry J. Kaiser Family Foundation, "Hospital Inpatient Days per 1,000 Population by Ownership Type," data for 2014, http://kff
.org/other/state-indicator/inpatient-days-by-ownership/?currentTimeframe=0&
sortModel=%7B%22colId%22:%22Location%22,%22sort%22:%22asc%22
%7D. On education, see National Center for Education Statistics (NCES), *Digest of Education Statistics*, table 303.70 (undergraduates) and table 303.80 (postbaccalaureate students), http://nces.ed.gov/programs/digest/d15/tables/dt15_303.70

.asp?current=yes and https://nces.ed.gov/programs/digest/d15/tables/dt15_303.80
.asp?current=yes.

2. This book focuses largely on US-based nonprofit organizations that register as public charities under Section 501(c)(3) of the Internal Revenue Code (IRC). There are roughly thirty types of tax-exempt nonprofit organizations outlined by the IRC, and 501(c)(3) organizations are the largest of those types; they account for roughly three-quarters of total nonprofit sector revenue. Donors can claim a tax deduction for making a contribution to a charitable organization, but they cannot do so for contributing to most other types of nonprofits, including labor unions, trade associations, and political organizations. In this book, we use the terms *charitable organization*, *nonprofit organization*, *charity*, and *nonprofit* more or less interchangeably. In each case, we mean entities that are tax-exempt charitable organizations.

3. "Alexis de Tocqueville: From *Democracy in America*," chap. 9 in *The Civil Society Reader*, ed. Virginia A. Hodgkinson and Michael W. Foley (Hanover, NH: University Press of New England, 2003), 123.

4. Ibid.

5. Brice S. McKeever, Nathan E. Dietz, and Saunji D. Fyffe, *The Nonprofit Almanac: The Essential Facts and Figures for Managers, Researchers, and Volunteers*, 9th ed. (Lanham, MD: Rowman and Littlefield; Washington, DC: Urban Institute Press, 2016), 87, figure 5.2, data for 2013; and Bureau of Economic Analysis, "National Data: Table 1.3.5—Gross Value Added by Sector," annual data for 2013, accessed April 27, 2017, http://www.bea.gov/iTable/iTableHtml.cfm?reqid=9&step=3&isuri=1&904=2013&903=24&906=a&905=2013&910=x&911=0.

6. Lester M. Salamon, S. Wojciech Sokolowski, and Associates, *Global Civil Society: Dimensions of the Nonprofit Sector*, vol. 2 (Bloomfield, CT: Kumarian Press, 2004), table 5, http://ccss.jhu.edu/wp-content/uploads/downloads/2013/02/Comparative-data-Tables_2004_FORMATTED_2.2013.pdf.

7. Robert D. Putnam, *Bowling Alone: The Collapse and Revival of American Community* (New York: Simon & Schuster, 2000).

8. Eleanor Brown and James M. Ferris, "Social Capital and Philanthropy: An Analysis of the Impact of Social Capital on Individual Giving and Volunteering," *Nonprofit and Voluntary Sector Quarterly* 36, no. 1 (2007): 85–99.

9. John J. Havens and Paul G. Schervish, "A Golden Age of Philanthropy Still Beckons: National Wealth Transfer and Potential for Philanthropy Technical Report," Boston College Center on Wealth and Philanthropy, May 28, 2014, Table 5, http://www.bc.edu/content/dam/files/research_sites/cwp/pdf/A%20Golden%20Age%20of%20Philanthropy%20Still%20Bekons.pdf.

10. Peter Dobkin Hall, "A Historical Overview of Philanthropy, Voluntary Associations, and Nonprofit Organizations in the United States, 1600–2000," in *The Nonprofit Sector: A Research Handbook*, 2nd ed., ed. Walter W. Powell and Richard Steinberg (New Haven, CT: Yale University Press, 2006), 38–39.

11. Paul Arnsberger, Melissa Ludlum, Margaret Riley, and Mark Stanton, "A History of the Tax-Exempt Sector: An SOI Perspective," *Statistics of Income Bulletin* (Winter 2008): 106.

12. Andrew Carnegie, *The Gospel of Wealth and Other Timely Essays* (New York: Century Co., 1901).

13. "Margaret Olivia Slocum (Mrs. Russell) Sage (1828–1918): Founder of the Russell Sage Foundation," Auburn University Digital Libraries, accessed November 30, 2015, http://diglib.auburn.edu/collections/sage/essays.html.

14. Karl Zinsmeister, "The Philanthropy Hall of Fame: Julius Rosenwald," Philanthropy Roundtable, accessed April 3, 2017, http://www.philanthropyround table.org/almanac/hall_of_fame/julius_rosenwald.

15. Peter M. Ascoli, *Julius Rosenwald: The Man Who Built Sears, Roebuck and Advanced the Cause of Black Education in the American South* (Blooming- ton, IN: Indiana University Press, 2006), 87. The quote is taken from a speech on May 18, 1911.

16. Peter M. Ascoli, "Julius Rosenwald's Crusade: One Donor's Plea to Give While You Live," *Philanthropy* (May–June 2006), http://www.philanthropyround table.org/topic/excellence_in_philanthropy/julius_rosenwalds_crusade.

17. Arnsberger, "History of Tax-Exempt Sector," 106, 108.

18. Unpublished analysis by Melissa S. Brown (manager, Nonprofit Research Collaborative).

19. "Our History," United Way, accessed November 30, 2015, http://www .unitedway.org/about/history; and David Rose, "A History of the March of Dimes," March of Dimes, August 26, 2010, accessed November 30, 2015, http://www .marchofdimes.org/mission/a-history-of-the-march-of-dimes.aspx.

20. Theodore Caplow, Howard M. Bahr, John Modell, and Bruce A. Chad- wick, *Recent Social Trends in the United States, 1960–1990* (Montreal: McGill- Queen's University Press, 1994), 341.

21. Giving USA Foundation, *Giving USA 2003: The Annual Report on Phi- lanthropy for the Year 2002* (Chicago: Giving USA Foundation, 2003), 200.

22. Commission on Private Philanthropy and Public Needs (Filer Commis- sion), *Giving in America: Toward a Stronger Voluntary Sector* (Washington, DC: Commission on Private Philanthropy and Public Needs, 1975), 1, 172.

23. Olivier Zunz, *Philanthropy in America: A History* (Princeton, NJ: Princeton University Press, 2012), 237; and Filer Commission, *Giving in America*, 231–233.

24. Filer Commission, *Giving in America*, 53.

25. Ibid.; and "1973 Filer Commission Defends Private Giving," Philanthropy Roundtable, accessed November 30, 2015, http://www.philanthropyroundtable .org/almanac/public_policy_reform/1973_filer_commission_defends_private_giving.

26. Zunz, *Philanthropy in America*, 240.

27. Ibid., 242.

28. Evangelical Council for Financial Accountability, "Seven Standards of Responsible Stewardship," accessed November 30, 2015, http://www.ecfa.org/ content/standards; and Presbyterian Mission Agency, "Stewardship Manual:

A Guide for Year-Round Financial Stewardship Planning," accessed November 30, 2015, http://www.presbyterianfoundation.org/getattachment/2a2140ca-8ac1 -47e5-8c8b-29c66be913a4/PCUSA-Stewardship-Manual.aspx. Both offer examples of contemporary stewardship standards.

29. Cheryl Chasin, Debra Kawecki, and David Jones, "G. Form 990," Internal Revenue Service (2002), accessed September 21, 2016, http://www.pgdc .com/pdf/CPEtopic02.pdf.

30. Arnsberger, "History of Tax-Exempt Sector."

31. "NSF and the Birth of the Internet," National Science Foundation, accessed July 5, 2017, https://www.nsf.gov/news/special_reports/nsf-net/textonly/90s.jsp.

32. On Ford, see Horace Lucian Arnold and Fay Leone Faurote, *Ford Methods and the Ford Shops* (New York: Engineering Magazine Company, 1915; reprint, New York: Arno Press, 1972), 111. On Carnegie, see Alfred D. Chandler, "The Beginnings of 'Big Business' in American Industry," *Business History Review* 33, no. 1 (1959): 1–31.

33. Jacob Harold (president and CEO, GuideStar), email correspondence with William F. Meehan III and Kim Starkey Jonker, December 12, 2016.

34. Arthur "Buzz" Schmidt, phone interview by Melissa S. Brown, October 15, 2015.

35. "GuideStar: A Brief History," GuideStar, accessed November 30, 2015, https://www.learn.guidestar.org/about-us/history.

36. "About Us," GuideStar, accessed September 22, 2016, https://learn.guide star.org/about-us.

37. GuideStar, *GUIDESTAR 2020: Building the Scaffolding for Social Change*, accessed September 27, 2016, https://learn.guidestar.org/hubfs/docs/ GuideStar_2020_Strategic_Plan.pdf.

38. Christine W. Letts, William P. Ryan, and Allen S. Grossman, "Virtuous Capital: What Foundations Can Learn from Venture Capitalists," *Harvard Business Review* (March–April 1997): 36–44.

39. Joel L. Fleishman, *The Foundation: A Great American Secret; How Private Wealth Is Changing the World* (New York: PublicAffairs, 2007), 262; and Caitlin Duffy, "Lessons in Foundation Transparency from Philamplify," *Transparency Talk* (blog), September 22, 2014, http://blog.glasspockets.org/2014/09/ duffy-22092014.html.

40. McKeever, Dietz, and Fyffe, *Nonprofit Almanac*, 87, figure 5.2, data for 2013.

41. Bureau of Economic Analysis, "Value Added by Industry," annual data for 2013, accessed April 27, 2017, https://www.bea.gov/iTable/iTable.cfm?ReqI D=51&step=1#reqid=51&step=51&isuri=1&5114=a&5102=1. The "value added" by an industry is the contribution of that industry to overall US GDP.

42. Henry J. Kaiser Family Foundation, "Hospital Inpatient Days."

43. McKeever, Dietz, and Fyffe, *Nonprofit Almanac*, figures 5.6. and 5.12.

44. Indiana University Lilly Family School of Philanthropy, *The 2013 Congregational Impact Study* (Indianapolis: Indiana University Lilly Family School

of Philanthropy), 23 (the study reports the median percentage); and McKeever, Dietz, and Fyffe, *Nonprofit Almanac*, figure 5.4.

45. Ann Goggins Gregory and Don Howard, "The Nonprofit Starvation Cycle," *Stanford Social Innovation Review* (Fall 2009): 49–53.

46. Ibid.

47. Ibid.

48. William J. Baumol and William G. Bowen, *Performing Arts—the Economic Dilemma: A Study of Problems Common to Theater, Opera, Music and Dance* (Cambridge, MA: MIT Press, 1966).

49. Jacob Harold (president and CEO, GuideStar) and Anisha Singh White (strategy manager, GuideStar), email correspondence with William F. Meehan III, February 1, 2016. Data provided by GuideStar and used with permission.

50. Kim Nyegaard Meredith (executive director, Stanford Center on Philanthropy and Civil Society), email correspondence with William F. Meehan III, January 31, 2016.

51. Giving USA Foundation, *Giving USA 2016: The Annual Report on Philanthropy for the Year 2015* (Chicago: Giving USA Foundation, 2016).

52. William F. Meehan III and Kim Starkey Jonker, 2016 Stanford Survey on Leadership and Management in the Nonprofit Sector, Stanford Graduate School of Business, 2016, engineofimpact.org/survey.

Chapter 1

1. The maxim is often asserted but does not apply uniformly. Other options and frameworks for corporate governance exist, as we discuss on our website (engineofimpact.org).

2. Kim Jonker and William F. Meehan III, "Mission Matters Most," *Stanford Social Innovation Review*, February 19, 2014, https://ssir.org/articles/entry/mission_matters_most, used with permission; and Kim Jonker and William F. Meehan III, "Curbing Mission Creep," *Stanford Social Innovation Review* (Winter 2008), used with permission. This chapter draws on these two articles by the authors.

3. Residents of Hull-House, A Social Settlement at 335 South Halsted Street, Chicago, Ill., *Hull-House Maps and Papers: A Presentation of Nationalities and Wages in a Congested District of Chicago, Together with Comments and Essays on Problems Growing out of the Social Conditions* (New York: 46 East Fourteenth Street Thomas Y. Crowell & Co.; Boston: 100 Purchase Street, 1895), 105.

4. Peter F. Drucker, *Managing the Non-Profit Organization: Principles and Practices* (New York: HarperCollins, 1990), 3.

5. William F. Meehan III and Kim Starkey Jonker, 2016 Stanford Survey on Leadership and Management in the Nonprofit Sector, Stanford Graduate School of Business, 2016, engineofimpact.org/survey.

6. Kim Starkey Jonker, William F. Meehan III, and Sakena Yacoobi, "Making Mission Matter," *Stanford Social Innovation Review*, webinar, June 18, 2014.

7. Chip Heath and Dan Heath, *Made to Stick: Why Some Ideas Survive and Others Die* (New York: Random House, 2007), 8.

8. "Our Mission," Elks National Foundation, accessed March 10, 2016, http://www.elks.org/ENF/mission.cfm.

9. Jonker and Meehan, "Mission Matters Most."

10. Geoffrey M. Kistruck, Israr Qureshi, and Paul W. Beamish, "Geographic and Product Diversification in Charitable Organizations," *Journal of Management* 39, no. 2 (February 2013): 515.

11. Brice S. McKeever, *The Nonprofit Sector in Brief 2015: Public Charities, Giving, and Volunteering* (Washington, DC: Urban Institute, 2015), accessed April 11, 2016, http://www.urban.org/sites/default/files/alfresco/publication-pdfs/2000497 -The-Nonprofit-Sector-in-Brief-2015-Public-Charities-Giving-and-Volunteering.pdf.

12. John Boli and George M. Thomas, *Constructing World Culture: International Nongovernmental Organizations since 1875* (Stanford, CA: Stanford University Press, 1999).

13. Meehan and Jonker, 2016 Stanford Survey on Leadership and Management in the Nonprofit Sector.

14. "About Us," CASA for Children, accessed January 6, 2016, http://www .casaforchildren.org/site/c.mtJSJ7MPIsE/b.5301303/k.6FB1/About_Us__CASA _for_Children.htm.

15. Tara Perry and Sally Erny (chief program officer, National CASA Association), phone interview by Kim Starkey Jonker and Devin Bruckner, March 4, 2016.

16. Ibid.

17. "Landesa's Impact," Landesa, accessed January 6, 2016, http://www .landesa.org/who-we-are/global-impact.

18. "Who We Are—Mission," Landesa, accessed July 5, 2017, http://www .landesa.org/who-we-are.

19. Jonker and Meehan, "Curbing Mission Creep." Kim Jonker and William Meehan III, "Rural Development Institute: Should It Tackle the Problem of the Landless Poor in India?" Case Study SM159A, Stanford Graduate School of Business (2007). Copyright © 2001 to 2015 by the Board of Trustees of the Leland Stanford Junior University. All rights reserved. Used with permission from the Stanford University Graduate School of Business. Kim Jonker and William Meehan III, "Rural Development Institute: Success in India," Case Study SM159B, Stanford Graduate School of Business (2007). Copyright © 2001 to 2015 by the Board of Trustees of the Leland Stanford Junior University. All rights reserved. Used with permission from the Stanford University Graduate School of Business. This paragraph and the subsequent discussion about Landesa draw on these studies.

20. Jonker and Meehan, "Curbing Mission Creep," 62.

21. Ibid.

22. Tim Hanstad, email correspondence with Kim Starkey Jonker, November 12, 2016.

23. World Bank, *India: Achievements and Challenges in Reducing Poverty* (Washington, DC: World Bank, 1997), xiv.

24. Jonker and Meehan, "Curbing Mission Creep," 62.

25. Ibid.

26. Ibid., 63.

27. Ibid.

28. "What We Do—Landesa in India," Landesa, accessed April 11, 2016, http://www.landesa.org/what-we-do/india.

29. "Mission Statement," American Museum of Natural History, accessed December 26, 2015, http://www.amnh.org/about-us/mission-statement.

30. Ellen V. Futter and Lisa J. Gugenheim (senior vice president, Institutional Advancement, Education and Strategic Planning, AMNH), phone interview by Kim Starkey Jonker, February 3, 2016.

31. Ibid.

32. Ibid.

33. "The Richard Gilder Graduate School Brochure," American Museum of Natural History, accessed July 5, 2017, http://www.amnh.org/our-research/richard-gilder-graduate-school/amnh-ph.d.-program.

34. "Inaugural Commencement," American Museum of Natural History, September 30, 2013, http://www.amnh.org/about-us/annual-report/online-annual-report-2014/inaugural-commencement.

35. The Kravis Prize Recipient Retreat discussion took place on April 19, 2013, in Claremont, CA.

36. "Who We Are—Mission Statement," Afghan Institute of Learning, accessed March 10, 2016, http://www.afghaninstituteoflearning.org/who-we-are.html.

37. "What We Do," Afghan Institute of Learning, accessed December 26, 2015, http://www.afghaninstituteoflearning.org/what-we-do.html. "The mission of AIL is to empower all Afghans by providing comprehensive, quality education, training and health services in order to foster self-reliance, critical thinking skills, community participation and economic independence thereby transforming lives and communities."

38. Erica Mills, "Great Mission, Bad Statement," *Stanford Social Innovation Review*, January 15, 2016, https://ssir.org/articles/entry/great_mission._bad_statement.

39. Ibid.

40. Madhav Chavan, conversation with William F. Meehan III and Kim Starkey Jonker, Kravis Prize Recipient Retreat, April 19, 2013, Claremont, CA.

41. Sakena Yacoobi, conversation with William F. Meehan III and Kim Starkey Jonker, Kravis Prize Recipient Retreat, April 19, 2013, Claremont, CA.

42. Gyles Daubeney Brandreth, ed., *Oxford Dictionary of Humorous Quotations* (Oxford: Oxford University Press, 2013), 31.

43. Steven A. Denning, email correspondence with William F. Meehan III and Kim Starkey Jonker, April 7, 2016.

44. Jonker and Meehan, "Mission Matters Most."

45. Ibid.

46. "FAQs," Pratham, accessed March 10, 2016, http://www.prathamusa.org/about-us/faqs.

47. "About Us," Pratham Books, accessed March 10, 2016, http://prathambooks.org/about-us.

48. Jim Collins and Jerry I. Porras, *Built to Last: Successful Habits of Visionary Companies* (New York: Harper Business Essentials, 1994), 73.

49. Drucker, *Managing the Nonprofit Organization*, 3.

50. Jonker and Meehan, "Curbing Mission Creep," 65.

Chapter 2

1. On the four-box growth-share matrix, see Martin Reeves, Sandy Moose, and Thijs Venema, "BCG Classics Revisited: The Growth Share Matrix," *bcg.perspectives*, June 4, 2014, https://www.bcgperspectives.com/content/articles/corporate_strategy_portfolio_management_strategic_planning_growth_share_matrix_bcg_classics_revisited. On the GE-McKinsey nine-box matrix, see Kevin Coyne, "Enduring Ideas: The GE-McKinsey Nine-Box Matrix," *McKinsey Quarterly*, September 2008, podcast, 14:39, http://www.mckinsey.com/business-functions/strategy-and-corporate-finance/our-insights/enduring-ideas-the-ge-and-mckinsey-nine-box-matrix.

2. Bruce R. Sievers, "Philanthropy's Blindspots," in *Just Money: A Critique of Contemporary American Philanthropy*, ed. H. Peter Karoff (Boston: TPI Editions, 2004), 131.

3. Henry B. Hansmann, "Economic Theories of Nonprofit Organization," in *The Nonprofit Sector: A Research Handbook*, ed. Walter W. Powell (New Haven, CT: Yale University Press, 1987), 31.

4. Ibid., 27–42.

5. The term *War on Poverty* refers to a series of laws proposed by President Lyndon B. Johnson and passed by Congress in 1964–1965. The term comes from President Johnson's 1964 State of the Union address wherein he remarked, "This administration today, here and now, declares unconditional war on poverty in America."

6. "Theory of Change Origins," Center for Theory of Change, accessed April 14, 2016, http://www.theoryofchange.org/what-is-theory-of-change/toc-background/toc-origins.

7. Andrea A. Anderson, *Theory of Change as a Tool for Strategic Planning: A Report on Early Experiences* (New York: Aspen Institute Roundtable on Community Change, August 2004), 2.

8. Carol H. Weiss, "Nothing as Practical as a Good Theory," in *New Approaches to Evaluating Community Initiatives: Concepts, Methods, and Contexts*, ed. James P. Connell, Anne C. Kubisch, Lisbeth B. Schorr, and Carol H. Weiss (New York: Aspen Institute Roundtable on Comprehensive Community Initiatives for Children and Families, 1995), 1:65–93.

9. Anderson, *Theory of Change as a Tool for Strategic Planning*, 2.

10. Paul Brest and Hal Harvey, *Money Well Spent: A Strategic Plan for Smart Philanthropy* (New York: Bloomberg Press, 2008), 2, 6.

11. Paul Brest, "Update on the Hewlett Foundation's Approach to Philanthropy: The Importance of Strategy," president's statement to *William and Flora Hewlett Foundation 2003 Annual Report* (Menlo Park, CA: William and Flora Hewlett Foundation, June 2004), x–xi.

12. Brest and Harvey, *Money Well Spent.*

13. Nonprofit Finance Fund, *State of the Nonprofit Sector: 2015 Survey*, 15, accessed September 26, 2016, http://www.nonprofitfinancefund.org/sites/default/files/docs/2015/2015survey_natl_full_results.pdf.

14. William F. Meehan III and Kim Starkey Jonker, 2016 Stanford Survey on Leadership and Management in the Nonprofit Sector, Stanford Graduate School of Business, 2016, engineofimpact.org/survey.

15. "Our Mission & Vision," CEO, accessed December 4, 2015, http://ceoworks.org/about/what-we-do/mission-vision.

16. "CEO Theory of Change," CEO, accessed December 4, 2015, http://ceoworks.org/about/what-we-do/ceo-model-3.

17. Cindy Redcross, Megan Millenky, Timothy Rudd, and Valerie Levshin, *More Than a Job: Final Results from the Evaluation of the Center for Employment Opportunities (CEO) Transitional Jobs Program*, Office of Planning, Research and Evaluation (OPRE) Report 2011-18 (Washington, DC: Office of Planning, Research and Evaluation, Administration for Children and Families, U.S. Department of Health and Human Services, January 2012), http://www.mdrc.org/sites/default/files/full_451.pdf.

18. Christian Henrichson and Ruth Delaney, *The Price of Prisons: What Incarceration Costs Taxpayers* (New York: Vera Institute of Justice, January 2012, updated July 20, 2012), http://www.vera.org/sites/default/files/resources/downloads/price-of-prisons-updated-version-021914.pdf.

19. Sam Schaeffer, email correspondence with Kim Starkey Jonker, November 22, 2016.

20. Tina Rosenberg, "Out of Jail, and Into a Job," Opinionator (blog), *New York Times*, March 28, 2012, https://opinionator.blogs.nytimes.com/2012/03/28/out-of-jail-and-into-jobs/?_r=0.

21. Schaeffer, email correspondence with Jonker, November 22, 2016.

22. "CEO Theory of Change," CEO.

23. Redcross, Millenky, Rudd, and Levshin, *More Than a Job.*

24. Rosenberg, "Out of Jail."

25. Tim Hanstad (cofounder and former CEO, Landesa), email correspondence with Kim Starkey Jonker, January 6, 2016. The five items summarized here are a paraphrase of Hanstad's email communication.

26. Roy Prosterman, phone interview by Kim Starkey Jonker, February 24, 2015.

27. Hanstad, phone interview by Kim Starkey Jonker, July 20, 2015.

28. Ibid.

29. Michael E. Porter, *Competitive Strategy: Techniques for Analyzing Industries and Competitors*, with a new introduction (1980; New York: Free Press, 1998).

30. Michael E. Porter, "The Five Competitive Forces That Shape Strategy," *Harvard Business Review*, January 2008. Copyright © 2008 by Harvard Business Publishing; all rights reserved.

31. Porter, "The Five Competitive Forces That Shape Strategy," editor's note.

32. Sharon M. Oster, *Strategic Management for Nonprofit Organizations: Theory and Cases* (Oxford: Oxford University Press, 1995), 29–30.

33. Jennifer Warren, "E. Palo Alto Murder Rate Worst in US; Drug Wars Blamed," *Los Angeles Times*, January 5, 1993, http://articles.latimes.com/1993 -01-05/local/me-833_1_east-palo-alto. The city had a population of 24,000 and forty-two murders.

34. Paul Krugman, "The Spiral of Inequality," *Mother Jones*, November– December 1996, 44.

35. William Meehan III and Pehr Luedtke, "Eastside College Preparatory School," Case Number SI13, Stanford Graduate School of Business (2001). Copyright © 2001 to 2015 by the Board of Trustees of the Leland Stanford Junior University. All rights reserved. Used with permission from the Stanford University Graduate School of Business. The subsequent discussion draws on the case study.

36. Eastside College Preparatory School, "Eastside College Preparatory School— Best Practices," 1, http://eastside.org/_pdfs/Eastside_Programs&Best_Practices.pdf.

37. Meehan and Luedtke, "Eastside College Preparatory School," 5.

38. Ibid., 14.

39. John A. Kastor, *Mergers of Teaching Hospitals in Boston, New York, and Northern California* (Ann Arbor, MI: University of Michigan, 2001), 20.

40. Ibid., 55.

41. Ibid., 19–20.

42. Ibid., 55–57.

43. Ibid., 58–78.

44. "About Partners HealthCare," Partners HealthCare, accessed March 29, 2017, http://innovation.partners.org/about/about-partners-healthcare.

45. Kastor, *Mergers of Teaching Hospitals*, 265–282.

46. Ibid., 271–282.

47. William F. Meehan, Katharina Schmitt, and Anne Lee, "The San Francisco Symphony," Case Number SM-63, Stanford Graduate School of Business (updated January 22, 2015). Copyright © 2001 to 2015 by the Board of Trustees of the Leland Stanford Junior University. All rights reserved. Used with permission from the Stanford University Graduate School of Business. The subsequent discussion draws on the case study.

48. Nine of the top ten major orchestras in the United States ran deficits in 2014. The Los Angeles Philharmonic is the only major orchestra in the United States that has been running a surplus, under unique circumstances (it is able to cross-finance from the Hollywood Bowl, a popular outdoor concert venue). In 2011, the Philadelphia Orchestra became the first top-tier orchestra to file for Chapter 11 bankruptcy protection.

49. Meehan, Schmitt, and Lee, "San Francisco Symphony," 5.

50. C. K. Prahalad and Gary Hamel, "The Core Competence of the Corporation," *Harvard Business Review*, May–June 1990, 79–91.

51. William F. Meehan and Davina Drabkin, "Equal Opportunities Schools: Finding the Missing Students," Case Number SM-240, Stanford Graduate School of Business (2015). Copyright © 2001 to 2015 by the Board of Trustees of the

Leland Stanford Junior University. All rights reserved. Used with permission from the Stanford University Graduate School of Business. The subsequent discussion draws on the case study.

52. Ibid., 2.

53. Ibid., 2–4; Reid Saaris (founder and CEO, EOS), email correspondence with Kim Starkey Jonker, April 4, 2017.

54. Meehan and Drabkin, "Equal Opportunities Schools," 5.

55. Ibid., 5–8.

56. Ibid., 8.

57. Carol S. Dweck, *Mindset: The New Psychology of Success* (New York: Random House, 2006), 6–7.

58. Reid Saaris, email correspondence with William F. Meehan III and Kim Starkey Jonker, March 22, 2016.

59. Ibid.

60. "AP/IB Excellence and Equity Project Enters 3rd and Final Year in 2015–2016," EOS, accessed April 28, 2016, http://eoschools.org/equityexcellence.

61. William F. Meehan III, Molly McNamee, and Deena Soulon, "The San Francisco Symphony," Case Number SM-63, Version A, Stanford Graduate School of Business (February 14, 2002), 5, 15.

62. San Francisco Symphony, *Financial Statement 2012–2013*, http://www.sfsymphony.org/SanFranciscoSymphony/media/Library/PDFs/Financials/SFS_Financials_201213.pdf.

63. James Heilbrun, "Baumol's Cost Disease," in *A Handbook of Cultural Economics*, ed. Ruth Towse (Northhampton, MA: Edward Elgar Publishing, 2011), 67–75.

64. Sheila Bonini, Emily Sophia Knapp, and William Meehan III, "Oregon Shakespeare Festival," Case Number SM 104, Stanford Graduate School of Business (October 18, 2002; revised January 30, 2014). Copyright © 2001 to 2015 by the Board of Trustees of the Leland Stanford Junior University. All rights reserved. Used with permission from the Stanford University Graduate School of Business. William F. Meehan and Emily Sophia Knapp, "Oregon Shakespeare Festival: The 2015–2025 Long Range Plan," Case Number SM-104B, Stanford Graduate School of Business (October 31, 2015). Copyright © 2001 to 2015 by the Board of Trustees of the Leland Stanford Junior University. All rights reserved. Used with permission from the Stanford University Graduate School of Business. These case studies provide details of OSF's strategic planning processes.

65. Zannie Giraud Voss and Glenn B. Voss, with Ilana B. Rose and Laurie Baskin, *Theatre Facts 2012: A Report on the Fiscal State of the Professional Not-for-Profit American Theatre*, Theatre Communications Group, 2012. TCG, a national organization of professional not-for-profit American theater organizations, gathered data from 178 of its members. Only 11 of these organizations had budgets of more than $20 million, and OSF's budget ($31.3 million) was well above the peer median. OSF maintains its size despite having comparatively low contributed income and average ticket prices. See Meehan, Knapp, and Bonini, "Oregon Shakespeare Festival," 3.

66. Meehan, Knapp, and Bonini, "Oregon Shakespeare Festival," 5–8. The case study provides details about the 2009–2013 planning process.

67. Meehan and Knapp, "Oregon Shakespeare Festival: The 2015–2025 Long Range Plan," 3–5.

68. Ibid., 4–5.

69. Richard M. Nixon, *Six Crises* (Garden City, NY: Doubleday, 1962), 235.

Chapter 3

1. Aspen Institute Program on Philanthropy and Social Innovation, "Advancing Evaluation Practices," special edition to the *Stanford Social Innovation Review*, accessed September 26, 2016, https://ssir.org/supplement/advancing_evalu ation_practices_in_philanthropy; and "Introduction to Evaluations," J-PAL, accessed September 26, 2016, https://www.povertyactionlab.org/research-resources/intro duction-evaluations. Both sources provide a good summary of this development and a broad overview of evaluation.

2. "Evaluations," J-PAL, accessed March 27, 2017, https://www.poverty actionlab.org/evaluations. See also J-PAL, *2012 Annual Report*, accessed September 22, 2016, https://www.povertyactionlab.org/sites/default/files/documents/2012 _Annual_Report.pdf.

3. "About," IPA, accessed March 27, 2017, http://www.poverty-action.org/ about.

4. "Impact Audit Standard," ImpactMatters, November 2016, accessed March 29, 2017, http://www.impactm.org/impact-auditing/standard.

5. "About 3ie," 3ie, accessed April 11, 2017, http://www.3ieimpact.org/en/ about/.

6. "About CrimeSolutions.gov," CrimeSolutions.gov, accessed February 25, 2016, https://www.crimesolutions.gov/about.aspx.

7. "Tools and Resources for Assessing Social Impact," Foundation Center, accessed November 1, 2016, http://trasi.foundationcenter.org/browse.php.

8. Bill Gates, "Bill Gates: My Plan to Fix the World's Biggest Problems," *Wall Street Journal*, January 25, 2013, https://www.wsj.com/articles/SB10001424127 887323253980457826178064828577O.

9. Joel Peterson, "Feedback Is the Breakfast of Champions: 10 Tips for Doing It Right," October 11, 2013, Peterson Partners (also published on LinkedIn), http://www.petersonpartners.com/feedback-is-the-breakfast-of-champions-10-tips -for-doing-it-right.

10. William F. Meehan III and Kim Starkey Jonker, 2016 Stanford Survey on Leadership and Management in the Nonprofit Sector, Stanford Graduate School of Business, 2016, engineofimpact.org/survey.

11. Nonprofit Finance Fund, *State of the Nonprofit Sector: 2015 Survey*, 22, accessed September 26, 2016, http://www.nonprofitfinancefund.org/sites/default/ files/docs/2015/2015survey_natl_full_results.pdf.

12. Laura Arrillaga-Andreessen with Melinda Gates, "Melinda Gates at the Philanthropy Summit 2015," Vimeo video of keynote address, 29:30, from Re-

cap of Stanford Center on Philanthropy and Civil Society (PACS) Philanthropy Summit 2015, September 30, 2015, accessed January 19, 2016, http://pacscenter .stanford.edu/recap-philanthropy-summit-2015.

13. Charity Navigator, *Results Reporting Concept Note: The Third Dimension of Intelligent Giving*, January 2013, accessed April 11, 2016, http://www .charitynavigator.org/__asset__/_etc_/CN_Results_Reporting_Concept_Note.pdf.

14. William Meehan III and Davina Drabkin, "Willow Creek Community Church: What Really Makes a Difference?" Case Number SM-198, Stanford Graduate School of Business (January 4, 2012), 1–22. Copyright © 2001 to 2015 by the Board of Trustees of the Leland Stanford Junior University. All rights reserved. Used with permission from the Stanford University Graduate School of Business. The subsequent discussion about Willow Creek Church is drawn from this case study.

15. Ibid., 1.

16. Ibid., 8–10.

17. Ibid., 15.

18. Ibid.

19. "Frequently Asked Questions—History," REVEAL for Church: Spiritual Life Survey, accessed January 20, 2016, http://revealforchurch.com/faqs.

20. Kathy Spahn, phone interview by Kim Starkey Jonker, September 23, 2015.

21. Ibid.

22. Bill Drayton and Diana Wells, interview by William F. Meehan III and Kim Starkey Jonker, February 11, 2016.

23. Ibid.

24. "Random Harvest: Once Treated with Scorn, Randomised Control Trials Are Coming of Age," *Free Exchange* (blog), from print edition *Economist*, December 14, 2013, http://www.economist.com/news/finance-and-economics/ 21591573-once-treated-scorn-randomised-control-trials-are-coming-age-random -harvest.

25. Ian Parker, "The Poverty Lab: Transforming Development Economics, One Experiment at a Time," *New Yorker*, May 17, 2010, http://www.newyorker .com/magazine/2010/05/17/the-poverty-lab.

26. Madhav Chavan, phone interview by Kim Starkey Jonker, March 10, 2016.

27. Kim Jonker and William F. Meehan III, "Clear Measurement Counts," *Stanford Social Innovation Review*, March 20, 2014, accessed January 19, 2016, http://ssir.org/articles/entry/clear_measurement_counts.

28. HKI, *Transforming Tomorrow: 2015 Annual Report*, accessed September 22, 2016, http://www.hki.org/sites/default/files/attach/2016/07/HKI_Annual_ Report_2015_Finalweb.pdf.

29. Thomas Goetz, "Harnessing the Power of Feedback Loops," *Wired*, June 19, 2011, http://www.wired.com/2011/06/ff_feedbackloop.

30. Jonker and Meehan, "Clear Measurement Counts."

31. Michael Faye and Paul Niehaus, interview by Kim Starkey Jonker, September 23, 2015.

32. Spahn, interview by Jonker.

33. Jonker and Meehan, "Clear Measurement Counts." The discussion of BRAC is drawn from this *SSIR* article.

34. Ibid.

35. Nico Pitney, "This Startup Gives Poor People a Year's Income, No Strings Attached," *Huffington Post*, June 4, 2015, updated September 8, 2015, http://www.huffingtonpost.com/2015/06/04/givedirectly-cash-transfers_n_7339040.html.

36. Tim Hanstad, phone interview by Kim Starkey Jonker, July 20, 2015.

37. Jonker and Meehan, "Clear Measurement Counts."

38. Ibid; and Vicky Colbert (founder and director, Fundación Escuela Nueva), phone interview by Kim Starkey Jonker, January 21, 2016.

39. "BAM—Becoming a Man," Youth Guidance, accessed November 4, 2016, https://www.youth-guidance.org/bam/.

40. Ibid.

41. Michelle Adler Morrison, interview by Kim Starkey Jonker at the Thrive Foundation grantee retreat, October 28, 2016.

42. Faye and Niehaus, interview by Jonker.

43. Cari Tuna, "Announcing a $25 Million Grant to GiveDirectly," Good Ventures, August 3, 2015, http://www.goodventures.org/research-and-ideas/blog/announcing-a-25-million-grant-to-givedirectly.

44. Kathy Spahn, email correspondence with Kim Starkey Jonker, November 13, 2016

45. Jonker and Meehan, "Clear Measurement Counts."

46. Ibid. The discussion of BRAC is drawn from this *SSIR* article.

47. Ibid.

48. Ibid.

49. "Building Stable Livelihoods for the Ultra-Poor," Abdul Latif Jameel Poverty Action Lab (J-PAL) and Innovations for Poverty Action (IPA) Policy Bulletin (Cambridge, MA: J-PAL and IPA, 2015).

50. "Graduation into Sustainable Livelihoods," Consultative Group to Assist the Poor (CGAP), accessed January 20, 2016, http://www.cgap.org/topics/graduation-sustainable-livelihoods. See also "Graduation into Sustainable Livelihoods," Microfinance Gateway, accessed January 20, 2016, http://www.microfinancegateway.org/topics/graduation-sustainable-livelihoods.

51. J-PAL, *2012 Annual Report*.

52. "Most Recently Registered Trials," American Economic Association's Registry for Randomized Controlled Trials, accessed April 8, 2017, http://www.socialscienceregistry.org.

53. J-PAL, *2012 Annual Report*.

54. Ibid.

55. Johannes Haushofer and Jeremy Shapiro, "Household Response to Income Changes: Evidence from an Unconditional Cash Transfer Program in Kenya," No-

vember 15, 2013, https://www.princeton.edu/~joha/publications/Haushofer_Sha
piro_UCT_2013.pdf.

56. Faye and Niehaus, interview by Jonker.

57. Ibid.

58. Pitney, "This Startup Gives Poor People a Year's Income."

59. Faye and Niehaus, interview by Jonker.

60. Alex Berger, email correspondence with William F. Meehan III and Kim
Starkey Jonker, April 12, 2016.

61. Ibid.

62. "Blue Meridian Partners," Edna McConnell Clark Foundation, accessed
February 1, 2016, http://www.emcf.org/capital-aggregation/blue-meridian-partners.

Chapter 4

1. Adam Ludwig, "Ashoka Chairman Bill Drayton on the Power of Social Entrepreneurship," *Forbes*, March 12, 2012, https://www.forbes.com/sites/
techonomy/2012/03/12/ashoka-chairman-bill-drayton-on-the-power-of-social
-entrepreneurship.

2. Keith H. Hammonds, "A Lever Long Enough to Move the World,"
Fast Company, January 1, 2005, https://www.fastcompany.com/52233/
lever-long-enough-move-world.

3. "Profiles in Giving: Roy Prosterman, Founder of Seattle-Based Landesa,"
Seattle Business Magazine, accessed February 25, 2016, http://www.seattle
businessmag.com/blog/profiles-giving-roy-prosterman-founder-seattle-based
-landesa.

4. Shivani Vora, "A Conversation With: Landesa Founder Roy Prosterman," *New York Times*, September 25, 2012, https://india.blogs.nytimes
.com/2012/09/25/a-conversation-with-landesa-founder-roy-prosterman/?_r=0.

5. Ibid.

6. Roy Prosterman, "Land Reform in Latin America: How to Have a Revolution Without a Revolution," *Washington Law Review* 42 (1966): 189–211.

7. Vora, "Conversation."

8. Ibid.

9. Felix Belair Jr., "Expert's Report Assails Saigon on Land Reform," *New
York Times*, March 6, 1968, 2L.

10. Roy Prosterman (founder and chairman emeritus, Landesa), phone interview by Kim Starkey Jonker, April 13, 2016.

11. Belair, "Expert's Report Assails Saigon on Land Reform."

12. Vora, "Conversation."

13. Prosterman, phone interview by Jonker.

14. Ibid.

15. Ibid.

16. Vicky Colbert (founder and director, Fundación Escuela Nueva), phone
interview by Kim Starkey Jonker, January 21, 2016.

17. Ibid.

18. Ibid.

19. Ibid.

20. "Clara Victoria Colbert," Ashoka Innovators for the Public, accessed February 25, 2016, https://www.ashoka.org/node/3460.

21. Colbert, phone interview by Jonker.

22. Duncan Campbell (founder, Friends of the Children), phone interview by Kim Starkey Jonker, November 18, 2015.

23. Helaina Hovitz, "Motivated by Dark Childhood, Entrepreneur Helps At-Risk Kids with 'Friends' Program," *Forbes*, June 18, 2014, https://www .forbes.com/sites/helainahovitz/2014/06/18/motivated-by-dark-childhood -entrepreneur-helps-at-risk-kids-with-friends-program.

24. Campbell, phone interview by Jonker.

25. Ibid.

26. Ibid.

27. "Profiles in Courage—About the Book," John F. Kennedy Presidential Library and Museum, 266, accessed February 25, 2016, http://www.jfklibrary .org/Research/Research-Aids/Ready-Reference/JFK-Quotations/Profiles-in-Cour age-quotations.aspx.

28. Sakena Yacoobi (founder and CEO, Afghan Institute of Learning), interview by Kim Starkey Jonker, April 5, 2016.

29. "The Spiritual Journey of Sakena Yacoobi," Vimeo video, 17:20, accessed February 26, 2016, https://vimeo.com/36786934.

30. Ibid.

31. Yacoobi, interview by Jonker.

32. Ibid.

33. Ibid.

34. Ibid.

35. Ibid.

36. Sakena Yacoobi, "In Afghanistan, Teaching Men That Education Is Not a Threat," *Christian Science Monitor*, February 19, 2015, http:// www.csmonitor.com/World/Making-a-difference/Change-Agent/2015/0219/ In-Afghanistan-teaching-men-that-education-is-not-a-threat.

37. Ibid.

38. Yacoobi, interview by Jonker.

39. Yacoobi, "In Afghanistan, Teaching Men."

40. Yacoobi, interview by Jonker.

41. Sakena Yacoobi, email correspondence with Kim Starkey Jonker, March 11, 2016.

42. Richard Adams, "Sal Khan: The Man Who Tutored His Cousin and Started a Revolution," *The Guardian*, April 23, 2013, https://www.theguard ian.com/education/2013/apr/23/sal-khan-academy-tutored-educational -website.

43. Sal Khan (founder, Khan Academy), phone interview by William F. Meehan III and Kim Starkey Jonker, February 12, 2016.

44. Salman Khan, "Let's Use Video to Reinvent Education," 2011 TED Talk, 20:27, March 9, 2011, accessed March 3, 2016, https://www.ted.com/talks/salman_khan_let_s_use_video_to_reinvent_education?language=en.

45. Khan, phone interview by Meehan and Jonker.

46. Bryant Urstadt, "Salman Khan: The Messiah of Math," *Bloomberg Business*, May 19, 2011, accessed February 26, 2016, http://www.bloomberg.com/bw/magazine/content/11_22/b4230072816925.htm.

47. Khan, phone interview by Meehan and Jonker.

48. Adams, "Sal Khan."

49. "How Did Khan Academy Get Started?," Khan Academy, accessed January 31, 2016, https://khanacademy.zendesk.com/hc/en-us/articles/202260104-How-did-Khan-Academy-get-started.

50. Khan, phone interview by Meehan and Jonker.

51. Ibid.

52. William F. Meehan III and Kim Starkey Jonker, 2016 Stanford Survey on Leadership and Management in the Nonprofit Sector, Stanford Graduate School of Business, 2016, engineofimpact.org/survey.

Chapter 5

1. "Casablanca (1942)—'As Time Goes By,' Music and Words by Herman Hupfeld," Reel Classics, accessed November 11, 2016, http://www.reelclassics.com/Movies/Casablanca/astimegoesby-lyrics.htm.

2. "What We Do," International Federation of Red Cross and Red Crescent Societies, accessed November 11, 2016, http://www.ifrc.org/en/what-we-do.

3. Bill Drayton, "A Team of Teams World," Ashoka, July 15, 2016, https://www.ashoka.org/en/story/team-teams-world.

4. "About Ashoka—Ashoka's Vision: Realizing the 'Everyone a Changemaker' World," Ashoka, accessed November 14, 2016, https://www.ashoka.org/en/about-ashoka.

5. "Help the World Play the New Game," Ashoka, accessed November 2, 2016, http://joinnow.ashoka.org.

6. Bill Drayton (founder and CEO, Ashoka) and Diana Wells (president, Ashoka), phone interview by William F. Meehan III, Kim Starkey Jonker, and Sheila Melvin, January 28, 2016.

7. "Every Child Practicing Empathy," Ashoka, accessed November 2, 2016, https://www.ashoka.org/focus/every-child-practicing-empathy.

8. Drayton and Wells, phone interview by Meehan, Jonker, and Melvin.

9. Ibid.

10. Ibid., and Bill Drayton and Diana Wells, phone interview by William F. Meehan III, Kim Starkey Jonker, and Sheila Melvin, February 11, 2016.

11. Drayton and Wells, phone interview by Meehan, Jonker, and Melvin, January 28, 2016.

12. Drayton and Wells, phone interview by Meehan, Jonker, and Melvin, February 11, 2016.

13. Ibid.

14. Ibid.

15. Holger Mueller, "Worldwide Human Capital Management in Less Than 90 Days: How FinancialForce HCM Was Implemented in 47 Countries in Less than Three Months," Case Study: Ashoka and FinancialForce.com, Constellation Research, February 9, 2016, https://www.constellationr.com/research/worldwide-human-capital-management-less-90-days.

16. Teryll Hopper, "Ashoka Expands Its Global Social Impact with Pro Bono Volunteers," *NetSuite Blog*, July 16, 2015, http://www.netsuite.org/ashoka-expands-its-global-social-impact-with-pro-bono-volunteers.

17. "Overview," ASER Centre, accessed October 28, 2016, http://www.asercentre.org/Survey/Basic/Pack/Sampling/History/p/54.html.

18. Ibid.

19. Rukmini Banerji, interview by Kim Starkey Jonker, September 13, 2016.

20. Ibid.

21. "Ensuring Data Quality," ASER Centre, accessed October 28, 2016, http://www.asercentre.org/p/136.html.

22. Peter F. Drucker, *Managing the Nonprofit Organization: Principles and Practices* (New York: HarperCollins, 1990), 3.

23. R. Michael Murray Jr. and Guillermo G. Marmol, "Leading from the Front," *McKinsey Quarterly* 3 (Summer 1995): 18–31.

24. Jim Collins, *Good to Great: Why Some Companies Make the Leap . . . And Others Don't* (New York: Harper Business, 2001), 44.

25. Jim Collins, *Good to Great and the Social Sectors: A Monograph to Accompany Good to Great (Why Business Thinking Is Not the Answer)* (Boulder, CO: Jim Collins, 2005), 34.

26. Ibid.

27. Marla Cornelius, Patrick Corvington, and Albert Ruesga, *Ready to Lead? Next Generation Leaders Speak Out* (San Francisco: CompassPoint Nonprofit Services, Annie E. Casey Foundation, Meyer Foundation, and Idealist.org, 2008).

28. Collins, *Good to Great and the Social Sectors*, 15.

29. Collins, *Good to Great*, 13.

30. William F. Meehan III and Kim Starkey Jonker, 2016 Stanford Survey on Leadership and Management in the Nonprofit Sector, Stanford Graduate School of Business, 2016, engineofimpact.org/survey.

31. Collins, *Good to Great*, 56.

32. Collins, *Good to Great and the Social Sectors*, 15.

33. Jeffrey Pfeffer and Robert I. Sutton, *Hard Facts, Dangerous Half-Truths, and Total Nonsense: Profiting from Evidence-Based Management* (Boston: Harvard Business School Press, 2006), 6, 8, 10.

34. Michael Faye, email correspondence with Kim Starkey Jonker, November 5, 2016.

35. Thomas J. Peters and Robert H. Waterman Jr., *In Search of Excellence: Lessons from America's Best-Run Companies* (New York: Harper & Row, 1982), 156, 292, 318.

36. Ibid., 318.

37. Nonprofit HR LLC, *2015 Nonprofit Employment Practices Survey Results*, 9–10, accessed November 10, 2016, http://www.nonprofithr.com/wp-content/uploads/2015/02/2015-Nonprofit-Employment-Practices-Survey-Results-1.pdf.

38. Kirk Kramer and Preeta Nayak, *Nonprofit Leadership Development: What's Your "Plan A" for Growing Future Leaders?* (Boston: Bridgespan Group, 2013).

39. Libbie Landles-Cobb, Kirk Kramer, and Katie Smith Milway, "The Nonprofit Leadership Development Deficit," *Stanford Social Innovation Review*, October 22, 2016, https://ssir.org/articles/entry/the_nonprofit_leadership_development_deficit.

40. Josh Solomon and Yarrow Sandahl, *Stepping Up or Stepping Out: A Report on the Readiness of Next Generation Nonprofit Leaders* (New York: Young Nonprofit Professionals Network, 2007).

41. Cornelius, Corvington, and Ruesga, *Ready to Lead?*, 22.

42. Wendy Kopp, interview by Kim Starkey Jonker, March 30, 2017.

43. "Our Commitment to Developing Leaders," Teach for America, accessed April 4, 2016, https://www.teachforamerica.org/about-us/careers/life-at-tfa.

44. Ibid.

45. "Leadership Approach," Global Health Corps, accessed April 4, 2017, http://ghcorps.org/why-were-here/leadership-practices.

46. Barbara Bush, email correspondence with Kim Starkey Jonker, April 8, 2017.

47. Ibid.

48. Bridgespan Group, *Finding Leaders for America's Nonprofits*, accessed November 10, 2016, https://www.bridgespan.org/bridgespan/Images/articles/finding-leaders/findingleaders.pdf.

49. Nonprofit HR LLC, *2015 Nonprofit Employment Practices*.

50. Landles-Cobb, Kramer, and Smith Milway, "Nonprofit Leadership Development Deficit."

51. Martin Dewhurt, Mathew Guthridge, and Elizabeth Mohr, "Motivating People: Getting Beyond Money," *McKinsey Quarterly* (2009), accessed April 4, 2016, http://www.mckinsey.com/insights/organization/motivating_people_getting_beyond_money.

52. Cliff Zukin and Mark Szeltner, *Talent Report: What Workers Want in 2012* (San Francisco: Net Impact, 2012), 10.

53. James K. Harter, Frank L. Schmidt, Emily A. Killham, and James W. Asplund, *Q12 Meta-Analysis* (Washington, DC: Gallup Consulting, 2006).

54. "The Role of Incentives in the Distribution of Public Goods in Zambia," Innovations for Poverty Action, accessed April 4, 2016, http://www.poverty-action.org/study/role-incentives-distribution-public-goods-zambia.

55. "Nurse Family Partnership International," Nurse Family Partnership, accessed April 4, 2016, http://www.nursefamilypartnership.org/communities/NFP-Abroad; and "Nurse Family Partnership Snapshot," Nurse Family Partnership,

accessed April 4, 2016, http://www.nursefamilypartnership.org/getattachment/ about/fact-sheets/NFP_February_2016_Snapshot-(6).pdf.aspx.

56. Woodrow "Woody" McCutchen, phone interview by Kim Starkey Jonker, December 8, 2014.

57. "Licentie VoorZorg in Duitsland ingetrokken" [Voorzorg's license for Germany withdrawn], VoorZorg Nieuwsbrief 11 (May 2013): 3, accessed January 25, 2016, http://nphf.nl/footage/fm/File/JDV%20VoorZorg%20bijl.

58. McCutchen, phone interview by Jonker.

59. Sarah Avellar, Diane Paulsell, Emily Sama-Miller, Patricia Del Grosso, Lauren Akers, and Rebecca Kleinman, *Home Visiting Evidence of Effectiveness Review: Executive Summary*, Report &2015-85a (Washington, DC: Office of Planning, Research and Evaluation, Administration for Children and Families, US Department of Health and Human Services, September 2015); US Department of Health & Human Service's Maternal, Infant, and Early Childhood Home Visiting Program, *Which Program Models Identified by HHS as "Evidence-Based" Are Most Likely to Produce Important Improvements in the Lives of Children and Parents?* (Washington, DC: Coalition for Evidence-Based Policy, August 2011); and Stephanie Lee, Steve Aos, and Annie Pennucci, *What Works and What Does Not? Benefit-Cost Findings from WSIPP*, Doc. No. 15-02-4101 (Olympia: Washington State Institute for Public Policy, February 2015).

60. HHS, *Which Program Models Identified by HHS?*

61. David F. Larcker, Nicholas E. Donatiello, William F. Meehan III, and Brian Tayan, 2015 Survey on Board of Directors of Nonprofit Organizations, Stanford Graduate School of Business and Rock Center for Corporate Governance, 2015, 2.

62. Meehan and Jonker, 2016 Stanford Survey on Leadership and Management in the Nonprofit Sector.

63. Kim Jonker and William F. Meehan III, "Nothing Succeeds like Succession," *Stanford Social Innovation Review*, March 12, 2014, http://ssir.org/articles/entry/ nothing_succeeds_like_succession. The discussion of BRAC draws on this article.

64. Ibid.

65. Ibid. The discussion of HKI draws on this *SSIR* article.

66. Ibid.

67. Ibid. The discussion of Landesa draws on this *SSIR* article.

68. Ibid.

Chapter 6

1. David F. Larcker, Nicholas E. Donatiello, William F. Meehan III, and Brian Tayan, 2015 Survey on Board of Directors of Nonprofit Organizations, Stanford Graduate School of Business and Rock Center for Corporate Governance, 2015, 22.

2. William Landes Foster, Peter Kim, and Barbara Christiansen, "Ten Nonprofit Funding Models," *Stanford Social Innovation Review*, Spring 2009, http:// ssir.org/articles/entry/ten_nonprofit_funding_models.

3. BRAC USA, "Delivering Results in the Fight Against Poverty: The Lessons of BRAC and Why They Matter Today," 1, accessed April 5, 2017, http://www.bracusa.org/wp-content/uploads/2017/02/BRAC_DeliveringResults.pdf; and Kim Jonker, "In the Black with BRAC," *Stanford Social Innovation Review*, Winter 2009, http://ssir.org/articles/entry/in_the_black_with_brac.

4. Jonker, "In the Black with BRAC."

5. Jim Thompson, phone interview by Kim Starkey Jonker, January 28, 2016.

6. Ibid.

7. William F. Meehan III and Kim Starkey Jonker, 2016 Stanford Survey on Leadership and Management in the Nonprofit Sector, Stanford Graduate School of Business, 2016, engineofimpact.org/survey.

8. BoardSource, *Leading with Intent: A National Index of Nonprofit Board Practices* (Washington, DC: BoardSource, 2015), 5.

9. Engine of Impact, engineofimpact.org.

10. Daniel Lurie, interview by Kim Starkey Jonker, August 26, 2015.

11. Marts & Lundy Special Report, "2015: New York City Board Giving, Adding Facts to Anecdotes," December 2015, 5, http://www.martsandlundy.com/wp-content/uploads/2015/12/NY_Board_Giving_2015_pages_FINAL.pdf.

12. Kim Jonker, William F. Meehan III, and Ernie Iseminger, "Fundraising Is Fundamental (If Not Always Fun)," *Stanford Social Innovation Review*, February 26, 2014, https://ssir.org/articles/entry/fundraising_is_fundamental_if_not_always_fun.

13. "Famous Cases & Criminals: Willie Sutton," Federal Bureau of Investigation, accessed April 5, 2017, https://www.fbi.gov/history/famous-cases/willie-sutton.

14. Giving USA Foundation, *Giving USA 2016: The Annual Report on Philanthropy for the Year 2015* (Chicago: Giving USA Foundation, 2016), 27. In using Giving USA data, we rounded the contribution amounts in each category, and thus the percentage figures that we provide differ slightly from figures in this report. The findings partly reflect the fact that an estimated $119 billion of the $373 billion in charitable giving went to religious congregations. That said, even if giving by living individuals accounted for all of that $119 billion, individual giving would still account for 57 percent of the remaining amount (roughly $254 billion).

15. William F. Meehan III, Kim Jonker, Ernie Iseminger, and Johann Koss, "The Fundamentals of Fundraising," *Stanford Social Innovation Review*, webinar, May 19, 2015.

16. Melissa S. Brown (manager, Nonprofit Research Collaborative), conversation with Kim Starkey Jonker, October 8, 2015.

17. Jon Durnford (analyst, Growth in Giving Initiative), personal communication with Melissa S. Brown, November 2, 2015.

18. Tom Wolfe, "Snob's Progress," review of *Cecil Beaton: A Biography*, by Hugo Vickers, *New York Times*, June 15, 1986, Sunday Book Review, http://www.nytimes.com/1986/06/15/books/snob-s-progress.html?pagewanted=all.

19. Council for Advancement and Support of Education (CASE), *The 2013 CASE Campaign Report: The 17th Analysis of the CASE Survey of Educational*

Fundraising Campaigns (Washington, DC: Council for Advancement and Support of Education, 2013), xi, figure A.

20. Brown, conversation with Jonker.

21. "Table 2.1—Returns with Itemized Deductions: Sources of Income, Adjustments, Itemized Deductions by Type, Exemptions, and Tax Items, by Size of Adjusted Gross Income, Tax Year 2014 (Filing Year 2015)," IRS Statistics of Income Division Tax, accessed November 2, 2016, https://www.irs.gov/uac/soi-tax-stats-individual-statistical-tables-by-size-of-adjusted-gross-income#_grp2; unpublished analysis by Melissa S. Brown. Itemized contributions include cash and noncash gifts deducted as charitable contributions, including contributions to donor-advised funds and foundations up to the limits allowed by law.

22. Nancy L. Raybin, phone interviews by Kim Starkey Jonker and William F. Meehan III, April 17, 2015, and October 19, 2015.

23. Bob Lasher, phone interview by Kim Starkey Jonker, August 13, 2015.

24. Ibid.

25. Ernie Iseminger, phone interview by Kim Starkey Jonker, May 29, 2015.

26. Nonprofit Research Collaborative (NRC), *Nonprofit Fundraising Study: Covering Charitable Receipts at Nonprofit Organizations in the United States and Canada in 2012*, March 2013, 27, http://npresearch.org/pdf/2013-reports/NRC-W_2013_FINAL.pdf.

27. Fundraising Effectiveness Project, *2015 Fundraising Effectiveness Survey Report* (Washington, DC: Association of Fundraising Professionals and Urban Institute, 2015), 13.

28. Iseminger, phone interview by Jonker.

29. Lasher, phone interview by Jonker.

30. Martin Shell, phone interview with Kim Starkey Jonker, March 24, 2016.

31. Christopher Hest, interview by Kim Starkey Jonker, September 15, 2015.

32. Anonymous donor, interview by Kim Starkey Jonker, September 12, 2015.

33. Lasher, phone interview by Jonker.

34. Hest, interview by Jonker.

35. Ibid.

36. NRC, *Nonprofit Fundraising Study 2012*, 30.

37. Hest, interview by Jonker.

38. Lasher, phone interview by Jonker.

39. Leslie Sara Gaviser and William Meehan III, "Tipping Point Community," Stanford Graduate School of Business, Case Study No. SI116, 2009; and Lurie, interview by Jonker.

40. Peter Panepento, "Connecting with Generation X: Charities Look for New Ways to Reach Out to the Under-40 Set," *Chronicle of Philanthropy,* June 25, 2009, https://www.philanthropy.com/article/Connecting-With-Generation-X/177013.

41. Lurie, interview by Jonker.

42. Ibid.

43. Penelope Burk, *The Burk Donor Survey: Where Philanthropy Is Headed in 2014* (Chicago: Cygnus Applied Research, 2014), 87.

44. Lasher, phone interview by Jonker.

45. "Hot Topic: Benchmarks," Association of Fundraising Professionals (AFP), posted July 2014, http://www.afpnet.org/BBTDetail.cfm?ItemNumber=26383.

46. Unpublished research by Melissa S. Brown (manager, Nonprofit Research Collaborative), in collaboration with the Association of Fundraising Professionals.

47. Nonprofit Research Collaborative, *Nonprofit Fundraising Study: Covering Charitable Receipts at U.S. Nonprofit Organizations in 2011*, April 2012, 11, http://www.afpnet.org/files/ContentDocuments/NRC_April_2012_FINAL%20v2 .pdf.

48. Jonker, Meehan, and Iseminger, "Fundraising Is Fundamental"; and Tim Hanstad, email correspondence with Kim Starkey Jonker, November 12, 2016.

49. Jonker, Meehan, and Iseminger, "Fundraising Is Fundamental."

50. Tim Hanstad, phone interview by Kim Starkey Jonker, October 11, 2016.

51. Jonker, Meehan, and Iseminger, "Fundraising Is Fundamental."

52. Chris Bischof, interview by Kim Starkey Jonker, May 21, 2015.

53. Lurie, interview by Jonker.

54. Iseminger, phone interview by Jonker.

55. Jonker, Meehan, and Iseminger, "Fundraising Is Fundamental."

56. Lasher, phone interview by Jonker.

57. Ibid.

58. Ann Goggins Gregory and Don Howard, "The Nonprofit Starvation Cycle," *Stanford Social Innovation Review*, Fall 2009, http://ssir.org/images/ articles/2009FA_feature_Gregory_Howard.pdf.

59. Nonprofit Finance Fund, *State of the Nonprofit Sector: 2015 Survey*, 7, accessed April 7, 2017, http://www.nonprofitfinancefund.org/sites/default/files/ nff/docs/2015-survey-brochure.pdf.

60. Ibid., 8.

61. Raybin, phone interview by Jonker and Meehan.

62. Brown, conversation with Jonker.

63. Shell, phone interview by Jonker.

64. Penelope Burk, *Donor-Centered Fundraising* (Chicago: Cygnus Applied Research, 2003), 87.

Chapter 7

1. BoardSource, *Leading with Intent: A National Index of Nonprofit Board Practices* (Washington, DC: BoardSource, 2015), 4.

2. David F. Larcker, Nicholas E. Donatiello, William F. Meehan III, and Brian Tayan, 2015 Survey on Board of Directors of Nonprofit Organizations, Stanford Graduate School of Business and Rock Center for Corporate Governance, 2015.

3. Ibid., 1, 3.

4. Stephen R. Covey, *The 7 Habits of Highly Effective People: Powerful Lessons in Personal Change*, 25th anniversary ed. (New York: Simon & Schuster, 2013), 73.

5. "About Us: GuideStar's Mission," GuideStar, accessed April 6, 2017, https://learn.guidestar.org/about-us.

6. "DataNerdInfographic," GuideStar, accessed April 7, 2016, http://www.guidestar.org/downloadable-files/DataNerdInfographic_FINAL.pdf.

7. Jacob Harold, phone interview by Kim Starkey Jonker, March 24, 2016.

8. "Mission and Values," Center for Global Development, accessed April 7, 2016, http://www.cgdev.org/page/mission.

9. "Evaluations of CGD," Center for Global Development, accessed April 7, 2016, http://www.cgdev.org/page/evaluations-cgd.

10. Ibid.

11. Cari Tuna, email correspondence with Kim Starkey Jonker, December 12, 2016.

12. BoardSource, *Leading with Intent*, 25.

13. Larcker et al., 2015 Survey on Board of Directors, 1.

14. Kim Jonker, William F. Meehan III, and Sakena Yacoobi, "Making Mission Matter," *Stanford Social Innovation Review*, webinar, June 18, 2014.

15. Mary Ellen Caron, phone interview by Kim Starkey Jonker, May 17, 2016.

16. "About Us: Mission, Goals and Values," Helen Keller International, accessed April 6, 2017, http://www.hki.org/about-us/mission-and-goals.

17. Kim Jonker and William F. Meehan III, "A Better Board Will Make You Better," *Stanford Social Innovation Review*, March 5, 2014, http://ssir.org/articles/entry/a_better_board_will_make_you_better.

18. Ibid.

19. Ibid. The discussion of Right to Play is drawn from this *SSIR* article.

20. Ibid.

21. Kim Jonker, William F. Meehan III, and Kathy Spahn, "Better Board Governance," *Stanford Social Innovation Review*, webinar, May 21, 2014.

22. BoardSource, *Leading with Intent*, 38, 27, 25, 22.

23. Ibid., 25.

24. Larcker et al., 2015 Survey on Board of Directors, 9, 1, 11.

25. Ibid., 1.

26. BoardSource, *Leading with Intent*, 3.

27. Jonker and Meehan, "A Better Board Will Make You Better."

28. Tommy Clark, phone interview by Kim Starkey Jonker, October 25, 2016.

29. Jonker and Meehan, "A Better Board Will Make You Better."

30. Ibid.

31. Larcker et al., 2015 Survey on Board of Directors, 2.

32. "Administration and Finances," Stanford University, accessed April 6, 2017, http://facts.stanford.edu/administration.

33. Isaac Stein, interview by William F. Meehan III, April 9, 2016.

34. William F. Meehan III and Kim Starkey Jonker, 2016 Stanford Survey on Leadership and Management in the Nonprofit Sector, Stanford Graduate School of Business, 2016, engineofimpact.org/survey.

35. Larcker et al., 2015 Survey on Board of Directors, 2.

36. BoardSource, *Leading with Intent*, 39, 23.

37. Marts & Lundy Special Report, "2015: New York City Board Giving, Adding Facts to Anecdotes," December 2015, http://www.martsandlundy.com/wp-content/uploads/2015/12/NY_Board_Giving_2015_pages_FINAL.pdf.

38. Chris Bischof, interview by Kim Starkey Jonker, May 21, 2015.

39. Mark Labberton, phone interview by Kim Starkey Jonker, December 29, 2015.

40. Susan Packard Orr, email correspondence with Kim Starkey Jonker, November 28, 2016.

41. BoardSource, *Leading with Intent*, 41.

42. Labberton, phone interview by Jonker.

43. Debbie Aung Din, Skype interview by Kim Starkey Jonker, October 31, 2016.

44. Jonker and Meehan, "A Better Board Will Make You Better."

45. Ibid.

46. Jonker, Meehan, and Spahn, "Better Board Governance," webinar.

47. Bischof, interview by Jonker.

48. Jonker, Meehan, and Spahn, "Better Board Governance," webinar.

Chapter 8

1. Aaron Hurst, "Demystifying Scaling: A Five-Part Series on Developing a Common Framework for Nonprofits to Scale for Impact," *Stanford Social Innovation Review*, part 1 (November 2, 2012), part 2 (November 13, 2012), part 3 (December 3, 2012), part 4 (December 20, 2012), part 5 (January 3, 2013); and Jeffrey L. Bradach, "Scaling Impact: How to get 100x the results with 2x the organization," *Stanford Social Innovation Review*, Summer 2010, https://ssir.org/articles/entry/scaling_impact.

2. Paul Carttar, "Why Don't the Best Nonprofits Grow?" *Harvard Business Review*, March 8, 2013, https://hbr.org/2013/03/social-enterprises-cant-grow-w; and Paul Bloom, "How to Take a Social Venture to Scale?" *Harvard Business Review*, June 18, 2012, https://hbr.org/2012/06/how-to-take-a-social-venture-t.

3. Diana Wells, email correspondence with Kim Starkey Jonker, November 11, 2016; "Ashoka Financial Statements, August 31, 2015, and Independent Auditor's Report, June 24, 2016," Ashoka Audit 2015, accessed April 7, 2017, https://www.ashoka.org/atom/3129; and "Frequently Asked Questions," Ashoka, accessed November 14, 2016, https://www.ashoka.org/faq.

4. Tim Hanstad, email correspondence with Kim Starkey Jonker, November 12, 2016; and Kim Jonker, William F. Meehan, and Ernie Iseminger, "Fundraising Is Fundamental (If Not Always Fun)," *Stanford Social Innovation Review*, February 26, 2014, https://ssir.org/articles/entry/fundraising_is_fundamental_if_not_always_fun.

5. Tim Hanstad, phone interview by Kim Starkey Jonker, October 11, 2016; and "Landesa," NGO Advisor, accessed October 5, 2015, https://www.ngoadvisor.net/ong/landesa.

6. Veris Consulting & Growth Philanthropy Network, "Executive Summary on the State of Scaling Among Nonprofits" (2013), 4, accessed March 8, 2016, http://www.verisconsulting.com/sites/default/files/thought-leadership/Stateof ScalingExecutiveSummary.pdf.

7. "Growth Share Matrix," *Economist*, September 11, 2009, http://www .economist.com/node/14299055.

8. See engineofimpact.org.

9. We are inspired by the well-known phrase "If you build it, he will come" from the 1989 movie *Field of Dreams*.

10. "Q&A; Health Care for the Poorest as a Central Human Right," *New York Times*, March 29, 2003, http://www.nytimes.com/2003/03/29/arts/q-a-health -care-for-the-poorest-as-a-central-human-right.html.

11. Dr. Martin Luther King Jr., "I've Been to the Mountaintop," speech delivered April 3, 1968, Memphis, TN, in *King Encyclopedia*, Martin Luther King Jr. Research and Education Institute, Stanford University, accessed November 15, 2016, http://kingencyclopedia.stanford.edu/encyclopedia/documentsentry/ ive_been_to_the_mountaintop.

12. See engineofimpact.org.

13. William F. Meehan III and Kim Starkey Jonker, 2016 Stanford Survey on Leadership and Management in the Nonprofit Sector, Stanford Graduate School of Business, 2016, engineofimpact.org/survey.

14. Ibid. For purposes of illustration, we have rounded percentage figures so that they add up to 100.

15. Jeffrey Bradach and Abe Grindle, "Transformative Scale: The Future of Growing What Works," *Stanford Social Innovation Review*, February 19, 2014, https://ssir.org/articles/entry/transformative_scale_the_future_of_growing_what_works.

16. Ibid.

17. Kevin Starr and Laura Hattendorf, "The Doer and the Payer: A Simple Approach to Scale," *Stanford Social Innovation Review*, August 21, 2015, https:// ssir.org/articles/entry/the_doer_and_the_payer_a_simple_approach_to_scale.

18. Ibid.

19. Ibid.

20. Ibid.

21. Ibid.

22. Roger L. Martin and Sally R. Osberg, with a foreword by Arianna Huffington, *Getting Beyond Better: How Social Entrepreneurship Works* (Boston: Harvard Business Review Press, 2015), 147.

23. Allen S. Grossman and V. Kasturi Rangan, "Managing Multi-Site Nonprofits," *Harvard Business School Social Enterprise Series No. 8* (2000), 9.

24. Ibid.

25. Ibid., 11–12.

26. Kathy Spahn, interview by Kim Starkey Jonker, May 20, 2015.

27. Paula Margulies, "Linda Rottenberg's High-Impact Endeavor," *Strategy and Business* 66 (Spring 2012), http://www.strategy-business.com/article/12106?gko=8b1a9.

28. Ibid.

29. Stephanie Strom, "Philanthropists Start Requiring Management Courses to Keep Nonprofits Productive," *New York Times*, July 29, 2011, http://www.nytimes .com/2011/07/30/business/philanthropists-start-requiring-management-courses-to -keep-nonprofits-productive.html; and "CEO Perspectives: Linda Rottenberg, Co-founder and CEO, Endeavor Global," Bridgespan Group (2011), accessed March 1, 2016, http://www.bridgespan.org/Publications-and-Tools/CEO-Executive-Director/ Nonprofit-CEO-Profiles/CEO-Perspectives-Linda-Rottenberg.

30. Matt Bannick, interview by Kim Starkey Jonker, April 4, 2016.

31. Linda Rottenberg, interview by Kim Starkey Jonker, March 20, 2016; and "Bain and Company Recognized for Its Pro-Bono Service on Behalf of Endeavor," Endeavor, accessed March 1, 2016, http://www.endeavor.org/in-the-news /bain-company-recognized-endeavor.

32. "Impact," Endeavor, accessed February 9, 2016, http://www.endeavor .org/impact.

33. William P. Ryan and Barbara E. Taylor, *An Experiment in Scaling Impact: Assessing the Growth Capital Aggregation Pilot* (New York: Edna McConnell Clark Foundation, December 2012), accessed March 1, 2016, http://www .emcf.org/fileadmin/media/PDFs/GCAPReport_Final.pdf.

34. Ibid.

35. "Youth Villages Inc.," GuideStar Nonprofit Profile Charting Impact Report, accessed April 7, 2017, https://www.guidestar.org/report/charting impact/576324247/youth-villages.pdf.

36. Sal Khan, phone interview by William F. Meehan III and Kim Starkey Jonker, February 12, 2016.

37. Ibid.

38. William F. Meehan and Georgia Levenson Keohane, "QuestBridge: A Search for Scale," Case Number SI-83, Stanford Graduate School of Business (January 19, 2011). Copyright © 2001 to 2015 by the Board of Trustees of the Leland Stanford Junior University. All rights reserved. Used with permission from the Stanford University Graduate School of Business. Information in subsequent paragraphs draws on this case study.

39. Ibid., 2.

40. Ibid., 25; "College Partners," QuestBridge, accessed April 7, 2017, https:// www.questbridge.org/college-partners.

41. Meehan and Keohane, "QuestBridge," 8.

42. Cecilia Corral, "Celebrating Our First Million Users!" CareMessage, September 19, 2016, https://blog.caremessage.org/celebrating-our-first-million -users-698f60d78c7a.

43. Mark Sullivan, "CareMessage Raises $6M for Text-Based Patient Outreach Platform," January 22, 2015, *Venture Beat*, January 22, 2015, http://venturebeat .com/2015/01/22/caremessage-raises-6m-for-text-based-patient-outreach-platform.

44. Kathy Spahn, email correspondence with Kim Starkey Jonker, November 11, 2016.

45. Analysis provided by Laurie E. Paarlberg, Bush School of Government & Public Service, Texas A&M University, March 13, 2016.

46. "2015 Online Giving Trends," Network for Good, accessed November 14, 2016, http://www.networkforgood.com/digitalgivingindex/2015-online-giving-trends.

47. Thomas Bidaux, "Kickstarter in 2015—Review in Numbers," Kickstarter, ICO Partners, February 9, 2016, http://icopartners.com/2016/02/2015-in-review.

48. Raj Punjabi, interview with Kim Starkey Jonker, October 11, 2016.

49. Ibid.

50. Peter W. Luckow, Avi Kenny, Emily White, Madeleine Ballard, Lorenzo Dorr, Kurby Erlandson, Benjamin Grant, Alice Johnson, Breanna Lorenzen, Subarna Mukherjee, et al., "Implementation Research on Community Health Workers' Provision of Maternal and Child Health Services in Rural Liberia," *Bulletin of the World Health Organization* 95 (2017), http://www.who.int/bulletin/volumes/95/2/16-175513.pdf; and Raj Punjabi, email correspondence with Kim Starkey Jonker, October 31, 2016.

51. "Lack of Access to Primary Health Services in Last Mile Communities Can Have Tremendous Global Consequences," Last Mile Health, accessed November 14, 2016, http://lastmilehealth.org/ebola-response.

52. Panjabi, interview by Jonker, October 11, 2016.

53. Kerry A. Dolan, "How Liberia Is Working to Deliver Healthcare to More Than a Quarter of Its Population," *Forbes*, August 12, 2016, https://www.forbes.com/sites/kerryadolan/2016/08/12/how-liberia-is-working-to-deliver-healthcare-to-more-than-a-quarter-of-its-population.

54. Kelly Wallace, "How to Make Your Kids Hate Sports Without Really Trying," *CNN*, January 21, 2016, http://www.cnn.com/2016/01/21/health/kids-youth-sports-parents.

55. Jim Thompson, phone interview by Kim Starkey Jonker, January 28, 2016.

56. Ibid.

57. Ibid.

58. Positive Coaching Alliance and LaPiana Consulting, "Positive Coaching Alliance Strategic Business Plan for Expansion" (April 2015), 17.

59. Thompson, phone interview by Jonker.

60. "Positive Coaching Alliance," New Berlin Soccer Club, accessed November 15, 2016, http://www.newberlinsoccerclub.com/page/show/80293-positive-coach-alliance.

61. "About Us," Pratham, accessed April 5, 2017, http://www.pratham.org/about-us/about-pratham; and "News," Pratham USA, accessed April 5, 2017, http://prathamusa.org/press/pratham-celebrates-20-years.

62. "FAQs," Pratham, accessed March 10, 2016, http://www.prathamusa.org/about-us/faqs.

63. Madhav Chavan, interview by Kim Starkey Jonker, March 10, 2016.

64. "Our Partners," Cassidy Trust, accessed March 7, 2016, http://www.cassidytrust.org/About/Partners.

65. ASER Centre, Monitoring, Measurement and Evaluation Unit, "Read India: Report 2014–15," accessed February 5, 2016, http://www.pratham.org/templates/pratham/images/Read_India_National_Report_2014-15.pdf.

66. "Citizen-Led, Household-Based Assessments Around the World," ASER Centre, accessed March 15, 2016, http://www.asercentre.org/p/76.html.

67. Chavan, interview by Jonker.

68. Rukmini Banerji, interview by Kim Starkey Jonker, April 22, 2015.

69. Rainer Maria Rilke, *Letters to a Young Poet*, originally published as *Briefe an einen jungen Dichter* (Leizpig: Insel Verlag: 1929).

Conclusion

1. "Alexis de Tocqueville: From *Democracy in America*," chap. 9 in *The Civil Society Reader*, ed. Virginia A. Hodgkinson and Michael W. Foley, Civil Society: Historical and Contemporary Perspectives (Hanover, NH: University Press of New England, 2003), 123.

2. Ibid., 126.

3. Susan Stamberg, "How Andrew Carnegie Turned His Fortune into a Library Legacy," *NPR Morning Edition*, August 1, 2013, http://www.npr.org/2013/08/01/207272849/how-andrew-carnegie-turned-his-fortune-into-a-library-legacy.

4. "1909: Eliminating Hookworm in the U.S.," Philanthropy Roundtable, accessed April 6, 2016, http://www.philanthropyroundtable.org/almanac/medicine_and_health/1909_eliminating_hookworm_in_the_u.s.

5. Joel L. Fleishman, *The Foundation: A Great American Secret; How Private Wealth Is Changing the World* (New York: PublicAffairs, 2007), 5.

6. Ibid., 122.

7. Melissa S. Brown, "How the 99% Give: Consequences for Philanthropy of the Concentration of Wealth" (conference presentation, Association of Fundraising Professionals, Hudson-Mohawk Chapter, Troy, NY, November 9, 2016). Data about giving in 2013 comes from Giving USA Foundation, *Giving USA 2016: The Annual Report on Philanthropy for the Year 2015* (Chicago: Giving USA Foundation, 2016) and IRS reports about deductions claimed on tax returns and by estates. Data includes individual giving and estimates for bequests. Melissa S. Brown & Associates (unpublished analysis).

Index

Page numbers in *italics* indicate material in figures.